MAPPING
CHINESE
RANGOON

Place and Nation among
the Sino-Burmese

JAYDE LIN ROBERTS

UNIVERSITY OF WASHINGTON PRESS
Seattle and London

Mapping Chinese Rangoon was published with the assistance of grants from the Charles and Jane Keyes Endowment for Books on Southeast Asia, established through the generosity of Charles and Jane Keyes, and from the Southeast Asia Center in the Jackson School of International Studies at the University of Washington.

UNIVERSITY OF WASHINGTON PRESS
www.washington.edu/uwpress

LIBRARY OF CONGRESS CATALOGING-IN-PUBLICATION DATA
Names: Roberts, Jayde Lin.
Title: Mapping Chinese Rangoon : place and nation among the Sino-Burmese /
  Jayde Lin Roberts.
Description: Seattle : University of Washington Press, 2016. | Includes
  bibliographical references and index.
Identifiers: LCCN 2016002910 | ISBN 9780295996677 (hardcover : acid-free paper)
Subjects: LCSH: Chinese—Burma—Rangoon—History. | Chinese—Burma—
  Rangoon—Social conditions. | Chinese—Burma—Rangoon—Ethnic identity.
  | Community life—Burma—Rangoon. | City and town life—Burma—
  Rangoon. | Ethnic neighborhoods—Burma—Rangoon. | Rangoon (Burma)—
  Ethnic relations. | Nationalism—Burma. | Nationalism—China. | Social
  change—Burma.
Classification: LCC DS530.9.R3 R63 2016 | DDC 305.8951/0591—dc23
LC record available at https://lccn.loc.gov/2016002910

The paper used in this publication is acid-free and meets the minimum requirements of American National Standard for Information Sciences—Permanence of Paper for Printed Library Materials, ANSI Z39.48–1984. ∞

For Lee and Owen, always

CONTENTS

PREFACE

Burma lingers. It troubles one's psyche with its contradictions—delighting one with its slowly decaying beauty while weighing one down with its suffering. I know Burma as a land of rich, tangled complexity where military generals oppressed the population through subtle and overt violence and where everyday people seemed to embody the quiet contentment taught in Theravada Buddhism. When I first arrived in Rangoon in 2006, the coexistence of these opposites seemed irreconcilable. My Western-educated intellect, trained in the scientific rationalism of post-Enlightenment thought, wanted clean categories and evidence of self-determination. Having grown up in the United States as a naturalized citizen, I had never been personally oppressed. I wondered how anyone could not stand up for his or her own rights, perpetuating military dictatorship through submissive inaction.

But the people of Burma do not have the luxury of absolutes. Right and wrong are context-specific. Dhamma/dharma, often translated as "the Buddhist conception of universal law," is believed to pervade all aspects of life. However, the consequences of moral and immoral action under that law are not always readily apparent or felt within a single lifetime. One is supposed to be patient and accommodating, accepting reality as it is while simultaneously working for change. From a purely Western-educated perspective, everyone in Burma was complicit in perpetuating military dictatorship, whether through docile acquiescence, as practiced by the poorest and least educated, or through subversive compliance, as practiced by those with the security to maneuver within regulations to create opportunities for themselves. However, I came to see that the singular and absolutist viewpoint of dominant Western intellectualism was not an appropriate lens for understanding Burma.

My graduate course in ethnographic methods had instructed me that the goal of fieldwork was to understand from within, not to appropriate knowledge. That admonition took on real, experiential meaning only after I had lived in Rangoon for a few months. In studying Burmese and conducting fieldwork, my task became achieving attunement with the local environment—the people and places—in order to see and gradually understand the multiple relationships in any given interaction or event. I came to see that paying bribes was not always motivated by weakness and that human agency could be exercised incrementally or even just within the confines of oneself. After all, I too paid the telephone repairman an extra fee to keep my phone operative. It had become common for government employees to create ways of earning extra money to supplement their meager wages. Similarly, when a township official came knocking on my door, I told her that I was a visiting relative, exactly as instructed by my landlady. It was not feasible to confront the system if I wanted to remain in Rangoon to complete my research. If I, a privileged Taiwanese-American researcher, could not stand up for myself, how could the local people?

Oppression in Burma is subtle and pervasive. As Aung San Suu Kyi wrote: "It is true that years of incoherent policies, inept official measures, burgeoning inflation and falling real income had turned the country into an economic shambles. But it was more than the difficulties of eking out a barely acceptable standard of living that had eroded the patience of a traditionally good-natured, quiescent people—it was also the humiliation of a way of life disfigured by corruption and fear."[1] The composure and contentment of almost everyone I met often masked the fear. However, when a new Burman friend came to my apartment at six thirty in the morning to return a gift because the book I had given her contained one photograph of Suu Kyi, I realized the depth of fear and resultant self-policing.

Under these circumstances, fieldwork could not take on the formal structure desirable in the ideal research project. People were reluctant to go on record with even the most innocuous comment. In addition, institutions of higher learning and research were barely functional after the State Law and Order Restoration Council (SLORC) shuttered and neutralized universities after the mass pro-democracy protests in 1988. Even institutions such as native place associations turned me away when I offered to teach English or Chinese. They did not need more Chinese teachers because trained teachers were dispatched from Yunnan by Hanban (the Chinese National Office for Teaching Chinese as a Foreign Language), and my American passport and visa requiring renewal every few months were potentially problematic. For example, while Europeans and Australians were allowed to study Burmese at the University of Foreign Languages, US citizens could not gain entry.

Fortunately, systematic ethnographic fieldwork is not dependent on official permission or support. Official permission often directly or indirectly constrains research to fit within the state discourse or dominant agenda. This was a particular concern in Myanmar under military rule. As my project was to understand how everyday Sino-Burmese live in Rangoon, I did not need access to government officials, the army, or the elite, all of whom have some stake in the dominant order. I could make myself known as a long-term visitor seeking to understand the Sino-Burmese ethos and prove myself trustworthy enough to be allowed into their lives.

I undertook this process by walking the same routes every day and visiting specific institutions such as the Hokkien Kuanyin Temple. In the morning, I made my way from Dagon Township to Chinatown (Tayout Tan) to observe the wet market on Eighteenth Street and then walked along Mahabandula Road before heading south on Sint Oh Dan Street to the Hokkien Kuanyin Temple. Along the way, I stopped for breakfast at various tea shops and chatted up vendors and customers who were willing to talk. At the temple, I had tea with members of the executive committee and talked with the various attendants who sold incense, maintained the incense urns, and kept the temple in functioning order. After visiting at the temple, I tried to gain entry into the numerous clan associations in Chinatown but succeeded only a few times, and with little to record because the elderly custodians either knew little or did not care to talk. In the afternoon, I walked around the core of downtown Rangoon, near Sule Pagoda, before heading to the Overseas Chinese Library in Chinatown to browse through its collection, meager though it was. In the evening, I observed the afternoon fruit market in front of the Cantonese Kuanyin Temple and then the night market on Mahabandula Road.

As fieldwork progressed, I was invited to join various regular activities such as singing practice at the Kien Tek Association and morning exercise at the Mahabandula Garden and Inya Lake Park. I was also invited to numerous Chinese New Year and anniversary banquets where Sino-Burmese Chineseness was put onstage. With persistence, I was also allowed to attend the practice sessions of some lion dance teams (women were said to be bad luck for the lions) and interviewed leaders in the Sino-Burmese community. These activities and volunteering for the hundredth anniversary celebration for the Myanmar Chinese Chamber of Commerce allowed me to participate more fully in the Sino-Burmese community, but, ultimately, I remained an outsider. Given the experience of all Burmese people (regardless of ethnicity) in the past five decades, trust is hard to earn, and my two years in the country hardly registered as a commitment to the Sino-Burmese people or to Burma/Myanmar.

To supplement the meager records in Rangoon, I undertook archival research at Xiamen University in China, a major center for research on overseas Chinese, in May 2008, and also interviewed Sino-Burmese in Macao and Hong Kong in September 2008 and in Taiwan in March 2009.

Since the 1980s, Burma scholars have used pseudonyms to protect their informants, cognizant of the dangers should the Myanmar government discover that a local person spoke to a foreign researcher. Stories abound of government officials following, interrogating, and even jailing Burmese people after they are seen talking to "suspicious" foreigners. Although the country has witnessed dramatic changes since the initiation of reforms in 2011, the Sino-Burmese I came to know between 2006 and 2009 remain cautious. After all, Thura Shwe Mann was stripped of his office as the chairman of the ruling political party in the middle of the night on August 12, 2015, and politics remain opaque. To respect their caution and uphold my original promise of maintaining their anonymity, I use pseudonyms throughout this book unless a person is known as a public figure, such as Daw Win Win Tint, "Myanmar's supermarket queen."

PERSONAL NAMES

Most Burmese people are known by common nicknames, such as Ma Kyi Kyi, Daw San San, Ko Lei, or U Kyaw. *Ma* and *Daw* are honorifics appended to female names. *Ma* is used for young women or between women of similar age, and *Daw* is used for mature women or those in a senior position. *Ko* and *U* are the honorifics appended to male names, with *Ko* for young men and *U* for mature men, following the same age-based hierarchy used for women. Among the Sino-Burmese (people of Chinese descent who identify with Burma), using Burmese names has become the standard practice since the anti-Chinese riots of 1967. Those born before 1967 were generally first given a Chinese name, which was sometimes transliterated into a Burmese name, such as Chen Yi-Sein becoming U Yi-Sein. Those born after 1967 were usually given both Chinese and Burmese names, but the Chinese name was known only among family members. For even more recent generations, such as those born in or after the 1980s, only Burmese names were given. Throughout this book, I follow the practice of my informants, using their Burmese or Chinese names according to how they refer to themselves and how they are generally known. However, in the Burmese naming system, there are no surnames to identify an entire family, so when referring to Sino-Burmese families, I use Chinese surnames romanized from their Hokkien pronunciation, unless a subject explicitly referred to himself or herself with standard Chinese (Mandarin) pronunciation.

Chinese in Burma once spoke mutually unintelligible languages (Hokkien, Cantonese, Hakka, and Yunnanese) and remained loyal to their native place identities until the Republic of China and the People's Republic of China exported their competing national ideologies via standard Chinese–medium education. That indoctrination did not last. In Rangoon, the Hokkien population has been dominant, so this book focuses on that subgroup. Unfortunately, there is no standard system for the romanization of Hokkien. Singapore, Taiwan, and southern Fujian Province in China (the source of the Hokkien language) have used different systems, and names were generally transliterated in an ad hoc manner. If people or organizations have already romanized their names, I follow their lead. If no prior romanization has been provided, I have transliterated their names according to the pattern most prevalent in Singapore: each syllable is rendered separately, with a space in between, and the spelling is more similar to the Wade-Giles system than to current standard pinyin. Although Peh-oe-ji, a system established by Christian missionaries, seems to be gaining followers, I have not adopted it because my informants, as non-Christians, are not familiar with this system, and the prevalence of diacritics in Peh-oe-ji makes it impractical for a book not focusing on linguistics.

PLACE-NAMES

Just as the Sino-Burmese have multiple names, places in Rangoon such as streets and temples are known by different names by different people, and some of these names have changed through time. Rangoon was planned as a British colonial capital, and its streets were named to designate the value of a street and recognize leaders in the colonial community. Street names such as Strand, Merchant, and Dalhousie are still well known, but most people refer to them by the post-1989 Burmese names specified by the military government. Unfortunately, the romanization of Burmese, like Hokkien, has yet to be standardized. The system in this book is based in part on John Okell's *Burmese: An Introduction to the Spoken Language* and San San Hnin Tun and Patrick McCormick's *Colloquial Burmese: The Complete Course for Beginners*.[2] However, to facilitate recognition, common place-names follow the usual spelling conventions. Finally, the streets in Tayout Tan (Chinatown) are also known by Chinese names, such as Guangdong Dadao (Canton Road) and Baichi Lu (One Hundred–Foot Street). The various names for the streets in Rangoon are provided in Map 1.

Similarly, the temples and associations discussed in this book often have multiple names. For example, the most enduring and significant place for the Sino-Burmese, the Hokkien Kuanyin Temple, is known by the following names: Kuanyin Ting and Kheng Hock Keong in Hokkien, Qingfu Gong in standard Chinese, and Tayout Hpongyi Kyaung and Kwamyin Medaw Hpayakyaung in Burmese. After introducing and explaining the various names, I employ the name most often used by the Sino-Burmese.

ACKNOWLEDGMENTS

In the process of writing about Burma and the Sino-Burmese, I have accumulated many debts. On the academic path, I could not have navigated the interdisciplinarity of my research without the guidance of Mary P. Callahan, Charles Keyes, and Robert Mugerauer. They not only pointed me toward the knowledge necessary to undertake rigorous and systematic fieldwork but also modeled the humanity and care that is central to producing meaningful analysis in the human sciences. I could not have asked for better guides. Without the linguistic foundation provided by my Burmese teachers and tutors, ethnographic research would have been impossible. For their patient and skillful teaching, I want to thank my *saya* and *sayamas*: U Saw Tun, Daw Yi Yi Win, Daw Than Than Win, Daw Ma Lay, and Ma Yu Yu Khaing. For their intellectual generosity, I thank U Thaw Kaung for our long conversations and the helpful sources; Patrick McCormick for sharing his knowledge of Burmese linguistics and history, for reading the entire first draft of this book, and for helping me with Burmese font and romanization; Daniel Abramson for hiring me as a research assistant to examine the architecture of the returned overseas Chinese in southern Fujian and thereby providing me with a base of knowledge that enabled more in-depth analysis into the built environment of the Sino-Burmese; and Tasaw Lu for her empathetic approach to fieldwork and for introducing me to Sino-Burmese people in Taipei.

On the path toward emplaced understanding, I am indebted to the people of Rangoon in general but specifically to the following: Yang Minquan, Yang Guorong, and Du Ziming, who should be recognized as local historians given their breadth and depth of knowledge about the Sino-Burmese; U Kyaw, Daw Tin Tin, and other members of the Sino-Burmese breakfast club for welcoming me into their circle and buying me numerous meals, including the best *mohinga* I have ever had; Ma Su and A Ko Gyi, who took me in as a relative, not just a tenant, and taught me subtly about Burmese and Muslim-Burmese culture; Daw Cho Cho and the Tuesday Vipassana meditation group, who provided a weekly reminder to strive for *myitta* in all of my actions, especially in intellectual pursuits that might be abstracted from the messy complexity of humanity; Anna Huang and Daw Myat Mon, who were not only fellow Vipassana yogis but also interlocutors for the Sino-Burmese community; and members of the Myanmar Chinese Mutual Aid Association, the Myanmar Chinese Chamber of Commerce, and the Myanmar Chinese Women's Association for opening your doors to me.

On the specific path of producing this book, I am grateful to Luo Lishi for producing the maps; Jiawen Hu for indexing; Jane Ferguson and Rhena Refsland for comments on an early version of the introductory chapter; Ian Holliday for encouraging me to publish; James Chin for sharing his knowledge of Malaysian Chinese culture; Jeff Malpas for assuring me that poetic language has a place in critical scholarship; Yomi Braester and Elizabeth Leane for last-minute assistance in refining the title of this book; Nick Cheesman for even more last-minute critique on my endnotes; the two blind reviewers for their helpful comments; Jane M. Lichty for copyediting; and Lorri Hagman and the staff at the University of Washington Press for their timely and professional assistance.

I want to thank the Blakemore Foundation for the financial support that made it possible for me to study Burmese in Rangoon and for extending my residence beyond one year due to the protest in 2007. I also thank the Fulbright Program for funding my fieldwork from 2008 to 2009. In addition, I would like to recognize at the University of Tasmania, the Institute for the Study of Social Change for supporting the creation of the three maps and the index for this book and the Faculty of the Arts Research Office for obtaining the permission to reproduce an 1895 photograph from the British Library.

This path I have taken would not have been possible if my parents, Chin and Linda Lin, had not emigrated from Taiwan, sacrificing their comfortable life to provide better opportunities for my brothers and me. Although neither of them had the luxury of pursuing higher education, they instilled in me an enthusiasm for learning that has served me well in every stage of my life. Throughout this process, many friends and family have provided support and relief when I needed it the most. They are Karin Eberhardt, John Buchannan, Francois Renaud and Yin Min Aye, Ma Khaing and U Kyaw Ngwe, Noy Thrupkaew, Anunta Intra-asksorn, Shane Suvikapakornkul, Silvia Pinto Masis, Isabel Selles, Jeff Cody, Rebekah Ingalls, Kateri

Snow, Charlotte Roberts, Steve Roberts, and Sara Wetstone. Finally, my deepest gratitude goes to Lee Roberts, whose intelligence and unbounded generosity supported me through this entire journey. Our partnership is the foundation of everything I do.

MAPPING CHINESE RANGOON

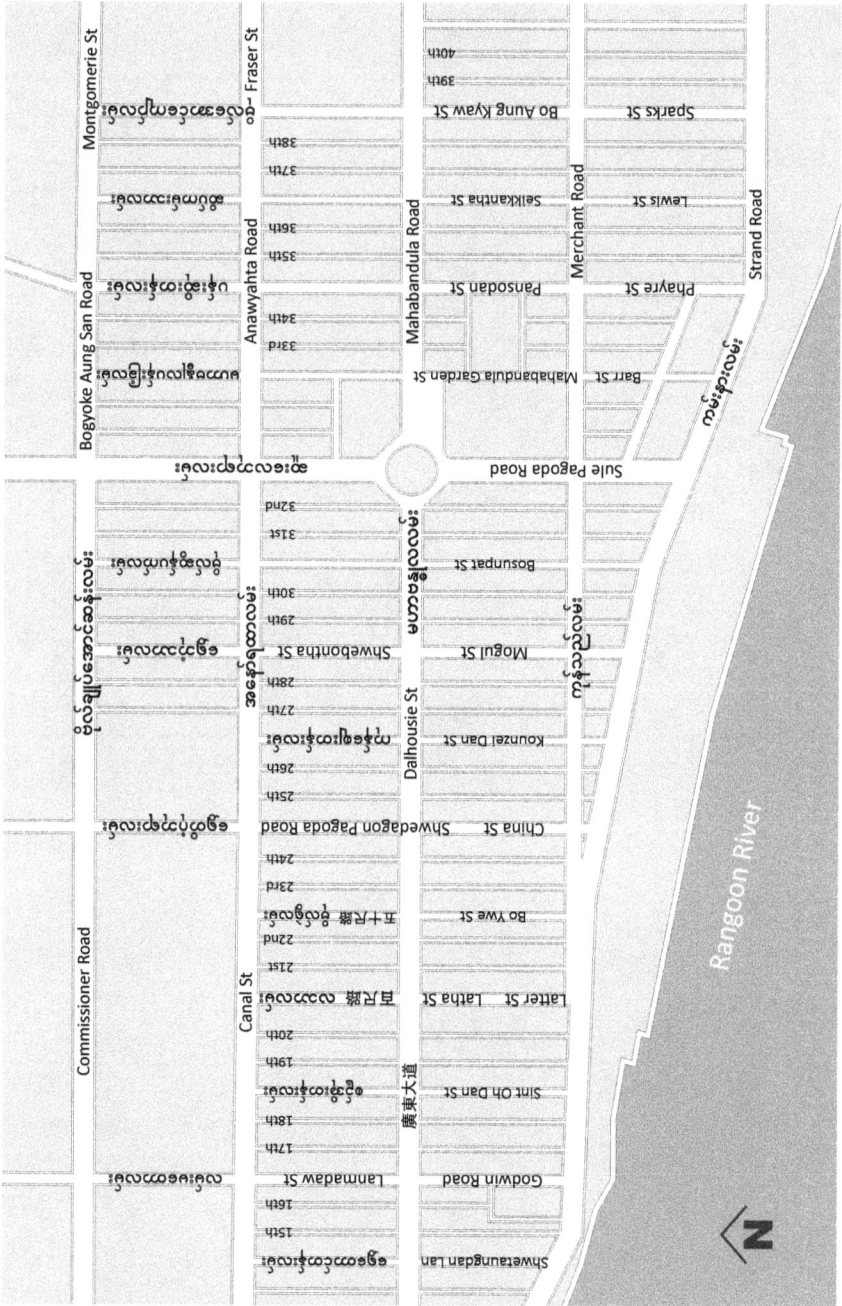

Map 1. Map of downtown Rangoon with historical, contemporary, and Chinese street names. Line work by Luo Lishi.

INTRODUCTION

Walking toward Understanding

WALKING toward the river on Sule Pagoda Road, the central axis of downtown Rangoon, now known as Yangon,[1] I was stopped in my tracks by a distinct rhythm: "Da—da-dong—dong—dong—dak-dong—dong—de-long-dong—dong-dong-dong-dong—dong-de-long-dong!"[2] Even though I was right next to a truck-size generator that seemed to envelop me in its diesel-fueled roar, the rumble of the drum and cymbals pierced through that sound barrier and pulled me back to the corner of Sule Pagoda Road and Bogyoke Aung San Road, away from the river and my destination: my Burmese tutorial. The drumming sounded distinctly Chinese to me, like the accompaniment to lion dancing, but in my four months of residence in Rangoon I had never heard of anyone doing lion dancing, much less seen a lion dance troupe. As I turned the corner on Bogyoke Aung San Road to chase after the drumming, the sound rushed past me. I glimpsed a truck with a golden lion head perched on top of the cab and the drummer and cymbal players standing in the midst of a lion dance troupe whaling away on their instruments.

Where had this lion dance troupe come from? Where were they going? Was such a public display of Chineseness advisable in a country run by generals who actively police public assembly and forbid any public expression that does not promote a singular Myanmar national identity? And why had I not heard about lion dancing in Rangoon after living in the city for four months and associating with the local Chinese?

This and other moments of puzzlement compelled me to walk the streets of Rangoon every day, to engage with the city and its people despite the stifling heat and broken sidewalks, in order to be present for any possible moment of unfolding. Between 2006 and 2009, when I was studying Bur-

3

mese and conducting my fieldwork, Burma/Myanmar was still under overt military rule. The residents of Rangoon neither offered unsolicited information nor answered questions directly, rendering life in the city largely illegible to an outsider. Even for a Taiwanese-American who was often mistaken for a local Sino-Burmese (a person of Chinese descent who was born in Burma, identifies with the country, and has chosen to remain), much was hidden, making my interpretations tentative and subject to error. I walked the streets as a fundamental practice in my research, to pursue a more attuned and emplaced understanding that would be continually reshaped in order to approach local self-understanding.

My goal was to study how the Sino-Burmese live in Rangoon and how they make a place for themselves. This place is not a territory. The reification of flexible spaces and places into territories, particularly national territories, is a persistent and thoroughly analyzed problem in Southeast Asia.[3] Rather, place is a located field of meaning, a common world that has been created through long-term interactions between a people and a geographical space. The question is not who the Sino-Burmese are as members of a static, irreversible category judged according to ethnicity or degrees of assimilation. That type of analysis has been undertaken by scholars such as Mya Than who divide the people of Chinese descent into two groups: ethnic Chinese and those who are so Burmanized that they are no longer Chinese.[4] More importantly, territory and ethnicity are inextricably tied to state violence in the Union of Burma/Myanmar and remain highly problematic concepts.[5] In a country where the identities and territories of different *tainyintha* (ethnic nationalities) have been perceived as a major threat to national unity, viable group identity for the descendants of foreigners has had to adopt different terms. In the case of the *tainyintha*, the immediate association between ethnic identity and territorial sovereignty has set up a nearly irreconcilable barrier to national reconciliation because *tainyintha* status demands the recognition of separate nations within the nation-state of Myanmar. In the case of the Sino-Burmese who are defined as foreigners, any claims to territory would destroy their chances of becoming a part of Burma. Their only option is to become as Burmese as possible without losing themselves. The question is how the Sino-Burmese dynamically maintain their lifeworld, responding to changing sets of economic, political, and social circumstances.[6] It is their identity as a way of being-in-relationship with others rather than a hollow ontological category. It is how they can become local, both Chinese and Burmese, through conscious and unconscious daily decisions that coalesce into an ethos, a grounded everyday Chineseness that is forced to contend with macro politico-economic forces.

While explaining my struggle to find Burmese words for *ethos* and *identity*, a Burmese scholar, Kyaw Yin Hlaing, suggested to me: "It's more like *Kokogo belo nale dele* ['How do I understand myself?' or 'How do people understand themselves?']."[7] Having my words reframed through the Burmese language reminded me that the ethos I sought was indeed a process: an understanding achieved by the Sino-Burmese in their relationship with a changing time and place and a non-appropriative understanding between me, the ethnographer, and the focus of my research, the Sino-Burmese. The ambition was neither to know the Sino-Burmese as a totalizable phenomenon nor to produce uncontestable knowledge. As Hannah Arendt has stated, this pursuit of understanding is an unending activity that attempts to activate the multiple meanings of things and these meanings are the unfolding of significance.[8] Accordingly, my fieldwork and this book constitute a spatial ethnography, an engaged interpretation of the complex Sino-Burmese ethos committed in writing.

Weaving through the upper, middle, and lower blocks of Rangoon, one is hard-pressed to identify with any certainty who is Chinese. Rangoon residents (Rangoonites) often state that Chinese have fairer skin, wear pants instead of *longyis* (Burmese men's sarongs), and "have that typical Chinese look about them" (without providing more details). However, these oft-cited ethnic markers are often misleading and even locals make mistakes. Many times, local people of Chinese descent said to me, "You must be Sino-Burmese" or "Just look at you, how could you be anything but Sino-Burmese." Others like my Muslim neighbors and random taxi drivers thought I was Shan or Akha (two of Myanmar's many ethnic nationalities).[9] These assessments about my identity point to the intersubjective nature of fieldwork. I was being studied as much as I was studying the Sino-Burmese and their city. As a Taiwanese-American, I was a curiosity because I appeared to be somewhat local but not quite.

These interactions also highlight the situatedness of understanding. On the immediate, commonsense level, my Chinese-looking face, accented Burmese, and physical presence in Rangoon suggested that there was a connection between me and the place: Rangoon and Burma. On a more subtle level, place is what we have in common, an "in-between [that] relates and separates men at the same time" like a table that is located between those who sit around it.[10] Place is where identity can appear, where differences must be confronted as people gather in a particular location and make sense of each other.[11] Furthermore, place is a mode of thinking that engages with the messy multiplicity in any given encounter rather than a controlled thought experiment based on preselected factors. There is no "pure vision" or absolute objectivity but a "situated impartiality" in which "the self does not move out of the world altogether but supplements her own view, her own experiences, by taking others' views into account."[12] It explicitly recognizes the interdependence between that which is seeking to understand and that which is being understood. This process can be likened to that of a surveyor who must repeatedly walk the terrain of an unknown land to map that region from within the region itself. "For such a surveyor, there is nowhere outside of the region itself from which an accurate topographical picture can be obtained. It is thus precisely through the surveyor's active involvement with the landscape that an accurate mapping is made."[13] Much like a surveyor, I am fully implicated in this ethnography, and the place of Rangoon is the source of my understanding.

LOCATING A PEOPLE IN BETWEEN

In contemporary Myanmar, anyone of Chinese descent is called Tayout, but no one is sure how many Tayout are in Rangoon or Burma as a whole. The most often quoted statistic has been about 3 percent of the national population, but Tayout in Rangoon say that is an underestimate. The obvious cause for this uncertainty is that since the colonial census of 1931, the post-1948 independent governments of Burma have yet to complete a national census.[14] The more subtle reason is that *Tayout* is ill-defined, with a variety of people from various places embodying different and often hybrid descent being perceived as somehow Chinese. *Tayout* is an exonym used by the Burmese to refer to the Chinese today.[15] G. H. Luce first posed the question of who and what is Tayout in 1959, but there has yet to be a definitive answer.[16] A persistent theory suggests that *Tayout* is derived from the transliteration of *Turk* or *Taruk* into the Burmese language, because the "Chinese" who invaded Burma in the thirteenth century were Mongols, also known as Turks. However, historians Michael Aung-Thwin and Goh Geok Yian have challenged this received knowledge first proposed by Arthur Purves Phayre, the first commissioner of Burma. Goh, through her examination of Burmese chronicles, found that since the thirteenth century Burman royalty have referred to the territory north of the Burman Buddhist sphere of influence and the different populations who resided in that area as Tayout.[17] This area, roughly the southern portion of contemporary Yunnan, is the most ethnically diverse province in contemporary China, where non-Han peoples had avoided centralized Chinese rule until the twentieth century.[18] The various Tibeto-Burman, Dai-Kadai, Austro-Asiatic, and Mongol populations were mostly ruled by local kingdoms and native chiefs, who exercised varying degrees of autonomy depending on the shifting power of the Han Empire.[19] Goh states, "Tayout as 'China' or 'Chinese' is likely a nineteenth- and twentieth-century modern construction imposed on earlier Burmese texts and past in general."[20]

This application of a single label to a diverse group of people is common throughout history, as seen in the western European appropriation of the term *Tartar* to refer to both Turks and Mongols and in the other exonym applied to Sino-Burmese, the name *Chinese* itself.[21] As numerous contemporary scholars have emphasized, China is not a monolithic place, nor do the people in the country constitute a homogenous whole.[22] However, thoughtful academic analyses seldom intervene in the shorthand conceptions employed in everyday life and popular media. For the Sino-Burmese in Rangoon, the labels *Tayout* and *Chinese* not only fail to recognize the linguistic, religious, and cultural differences between the three main groups that have settled in the city—Hokkien, Cantonese, and Hakka from southeastern China, not Yunnan Province—but they also conflate this diverse population with the nation-state actions of the People's Republic of China and the supposed economic dominance of the overseas Chinese network.[23]

In foregrounding the generalizing tendency of the labels *Tayout* and *Chinese*, I am not asserting that contemporary Sino-Burmese see no connections between themselves and China. Rather, I am highlighting differences between the more intimate cultural identification among a group of people such as the Hokkien and Cantonese and the more abstract political identification among the so-called Chinese. Furthermore, the naming of the Tayout serves as a ground upon which to understand the diversity of Sino-Burmese in the context of the tremendous ethnic diversity and identity politics within Burma. Whereas the ideological claim to identity among the *tainyintha* has served as an effective call to warfare, the Sino-Burmese understanding of self has eschewed ideology and contented itself with ethos, the actual practices of everyday life.

Sino-Burmese have generally avoided the state and shied away from politics. However, the definition of the Union of Burma/Myanmar as a territorially bound nation-state composed of officially recognized *lumyo* (biologically determined "kinds of people" or races) or *tainyintha lumyo* (sons or offspring of the geographical division or ethnic nationality) has dictated the terms of national membership.[24] Soon after the founding of independent Burma in 1948, the Union Citizenship Act of 1948 stipulated that anyone who was part Burmese by blood, inclusive of the recognized ethnicities, was granted citizenship. However, these ethnicities were restricted to the "'indigenous races of Burma' [which include] Arakanese, Burmese, Chin, Kachin,

Karen, Kayah, Mon or Shan race[s] and such racial group[s] as [have] settled in any of the territories included within the Union as their permanent
home from a period anterior to 1823 A.D."[25] This meant that descendants
of Chinese immigrants were defined as nonindigenous or alien residents
with questionable legal status.[26] A new constitution in 1974 followed by the
Burma Citizenship Law of 1982 further restricted citizenship; however, the
1948 and 1982 laws were never fully implemented.[27] But even if they had
been, they would not have challenged the Sino-Burmese understanding of
self, because their primary source for individual and group identity has been
the family and, by extension, the clan and native place, not legal belonging
in a state.

Since the colonial era, the governments of China and Burma/Myanmar
have failed to provide consistent and tangible support to the Sino-Burmese,
leaving them to fend for themselves. Many Sino-Burmese Rangoonites
remarked that neither the People's Republic of China nor the Republic of
China assisted them in their times of need, that they have had no *kosuan*
(literally "mountain to lean on," meaning a powerful defender).[28] Until the
last two decades of the Qing dynasty (1644–1911), overseas travel was officially forbidden, rendering any Chinese person caught outside of or returning to China a criminal. Accordingly, commercial ventures abroad were not
supported, and sojourners who succeeded were not recognized. However,
during the decline of the Qing, court mandarins began to see overseas Chinese merchants as sources for the financing and industrialization necessary to modernize China. They courted wealthy merchants throughout the
Nanyang region (or the Southern Ocean, now known as Southeast Asia)
and issued mandarin titles in exchange for money.[29] Revolutionaries such
as Sun Yat-sen also targeted overseas Chinese to bankroll their revolution,
and the governments that arose after the overthrow of the Qing dynasty—
the Nationalist Party and later the Chinese Communist Party—both sought
overseas Chinese support not only financially but also politically.[30] For
Sino-Burmese Rangoonites, China's export of political ideology created a
complex and contested national Chinese identity that took hold around the
1950s but dissipated after the 1967 anti-Chinese riots.

Given the regional particularism within Chinese society and the historical disappointments outlined above, overseas Chinese have exhibited a distrust of politics. As Anthony Reid has stated, "Chinese migrants had learned
from long experience to expect little of governments, and to rely much on
the networks of kinship, culture, and trust."[31] This defining characteristic of
the Sino-Burmese and other hyphenated Chinese explains not only how the
Sino-Burmese in Rangoon have been able to survive but also how some have

managed to thrive through place-based and kin-like relationships within their adopted home, Burma.

Similarly, the governments of Burma/Myanmar have alienated the Sino-Burmese. Although the first independent Parliamentary government (1948–58) was relatively liberal in its approach toward foreigners, Sino-Burmese have been regarded as essential outsiders whose nonindigenous status renders them suspect. On December 11, 1979, U Ne Win, then chairman of the ruling Socialist Party, said: "Because of their mixed parentage, the descendants of alien-Burmese unions, like full aliens, could not be fully trusted because of their alleged foreign contacts and possible external economic or political interests."[32] However, in a country where everyone, regardless of ethnicity, has suffered under government mismanagement and direct oppression, distrust of the state is pervasive. A well-known trope among the Burmese states, "There are five enemies: water, fire, kings, thieves and ungrateful heirs."[33] This concise statement clearly communicates the apprehension toward politics in Burmese culture, not only under the various troubled and unjust governments in modern Burma but also during the reigns of Burman kings. The rule of kings or government is compared to natural disasters that can render human society helpless. The state of Myanmar has yet to become a government of and by the people and therefore remains an inescapable, often overpowering force that must be tolerated.

Under these circumstances, the Sino-Burmese have lived in between states, cognizant of the insecurity in their unclear political status but also aware of the economic and social possibilities in this gray zone between two oppressive states. They have been forced to contend with the economic and political fluctuations within and between China and Burma but have maneuvered through these challenges by avoiding the state.

LOCATING MEANING IN PLACE

The in-between that the Sino-Burmese in Rangoon occupy is unstable and unbounded but not ungrounded.[34] As a nonindigenous population with no right to a territory under Burmese law, Sino-Burmese have had to make flexible places that are meaningful and sustainable without threatening the state through claims of permanent territorial boundaries. Their everyday actions have been *spatial practices* that incrementally "secrete a society's space" through a dialectical process that both propounds and presupposes space.[35] In this dialectical process Sino-Burmese Rangoonites have become a part of the city and the city has become a part of them. As Edward S. Casey explains, "Bodies and places are as inseparable as they are distinguishable. . . . Just as a place is animated by the lived bodies that are in it, a lived place animates these same bodies as they become implaced there."[36]

To understand the emplaced Sino-Burmese, place-based research is necessary to uncover the connections that are actually operative on the ground and the meaning in those connections. How do the Sino-Burmese in Rangoon understand themselves in relationship to their neighbors (Burmese, Indo-Burmese, and Yunnanese), to the city they live in, and to different types of Chinese outside of Rangoon (domestically and internationally)? Furthermore, how is this self-understanding lived out in everyday life and manifested in the built environment, in the place that is Rangoon?

Place, on the societal scale, is a locus of conflicting forces. It opens up a space for multiple forms of engagement that can be simultaneously alienating, welcoming, and open to new possibilities. As in a capital city such as Rangoon, place can be a dehumanizing power structure that seeks to order heterogeneous lifeworlds through abstract planning. This rational structure dominates its residents, constraining their actions within a predetermined street grid and frames their perceptions of that prescribed world. However, the people living within this space can gradually reshape their environment, appropriating it through small measures, to make a place for themselves even if that place is contradictory and never free of powerful limitations.[37] At the scale of the individual, Rangoon residents layer meaning into a street or a street corner through their daily travels and the inevitable stop for a chat with a friend over a cup of *lahpet-yei* (Burmese tea). In urban environments, place can also be seen as a landscape of modernity wherein the discord of displacement wrestles with the yearning for home and where destruction can be an unavoidable step toward creating a place for the future. "Place," as phrased by Timothy Oakes, "can be read as a geographical expression of modernity's paradox—that tension between progress and loss—a creative yet ambivalent space carved out somewhere between the oppressiveness of the new order and the imprisonments of tradition."[38]

For the Sino-Burmese and other residents in contemporary Rangoon, the increasingly dramatic changes since 1990 have heightened their awareness of the differences between modernity and tradition. Nearly every Rangoon resident I spoke with said, *Myanmapyi/Bamapyi-ga khit ma hmi bu* (Myanmar/Burma is not modern [literally "not meeting the times"]). As rows of colonial-era houses have been demolished to make space for high-rise condominiums, the contrast between the old and the new has become more glaring. Residents lament that Rangoon was once a major transportation hub, home of the first modern airport in Southeast Asia, and speak about the city and the country as a whole in terms of loss. For the educated elite in Rangoon, this loss is doubly poignant because they see themselves as residents of a once modern city that is now decades behind its more economically and technologically developed neighbors.

In 1852, after the Second Anglo-Burmese War, the English East India Company decided to transfer its center of operations from Moulmein to Rangoon and set about creating a colonial port that would promote trade and instigate a British world order. The form of the city was to become a physical manifestation of governmental rationality. Following the precedent set in Singapore, a grid of major and minor streets along with a hierarchy of land lots was superimposed onto the loosely organized town that was Rangoon. Before 1852, Rangoon was a sleepy harbor settled by farmers and seasonal traders, known for the annual Buddhist festival centered on the Shwedagon Pagoda. The rational Cartesian plan proposed by Dr. William Montgomerie and Lieutenant Alexander Fraser was based on nineteenth-century European concepts of city planning and was supposed to civilize its residents, both local and foreign.[39] The belief was that a properly designed city, with its functions clearly legible and its environs hygienic, would promote progress and prosperity, even in the most remote backwaters. However, the British modernized Rangoon only to the extent that was profitable for the empire and excluded nearly all of the local Burmese population in the process. Even after Rangoon was named the capital of British Burma in 1885, the city served its foreign population—British, European, Armenian, Indian, Chinese, and others—at the expense of the locals.

The modernization that was reinitiated around 1990 is still exclusive, but it held out the promise of a functional urban infrastructure that would raise the standard of living for all residents. Several automobile overpasses have been built, major streets repaved, and high-rise towers constructed, but as yet the benefit to Rangoonites remains debatable. The driving forces of modernity—rationality, standardization, and development—are in the process of destroying old neighborhoods to build tall buildings and relocating traditional open-air markets into enclosed warehouses. This accelerated pace of change is compelling Rangoonites to reshape their lives in order to meet the challenges of the times. However, the Cartesian grid of the city, coupled with colonial property laws that are still enforced, continues to regulate the patterns of everyday life and limits pursuits for a better future. Nonetheless, some residents have pushed at the edges of the colonial grid through actions such as transforming a street into a living room in order to celebrate Chinese New Year, while others have broken through the confines of colonial lot sizes to build shopping centers that proclaim modernity and encourage "modern" consumption patterns, incidentally creating new social and community spaces.

<h2>LOCATING THE SINO-BURMESE</h2>

In locating the Sino-Burmese, they must be positioned in both place and time. Multiple political, economic, and societal forces operating at local, national, and international scales have affected how people of Chinese descent have understood themselves. According to the parameters of assimilation, one could argue, early migrants who settled in Rangoon before the twentieth century had ceased to be Chinese through intermarriage and adoption of local customs. They might be labeled as *Tayout-kabya* (mixed/half Chinese).[40] However, the Sino-Burmese in Rangoon are still seen as somehow Chinese even if they do not speak any of the common local Chinese languages (Hokkien, Cantonese, Hakka, and standard Chinese [Mandarin]) and never participate in the celebration of Chinese holidays. More importantly, the Sino-Burmese themselves have adjusted their self-understanding and self-representation in response to the changing political and economic conditions. They have maintained and retrieved aspects of their Chinese heritage as circumstances have allowed, not as a matter of expedience but as a way of living.

Descendants of Chan Mah Phee, a Hokkien merchant who landed in Rangoon in 1872 and married a Mon woman, Daw Aye Myat, recognize their Chinese descent and still address one another by Hokkien familial terms such as *tua-go* (eldest brother) and *san-gaw* (third aunt on the father's side).[41] Similarly, some third- and fourth-generation Sino-Burmese who do not have Chinese names are rediscovering their Chinese heritage through rituals at the Hokkien Kuanyin Temple and through lion dancing. Some are even studying standard Chinese through the night and weekend schools organized by the Kuanyin Temple and native place associations. These practices became possible in post-1990 Myanmar because the military government decided to open its national borders to encourage economic development. Under the prior Socialist regime (1962–88), the Sino-Burmese suppressed their Chineseness because the 1967 anti-Chinese riots clearly marked them as foreigners who could be summarily driven out of the country.

Unfortunately, outside of Burma, the Sino-Burmese do not have another place to call home. Writings that conceive of Chinese overseas as a global diaspora lead to an erasure of local differences and an overemphasis on the power of the overseas Chinese network in Southeast Asia. This is particularly misrepresentative of Sino-Burmese Rangoonites, who were effectively cut off from overseas Chinese commerce during the Burmese Socialist period and remain on the periphery of transnational business despite their efforts to attract investment. As the owner of a pharmaceutical company said to me: "Other Chinese people don't know about us. If you don't have good connections, you can't do big business. In the beginning, I couldn't access many of the opportunities because the overseas Chinese who came to Rangoon didn't know who I was. So if I wanted to do import and export, I had to get a letter of credit, which is a lot of hassle in a country like Burma where the banking system is no good."[42]

Unlike the Chinese in Thailand, Malaysia, Indonesia, and the Philippines, the population in Burma has had restricted access to trade and remained small in number since the colonial era.[43] They never became the wealthy intermediaries for the British as they did in the Straits Settlements (Penang, Melaka, and Singapore, also known as British Malaya). Indian entrepreneurs, having endured over a hundred years of colonial rule, were much better versed in English ways and more able to capitalize on colonial commerce.[44] "The Indian middle class had the strongest hold on foreign [and domestic] trade of any group in Burma."[45] By the 1940s, Indian firms controlled about 50 percent of Burma's import trade and operated large shops and industries throughout the country.[46] Within Rangoon, they owned the largest share of property, surpassing the British, even though the British dominated in the most lucrative businesses such as oil and banking. Furthermore, Burma was incorporated into the empire as a province of British India and administered from Calcutta, tying the political and economic fate of Burma to India. The labor shortage and commercial opportunities in Burma brought to the country over one million Indians, who entered not as immigrants but as residents moving from one district to another.[47] By 1931, over half the population of Rangoon, the commercial and administrative capital, was Indian, and the lingua franca of the city was Hindi, not English or Burmese.[48] In dramatic contrast, for the 1,017,825 Indians in Burma in 1931, there were only 193,589 Chinese.[49]

Among Chinese migrants before World War II, most settled in Rangoon by default, not by choice. Having tried and failed in other ports such as Singapore, Melaka, Penang, and Moulmein, they trickled into the newest British port as skilled laborers and small-time traders. Unlike Manila, Bangkok, and the Straits Settlements, Rangoon was not known as a land of opportunity for the Chinese; rather, it was called the "port of last resort/hope" (*juetougang*).[50] For destitute peasants who sought to escape food scarcity and instability in southeastern China, there was little attraction to Burma, where Indians saturated the coolie labor market. For enterprising Chinese, the dominance of moguls from Bengal, Bombay, Gujarat, and other places left little room for the Chinese to compete. A few notable merchants such as Chan Mah Phee managed to succeed through perseverance, but most relied on associational connections with established Chinese communities in Penang and beyond to gain a foothold. But even those who succeeded commercially could not compete directly with the Indian businesspeople who dominated regional trade and shipping.[51] Instead, the Chinese focused on the local Burmese market, operating small shops and other businesses, one tier below large Indian enterprises.

Sino-Burmese who live in Rangoon today are generally the descendants of immigrants from Guangdong and Fujian Provinces who landed in the city after the British defeated the Konbaung dynasty in 1885. According to Sino-Burmese historian Chen Yi-Sein (known as U Yi Sein in Burmese), Cantonese shipbuilders and carpenters arrived first in the eighteenth century, followed by Hokkien traders (from Fujian) in the nineteenth century.[52] In the nineteenth century, Burmese people came to refer to the Cantonese as *let-to* or *eingyi-do* (short sleeve), because they were artisans who generally wore short-sleeved shirts and short pants, and to the Hokkien as *let-shei* or *eingyi-shei* (long sleeve), because they were merchants who usually wore long-sleeved shirts and trousers. Unlike *Tayout*, these exonyms point specifically to the above two cultural linguistic groups rather than to China or the Han in general. *Let-to* and *let-shei* are also place-specific, referring only to the Cantonese and Hokkien in Burma and perhaps more narrowly to those in Rangoon. Chen, a rare historian literate in Burmese, Chinese, and English, was preparing to publish a book on the history of the Sino-Burmese, but he passed away in 2005 without producing this work.[53] However, Chen stated in earlier writing that both the Cantonese and the Hokkien likely entered Burma through Rangoon and arrived via European settlements in the Strait of Malacca.[54]

Other Chinese entered Burma from the north. These were itinerant Yunnanese and Muslim traders on the centuries-old Tea Horse Road (Chamadao).[55] They traded and resided in the borderlands between China, Burma, and Thailand before nation-state boundaries were imposed through colonial rule and have continued to prioritize their local and flexible self-identification over national identities. Some such as the Akha (known as Hani in China) have identified themselves as Akha, Shan, and Chinese depending on their physical and social location at the moment of self-identification.[56] Others have referred to themselves as Kachin and Shanba Tayout depending on the circumstances. While eating noodles at a Kachin restaurant in Dagon Township, I was surprised when one of the shop owners offered a red envelope to a lion dance team. When I asked why the owner had done so, she said that she is "Shanba Tayout" from Upper Burma and that although they do not maintain much of Chinese tradition, they still celebrate Chinese New Year.[57] Up until that day, she had identified herself to her customers as Kachin. Indeed, there are two categories that contemporary Sino-Burmese seem unable to define with any certainty: Shanba and Shan Tayout. In general, they describe someone as Shanba if that person is from a remote or mountain area and label someone as Shan Tayout if that person is from Shan State. Victor Purcell, in his brief study on the Chinese in Burma, used the labels "Shan Chinese" and "Mountain Chinese," also without clear definitions.[58] These people appear to be Yunnanese, Panthay (Chinese Muslims), and/or Shan who had lived and traded in the borderlands or migrated into Burma from the north. Their particular history and interactions with Burma lie beyond the scope of this book, but it is important to note that they are never referred to as *let-shei*. This term, which could have been interpreted as a general reference for all Chinese traders regardless of native place, is instead specific to Chinese traders who arrived from the south by sea.

Much remains hidden in the history of the Sino-Burmese. Other than Sino-Burmese scholars such as Chen Yi-Sein and Taw Sein Ko, few have tried to piece together the fragmentary sources that might explain the past of the Hokkien, Cantonese, Hakka, Yunnanese, and Panthay in Burma. Contemporary scholars such as Chang Wen-Chin, Duan Ying, Fan Hongwei, Li Yi, and Daw Win have begun to examine both the colonial and postcolonial histories of these different populations, but the field of Sino-Burmese studies is in its infancy.[59] Therefore, this book focuses on the Hokkien as the majority population who have largely shaped what it means to be Sino-Burmese in Rangoon.[60] Many Sino-Burmese Rangoonites said that the Hokkien population dominated historically and, as evidence, pointed to large clan houses built by Hokkien people such as the Liong San Tong (Khoo and Chan Clan Hall) and the Kiu Liong Tong (Lim Clan Hall). They also commented that the most powerful families were Hokkien, the Yeoh and the Lim, and that everyone in Tayout Tan (Chinatown) spoke Hokkien (known as Minnan in standard Chinese) even if they were Hakka or Cantonese.[61]

In this partial retelling of the past that foregrounds contingency, the perspective of the Hokkien Sino-Burmese is given primacy despite the omissions and occasional inconsistencies in their narratives. As defined by the Sino-Burmese, they are early settlers whose forefathers arrived before British and Indian colonialists.

Because China and Burma are neighbors sharing a border, natu-
rally the Chinese are probably the earliest foreigners to settle in
Burma. But it is actually not possible to verify the year of entry.
Perhaps the Chinese traveling by land entered Burma earlier
than those entering by sea. Those entering Burma by land were
Yunnanese, whereas those entering by sea were Cantonese and
Hokkien.

   During the Yuan, Ming, and Qing dynasties (1280–1911), relations between China and Burma improved. Although there were
several wars, in truth, people despise war, and Chinese soldiers
built a huge water engineering project for the Burmese people,
the Thindwe Canal. In addition, some soldiers remained in
Burma and married local people. After several years, they naturally became *one of the ethnic nationalities in Burma*. Some say
that the city and palace of Mandalay are the products of Chinese
labor.[62]

In this representation of the past, the Sino-Burmese recognize the complex
history between Burma and China but emphasize that the Chinese were one
of the first foreign populations to settle in Burma. By proclaiming this first-
to-arrive status, they distinguish themselves from the British and Indian
populations, who have been portrayed respectively as abusive colonial
masters and colonial collaborators. In this rhetoric of naturalization, the
Chinese also try to write themselves into the history by participating in an
engineering project and inserting themselves into a foundational moment
in Burma's history, the creation of Mandalay. This claim of early, implicitly
precolonial arrival is a response to the Union Citizenship Act of 1948. By
defining indigenous people as those who settled in Burma before the First
Anglo-Burmese War in 1824, the independent government of Burma was
symbolically and literally repudiating colonial rule, excluding foreigners as
interlopers with no place in Burma. In actual practice, the 1948 act provided
other conditions for acquiring citizenship, making it possible for Chinese
people to continue living in Burma with few impediments. According to Fan
Hongwei, over 50 percent of the Chinese population qualified for citizenship in the 1950s.[63] A much more exclusive citizenship law was written in
1982, but even during the writing of the above passage in 1961, the authors
were aware of the danger of being perceived as nonindigenous migrants.
They portrayed themselves as "one of the minority nationalities in Burma"
despite the fact that the various governments of independent Burma have
categorized Chinese people as foreigners.

In narrating their history, the Sino-Burmese define themselves not only as early settlers but also as *pauk-hpaw* (kinsfolk) to the Burmese. The origins of the Burmese word *pauk-hpaw*, transliterated as *baobo* in standard Chinese, have yet to be identified, but every Burmese, regardless of ethnicity, knows that *pauk-hpaw* is reserved for Chinese people, applicable to no other immigrant population. In the standard and widely used Myanmar-English dictionary published by the Department of the Myanmar Language Commission, *pauk-hpaw* is defined as (1) "sibling" and (2) an "intimate and affectionate term conferred to the Chinese by the Myanmar people."[64] The veracity of the second statement could be contested given the complex and occasionally conflicted relationship between the different Chinese and indigenous populations in Burma. In addition to the 1967 anti-Chinese riots, there has been palpable and increasing anti-Chinese sentiment in Upper Burma. Mya Maung, a professor of finance and a Burmese dissident, described the growing population of Chinese in Mandalay as illegal aliens who threaten to Sinicize Burma's cultural heartland.[65] Although Mya Maung's rhetoric is alarmist, Mandalay-based authors have written a number of short stories that reveal the tension between the Chinese and the Burmans, Burma's dominant ethnicity. A shared theme among these stories is the ballooning Chinese wealth that is inflating property values in Mandalay and smothering Burmese tradition.[66]

The supposed intimacy between the Chinese and the Burmese is also questionable because the above definition is printed in a dictionary produced by the Ministry of Education, an official organ of the post-1988 military government, the State Law and Order Restoration Council also known as the State Peace and Development Council (SLORC/SPDC). Whereas the pre-1988 governments of Burma maintained a delicate neighborly relationship with the People's Republic of China out of fear of Chinese encroachment, the SLORC/SPDC needed to secure and consolidate China's support politically and economically. According to political scientist Maung Aung Myoe, the SLORC/SPDC did so through multiple means, including censoring print media discussions about China's growing influence and the increasing wealth of Chinese residents in Mandalay and Upper Burma.[67]

The nature of the relationship between the dominant Burman population and the Sino-Burmese has changed through time and varied according to place. The above analysis does not deny any affection between these two groups but emphasizes the diversity among the Tayout people and their different interactions with Burmans in Upper Burma versus Lower Burma. Resentment toward the broad category of Tayout in Upper Burma was fueled by the dramatic influx of Chinese-looking people into Mandalay from 1989 onward.[68] Burman residents of Mandalay identified these people as strangers and assumed that they were Chinese. According to Maung Aung Myoe, many of the Chinese-looking people were long-term residents in Burma or members of indigenous ethnic groups such as Kokang, Wa, and Akha.[69] Given the historic porosity of the China-Burma and Thailand-Burma borders and the long residence of groups such as the Akha, Lisu, and Kachin, Maung Aung Myoe's considered analysis is significant. However, the pervasive rumor was that the recent arrivals were Yunnanese who had illegally purchased national resident cards, which signify proof of Myanmar citizenship.[70]

The situation in Upper Burma demands further research and the question of the Yunnanese concerns Tayout everywhere, even in Lower Burma. There has been a noticeable increase in the number of so-called Yunnanese in Rangoon, and their business practices trouble the Hokkien Sino-Burmese. In discussing the different groups of Tayout in Burma, an elder in the Teng clan said: "Yunnanese dare to do anything. They are not afraid to break the law. Hokkien are more conservative. We do things by the rule."[71] This Teng clan member was referring to the drug trade undertaken by infamous Chinese from the border region, such as Law Sit Han (also known as Lo Hsing-han) and Khun Sa (also known as Zhang Qifu). Although the Yunnanese are also known as Tayout/Chinese, Hokkien Sino-Burmese do not see themselves as belonging to the same group. Similarly, for Rangoon residents in general, Yunnanese are the other, recent immigrants who are insensitive to the local culture. Several informants commented that unlike the local Tayout, "the Yunnanese don't even know how to speak Burmese."[72] Given these attitudes among the Sino-Burmese and Burmese populations, and the illicit connections between some Yunnanese and the top generals in the former military government, the Yunnanese population is only considered in this analysis if their actions or reputation directly influence the lives of the Hokkien Sino-Burmese.

For Hokkien Sino-Burmese, there is a sense of nostalgia regarding the term *pauk-hpaw* because it once expressed the close, kin-like relationship between themselves and their Burman neighbors. Since the 1950s, Burmese governments have consistently used *pauk-hpaw* as a tool of bilateral diplomacy with the People's Republic of China and the repeated rhetoric of *pauk-hpaw* relations has largely drained the word of its meaning.

> [In the past] being called *pauk-hpaw* was so full of feeling, intimate and natural, without a trace of bureaucratic speech.
>
> A while ago, I bumped into Ko Htunla at the market. We are about the same age. He is the son of U Bo U, my father's good

friend from our old village. Now, like me, his old age is showing. We went to a tea shop to chat about old times, but I have always felt that we do not have the deep friendship that U Bo U and my father shared.

U Bo U passed away twenty years ago, but he left a very deep impression on me. When U Bo U came to Rangoon, he always came to our house and always placed me affectionately on his lap, calling me *Pauk-hpaw le, pauk-hpaw le* (little *pauk-hpaw*).[73] Before we moved to the city, we lived in a remote village. I was born there, and U Bo U was our neighbor. Our houses shared a wall, and we were like one big family.

In the past few years, we seem to hear *pauk-hpaw* more often again, but this *pauk-hpaw* sounds like officialese, devoid of the natural feeling of intimacy that I felt in my youth.[74]

In this reminiscence posted on the Myanmar Chinese website, the author commented on the distance between himself and an old family friend who is Burman. This reflection could be interpreted not only as the reserve between two individuals but also as the growing distance between Chinese and Burmese people within Burma. Although Sino-Burmese and Burmese Rangoonites live peaceably side-by-side, there is sometimes a quiet sense of guardedness or alienation. Commenting on his essay in person, the Sino-Burmese author lamented that *pauk-hpaw* no longer retained the old feeling of closeness because the military government had overused the term in its diplomatic correspondence with China. He longed for a bygone era in which Sino-Burmese and Burmese were genuine friends and, in expressing this longing, indirectly attributed the loss of closeness to the actions of the SLORC/SPDC. Whether or not Sino-Burmese and Burmese lived like brothers before military rule is difficult to assess. Different people in different circumstances likely had different perceptions. However, the sense of distance and guardedness was probably applicable to everyone living under the junta. Many Rangoonites (Burman, Karen, Indo-Burmese, and Sino-Burmese) said that although material conditions were often worse during the Socialist period, everyone suffered and that suffering brought them together. In addition, the Socialist government may have failed to provide basic services for the populace, but it did not police the people to the extent that the SLORC/SPDC did. In this context, the loss expressed by the above author represents a general malaise. As a Sino-Burmese man, he not only suffered the pervasive oppression meted out by the SLORC/SPDC, but he had the additional burden of being somehow associated with China, the nation-state that openly supported the military government and thereby enabled (and, as many say, perpetuated) the junta's rule.

China, the nation-state, and its relationship with the SLORC/SPDC are seen as greedy and immoral. By association, large businesses that are obviously successful are often assumed to be Chinese-, Indian-, or military-owned. This common perception is grounded in reality because the most profitable industries (natural gas, rare minerals, and hydropower, to name a few) are monopolized by the top ranks of the military and by joint ventures or backroom deals between top generals and state-sponsored companies from China.[75] The problem for the Sino-Burmese lies in the inaccuracy of the terms *Chinese* and *Tayout* and the negative associations readily evoked when the topics of China and Chinese businesses appear in the news or in daily conversations. At least since 1988, the opaqueness of military-owned and military-affiliated businesses, coupled with extensive censorship, has left the people of Burma guessing about who owns what. Moreover, the conspicuous wealth of the generals and crony businessmen such as Tay Za (Burman) and Law Sit Han (Kokang) has elicited a pervasive sense of inequity in the populace, rendering all successful businesses suspect. Other than obvious crony corporations such as Tay Za's Htoo Group and Law Sit Han's Asia World, Rangoonites speculate that companies such as Shwe Taung and Pun Hlaing Golf Estate are Indian- or Chinese-owned and comment that no one could become rich without special connections with the generals.

With China looming over Burma, the challenge for Sino-Burmese people is to be seen as a local population of hybrid Chinese, as both Chinese and Burmese, and to inhibit the immediate association between themselves and China, the nation-state, without forsaking their cultural heritage. For Sino-Burmese in Rangoon, this less dichotomous identity is not an expedient self-representation but a lived reality, an ethos, built up through decades of dwelling in Rangoon. Like their fellow residents, they have endured the multiple trials of Burma's colonial and postcolonial history, at times benefiting from their transnational connections but rarely supported by the Chinese government, whether that was the Qing Empire, the Republic of China, or the People's Republic of China.

Throughout their long residence in Rangoon, the Sino-Burmese have managed a degree of mobility. Most were able to evacuate when the Japanese invaded in 1942 and then were able to return in 1945, at the end of World War II. Nationalization and the anti-Chinese riots of the 1960s drove some to China, Hong Kong, Taiwan, and farther afield, but those Sino-Burmese would not be able to return until the 1990s. Since the 1990s, some Sino-Burmese have been able to journey abroad or send their children overseas to study. However, their travels have been far from smooth. Citizenship, especially as represented in the form of the Myanmar passport, has been a necessary nuisance, not a foundation of rights. As told to me by an elderly Sino-Burmese woman, other governments and people think little of Burma/Myanmar. "I went to Fujian once. When I was going through immigration in Xiamen Airport, the officer yelled at me. He showed me no respect because I hold a Myanmar passport. We Chinese from Burma get no respect."[76] Fujian/Hokkien Province is the native place for all Hokkien people. According to Han tradition, one's ancestral native place is one's eternal home regardless of physical and temporal distance. Those who have sojourned overseas and the children of those sojourners are supposed to be able to return home as welcome members of the family.

China, their ancestral homeland, has at times recognized the Sino-Burmese as country cousins from an undeveloped country, at times courted them as potential supporters of competing regimes (Nationalist versus Communist China), and at times ignored them as unattractive partners in promoting a Greater China that theoretically encompasses all populations of Chinese around the world.[77] Unlike the high-flying transnational Chinese in Hong Kong who used foreign passports as insurance against Mainland Chinese rule, most Sino-Burmese in Rangoon have been unable to escape the political and economic constraints of Burma.[78] Like their fellow Rangoonites, they were effectively cut off from the world during the Socialist period and remained on the margins of overseas Chinese networks even after the military government liberalized the national economy in the 1990s.

MAPPING THE PATH FORWARD

In tracing the places of the Hokkien Sino-Burmese, national, regional, and historical contexts are essential for an emplaced understanding. The Sino-Burmese in Rangoon encountered significant turning points in 1852 (the founding of colonial Rangoon), 1911 (the founding of the Republic of China), 1948 (Burmese independence), 1949 (the founding of the People's Republic of China), 1963 (nationalization under the Socialist government), 1967 (the anti-Chinese riots), 1990 (the opening of the Myanmar economy), and 2011 (political reform). Rather than a chronological narrative that might suggest a sense of orderly progression, which is not present in the Sino-Burmese people's improvised response to their physical, social, and political environment, this book examines each of these historical events in the particular places where their lives were defined and actively redefined.

Fieldwork for this spatial ethnography was undertaken between 2006 and 2009 before President Thein Sein initiated political and economic reforms in 2011. The national shift toward a more democratic state caught all Burma watchers by surprise, even the most seasoned scholars. As this book focuses on the Sino-Burmese who have played a notable role in the economic growth of Myanmar since 1990 and who are generally seen as an entrepreneurial class with transnational connections, I provide some analysis regarding their position in post-2011 Myanmar in the concluding chapter. However, as already stated, the Sino-Burmese in Rangoon are not members of overseas Chinese conglomerates. They remain traders, not financiers or capitalists. Indeed, even with Myanmar as the next untapped market in the global neoliberal economy, they are unlikely to be invited to join the elite. Conglomerates from Thailand, Malaysia, Hong Kong, and other overseas Chinese power centers are more likely to establish connections with Yunnanese Chinese who have existing ties with the top generals.[79]

Some Hokkien Sino-Burmese have built successful businesses such as City Mart and Sein Gay Har shopping centers, but their financial clout pales in comparison to Asia World or the Max Myanmar Group, which are widely known as crony companies. Furthermore, while financially successful Hokkien families are more visible in Rangoon's urban landscape, there are many impoverished Hokkien Sino-Burmese whose Chinese descent has yet to provide them with monetary benefits. They live in rudimentary housing in Sanchaung and Kyimyindaing Townships or outside the urban core in South Okkalapa and North Okkalapa, where the Yayway Cemetery is located.[80]

For the Sino-Burmese, making money has been the main, if not the only, way to exercise some control over their lives. They are caught between two oppressive states and generally distrustful of politics, and money has provided the security to build better futures, even if the pursuit of money has required calculated risks in the gray and black markets. As much as possible, this spatial ethnography is told from their perspective as those whose well-being has and remains at stake.

CHAPTER ONE

HYBRID CHINESE PLACES IN A FORMER COLONIAL CAPITAL

ALTHOUGH Rangoon was designed by the British as a grand commercial and administrative center to inspire awe, the Rangoon of today evokes little of that grandeur in its damp decay. Navigating my way through the city, I focused much of my attention on the ground to avoid stepping into gaping holes or tipping up a loose paver and thereby falling into the fetid sewage that ran just below the sidewalks. In addition, there were usually street vendors who had spread their wares halfway across the sidewalk and shoppers who stopped or crouched down to examine potential purchases, further limiting the space for movement and requiring even more vigilance. In this maze of obstacles where I was rarely able to look up, the neoclassical, Victorian, Queen Anne, and eclectic Western-influenced architecture was rendered a faint, moldy, and only half-noticed backdrop. At eye level, the brick and masonry work of colonial architects and builders was mostly masked by rusty metal gratings, layers of flaking paint, and false modern facades that had been hastily attached to create new shop fronts and small eateries. The few structures that retained their original Italianate or Renaissance facades were well worn, with softened corners and surfaces stained with soot, mold, and betel nut spit. These streets and sidewalks that were once designed to facilitate the movement of goods and people in order to produce profits for the British Empire now seemed intent on thwarting everyday movement and commerce.

Despite these challenges, Rangoon residents traverse the streets of the former colonial capital with aplomb, apparently unperturbed by the broken sidewalks, tangled webs of electrical wires, and potholed roads. Under the willful neglect of the municipal and national governments, the degradation of Rangoon's urban environment is only one of a number of obstacles confronting their daily lives. Compared to infrastructural issues such as frequent power outages, inconsistent water supply, and clogged sewers, the aesthetics and functionality of Rangoon's streets are minor nuisances.[1] Everyone, regardless of ethnicity or descent, has learned to make do with the limited services provided by the government.

This making do is not the passive acceptance of the dominant power structure but the use of creative tactics to sustain life in the interstices. As defined by Michel de Certeau, *tactics* are the makeshift maneuvers of the disenfranchised, exercised within strong constraints, to create momentary opportunities. In contrast, *strategies* are the comprehensive plans and policies of the powerful that seek to define absolute order and regulate physical and social space.[2] In Rangoon, the unequal relations between the government (both colonial and postindependence) and its subjects are evident in the rational, rectilinear downtown core and the way contemporary Rangoonites inhabit and modify that rigid framework.

RANGOON: THE MODERN COLONIAL CAPITAL

Rangoon was explicitly designed as a capital city to serve the needs of the colonial state: to encourage trade and instigate order in a newly conquered territory. By the early part of the twentieth century, Rangoon was usually described by British officials as "the only large Indian city which has grown up on a scientific plan" and was rated as "a study of modern urban development."[3] However, through the eyes of the colonized, Rangoon was a doubly colonized city that was artificially implanted. Passing through the city in 1916, Indian Nobel laureate Rabindranath Tagore wrote: "This city has not grown like a tree from the soil of the country . . . [it] floats like foam on the tides of time. . . . I have seen Rangoon, but it is mere visual acquaintance, there is no recognition of Burma in this seeing . . . the city is an abstraction."[4] He lamented that colonial commerce had dominated and determined the character of the city and noted that Indians, as the overwhelming majority, had essentially colonized the Burmese once more, almost in lockstep with the British Raj. As a later conquest of the British Empire, Burma was ruled according to the precedents established in British India, and its capital, Rangoon, was laid out according to so-called scientific principles that had been formulated to solve the environmental and public health problems of nineteenth-century London. The Industrial Revolution, along with other factors, led to a dramatic increase in London's population, which overwhelmed the capacity of the city to serve its residents and resulted in unsanitary slums, air pollution, increased crime, and rampant spread of disease. To solve these problems, Victorian reformers and government officials applied the science of their day, advocating wide and straight streets that could become the tools "to rout dangerous vapours as well as dangerous criminals."[5] These principles were applied indiscriminately to Rangoon as British officials sought to create an international port befitting and benefiting the empire.

As with many colonial and capital cities such as Bombay, New Delhi, Singapore, and Brasilia, the conquered landscape was seen as a tabula rasa to be shaped at will in service of the ruling elite. The physical form of Rangoon would be molded not only to reshape the native environment that was seen as primitive and unsightly but also to transform the indigenous people into proper British subjects. The order of Rangoon society would be determined by the rational order of the city. Veiled behind the pragmatic goals of promoting trade in order to increase England's dominance in the world economy and rendering the city more easily ruled through scientific rationality, the design of Rangoon was to transpose British civility to a colonial outpost, to encapsulate all the colonial territories into the British world order.[6]

Rangoon and Lower Burma as a whole were seized by British forces during the Second Anglo-Burmese War, which started in April 1852. Even before the first commissioner, Colonel Arthur Purves Phayre, arrived in December 1852, the riverfront had been identified as the source of future growth and planned accordingly. The first plan proposed by Dr. William Montgomerie, the superintendent surgeon during the war, reveals that the implicit approach to city design was to surgically remove undesirable elements. This plan was later modified by Lieutenant Alexander Fraser and submitted to Colonel Phayre for consideration. Both officers advocated a rational gridiron plan composed of wide streets to avoid the congestion that was seen as the root cause of inefficient transportation and inadequate sanitation. They, along with their brethren in England, saw the need to discourage the spread of bodily disease and societal disease—illness and crime—through proper city planning. This grid plan mandated a wide strand along the river that would be 150 feet wide and another main road that ran from the wharf north to the Shwedagon Pagoda that would be 100 feet wide. Phayre agreed with this layout that emphasized the riverfront strand and wrote to his superior in Calcutta that the design of Rangoon would be "with reference to the lines of these two [main] roads, which will run at right angles. At intervals of about 750 feet there will be roads of 100 feet broad, running from the strand road north, and intersected by roads of similar width running east and west. The intervening spaces between these main roads will be divided by three roads of 30 feet width each."[7] Phayre also decided that wider streets would be named and narrower streets numbered, clearly marking the hierarchical spatial order imposed on the city (Map 1). This grid of major and minor streets was not unique to Rangoon, for Dr. Montgomerie, having previously served in Singapore, based his schematic design on the latter's form. As with Singapore, the strand in Rangoon was seen as the public face of the city that would properly impress travelers and "spur an aesthetic response which would reinforce the solidity and permanence of its European and commercial quarter."[8] This grand facade's audience was other Europeans arriving by sea, not the local inhabitants, just as the promotion of trade was intended to benefit European and other foreign merchants, not the local Burmese.

The network of regular streets not only made Rangoon visually more aesthetic, more in line with good taste; it also rendered the city more readily ruled, more legible within British conceptions of order and manageability.[9] Wide and straight streets provided few hideouts for potential criminals, and the clear lines of sight made it easier for police to capture *dacoits* (bandits). This rectilinear grid also produced standard lots that could be systematically sold and taxed or otherwise regulated. Soon after arriving in Rangoon, Phayre declared all land in and around Rangoon government property, citing the destruction of Rangoon immediately before the war in 1852 as just cause for assuming state ownership. On this conveniently blank slate, Fraser and Phayre planned 25 blocks that were subdivided into 172 lots per block, which resulted in 4,300 lots that would be available for sale. They assigned an alphabetical letter to each block, and the lots within these blocks were numbered, creating an ultimately orderly system through which to govern the city.[10] "Phayre and his officers would have absolute knowledge of the town's geography, conveniently reduced to numbered and lettered parcels which could be quickly located on a map and readily understood."[11] Furthermore, Phayre's ruling on property rights meant that the government would supervise and direct the distribution of all land. "Private citizens were only allowed on their new property by the grace of the government's law. Living and building in the town was being made constantly available to government scrutiny."[12]

In fact, these lots were divided into five different classes, with the lots closest to the river, along Strand Road, commanding the highest prices. The riverfront, the most valuable property, was reserved for official buildings that would present a majestic facade to Europeans arriving by sea. The next three classes of property were valued according to their distance from the river and proximity to existing wharves.[13] In addition, specific requirements were dictated for different classes. All buildings in the first-class lots near Strand Road and in the business district had to be made of brick, with

CHAPTER ONE

pukka or tiled roofs.[14] Regardless of class, all owners of all lots would have to build "a good and substantial bona fide dwelling house or warehouse" within one year of purchase or the property would be confiscated.[15] This latter regulation was initially implemented to prevent speculative buying but also to mandate a particular kind of physical and social environment. Only the wealthy could afford to both buy a lot and build on it according to regulation. Brick was not a common material in Rangoon and required significant skill and investment to produce. The local building materials of bamboo and thatch were deemed too flimsy and primitive, counterproductive toward creating an orderly society. Phayre and his officers thought that living in more substantial houses that had to be purchased or rented would teach the Burmese to value personal property and take proper measures, using doors and locks, to protect their possessions. They were frustrated with the high incidence of theft and placed blame on the Burmese, who were seen as incapable of comprehending the standards of prevention or protection. Rangoon's magistrate wrote, "Until their unsubstantial tenements of bamboo and leaves are replaced by houses capable of resisting the efforts of burglars and thieves, by the simple process of locking the door, we cannot expect that temptation will be less strong."[16] These stipulations were a means to maintain control over the real estate in Rangoon and to mold proper British subjects.

This spatial and legal structure instituted a new social order that would have been completely alien to the local residents. Before the British designated Rangoon as their center of operations in 1852, Rangoon was a loosely organized town that had grown organically around the swamps and hills in the area (Map 2). Historically, this town was ruled by the Mon people and was known as Lgung or Dagung, which became "Dagon" in Burmese. In 1755, Alaungpaya, a Burmese king, conquered the town and renamed it Rangoon, meaning "the end of strife" in the Burmese language, to mark the cessation of warfare between the Burmans and the Mon. Although Rangoon served as a port for the Konbaung dynasty (the last Burmese kingdom, 1742–1885), it never rose to prominence as a regional port because it was prone to flooding and because the trade of silk and spices bypassed Burma, going straight from Java and Melaka to Calcutta.[17] In addition, the town was never significantly built up, because ports and trade towns in Southeast Asia were generally conceived of as temporary places that expanded and contracted according to the vagaries of trade.[18] A stockade with a *wungyi* (minister) had been established next to Rangoon River, but there were few buildings and the irregularity of the sparsely populated town struck the British as sadly inadequate.[19]

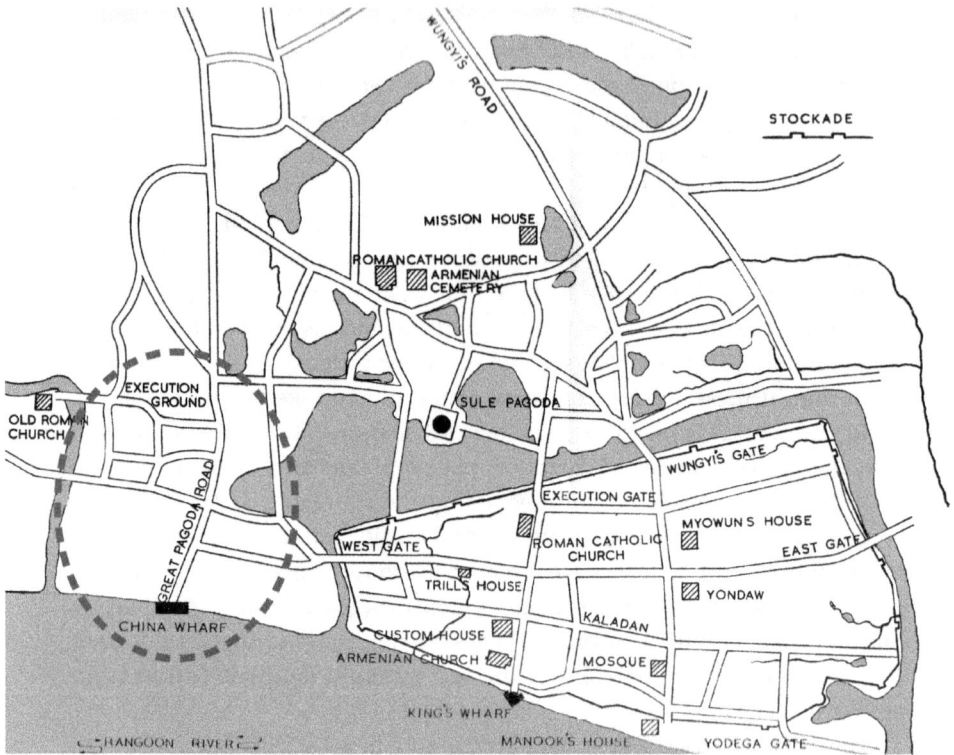

Map 2. Alaungpaya's town showing precolonial Chinese settlement.
Based on B. R. Pearn, *A History of Rangoon*.

For those who moved to British Rangoon from central Burma, the city would have been just as alienating. The only planned cities in precolonial Burma were sacral cities such as Mandalay, which was explicitly laid out in the form of a mandala to represent the cosmic order on earth and thereby proclaim the legitimacy of the Burman kings.[20] In contrast, the rectilinear grid of Rangoon was focused on the secular power of commerce and the authority derived from international capitalism and wealth. Almost everyone came from villages that were oriented toward the local Buddhist monastery, which was placed at the head of the village, and where the location of one's home was determined not by law or a foreign government but by the natural resources in the area.[21] In this context, the straight avenues and strictly delimited lots of Rangoon would have imposed an order unlike any the Burmese had experienced. Furthermore, Burmese people were mostly excluded from the planned city because the pricing of the lots, combined with the building requirements and taxation, rendered the properties pro-hibitively expensive. In theory, the parcels in the northernmost area near Montgomerie (now Bogyoke Aung San) Road were priced for commoners, but no Burmese could afford to buy lots within the planned city and instead squatted on unoccupied land.[22] Eventually, Phayre changed the regulations in 1854, making it possible for Burmese people to rent rather than buy land from the government, but in exchange they were further subjugated by the colonial system.

Similarly, the Chinese who migrated to Rangoon found themselves con-strained by the city's spatial, economic, and legal structure. However, unlike the more disadvantaged Burmese, Chinese migrants managed to insert themselves into the urban fabric through incremental tactics. Cantonese artisans had been traveling to and settling in Rangoon since the eighteenth century and were followed by Hokkien merchants in the nineteenth century, but their numbers remained small until the British established Rangoon as their center of operations. Like the Burmese and Indian migrants, Chinese sojourners moved to the modernizing port to take advantage of growing economic opportunities. Trade in commodities grew rapidly after the Brit-ish seized Rangoon and Lower Burma, but the sparsely populated country was unable to meet the increasing demand for labor. Therefore, migrants were welcomed from all quarters, leading to a surge in the population of Rangoon, from about 10,000 residents before 1852 to 134,176 in 1881 and 248,060 in 1901.[23]

CHINESE PLACES

In the precolonial Rangoon of 1795, China Wharf had already been estab-lished in an enclave west of the main town. This wharf was built by Chinese traders who sailed small junks carrying fifty tons or less and who enjoyed greater freedom to trade due to the small size of their vessels. Chinese junks could pass Monkey Point, the gateway into Rangoon, without paying tariffs, while larger British ships had to undergo official inspection.[24] Not much is known about these Chinese except that most migrated north from the Straits Settlements.[25] They settled in an area west of Rangoon, separated from the town by a marsh and Tatgale (also known as Tackley), a neigh-borhood where prostitutes and undesirables lived (Map 2).[26] Although con-temporary Sino-Burmese claim that their predecessors were friends of the Burmese, the location of their forefathers' residences in precolonial Rangoon would indicate otherwise. Unlike the Armenians, who had a church, and the Muslims, who had a mosque within the walled town, the Chinese lived in a separate quarter, on the other side of the river, with the prostitutes, near the execution ground.[27] This area around China Wharf would become the home district for Chinese people in Rangoon and was known as Tenglang-pou (Tang People Hill) by the Hokkien, Tongjangaai (Tang People Street) by the Cantonese, China Quarter by the British, and Tayout Tan (China Street or, as more commonly translated, Chinatown) by the Burmese.[28]

In colonial Rangoon, the number of Chinese increased from almost 3 percent of the population in 1881 to 4.5 percent in 1901 and 8.9 percent in 1911, but they were consistently overshadowed by the Indian population, which reached 56 percent in 1911.[29] Nonetheless, enterprising migrants, usually with connections in Penang, were able to establish themselves in niche markets, just as their predecessors had been able to compete with the British by sailing smaller ships.[30] Forming family- and clan-based businesses, they profited in the lucrative rice market by focusing on domestic rather than international trade because large-scale milling and exporting were dominated by Indian and British franchises. Similarly, they served as second-tier middlemen in the import of luxury goods, buying from Indian and British companies, to sell in the domestic market. Much more research must be done to uncover the history of the Chinese in colonial Burma, but the continued presence of prominent clan halls, religious structures, and other establishments indicates a past of financial and social success.

Although Strand Road was reserved for official European institutions, Chinese clans and businesses managed to secure lots in the western section, five blocks beyond the western edge of the city's administrative and banking center. This was the area near the old China Wharf, which was many blocks beyond the main wharves and therefore removed from the official maritime procession into the city. Nonetheless, this section of Strand between Shwedagon Pagoda Road (once China Street) and Lanmadaw (formerly Godwin) Street was still a part of Rangoon's riverfront facade, making the placement of Chinese buildings along this road significant. Although much more modest than the imposing colonial structures to the east, Sit Tek Tong (Fig. 1.1) and Tse Iong Tong (clan halls) and the Hokkien Kuanyin Temple, all with their upturned ornamented roofs, stand out along the shoreline, marking this area of the city as distinctly Chinese.

This neighborhood between Shwedagon Pagoda Road and Lanmadaw Street, from east to west, and Strand Road and Anawrata (formerly Canal) Street, from south to north, constitutes the historical and contemporary core of Tayout Tan. It was logical that Chinese migrants would continue to congregate around China Wharf, the site of earliest settlement, but the location of different ethnic neighborhoods reveals a critical spatial hierar-

1.1   Sit Tek Tong (clan hall) on Strand Road. Photograph by Lee Roberts, used by permission.

chy in the city (Map 3). The British placed themselves at the center of power, inscribed over the precolonial fortified port. Although it took about two decades to complete the land reclamation and engineering work in order to build on Rangoon's marshy soil, this area was eventually filled with imposing courthouses, banks, and international companies. Indians were in the next zone to the west, adjacent to Sule Pagoda, the heart of the planned city. Muslim Indian merchants dominated the real estate market. Many purchased lots near Sule Pagoda and built two large mosques along with numerous Indian businesses and residences, all centered on Shwebontha (formerly Mogul) Street. During the colonial era, the corner of Mogul and Merchant Streets served as the de facto stock exchange and the center for buying and selling rice, Burma's primary export.[31] The location of these primary and lucrative businesses within the Indian neighborhood illustrates their commercial dominance in Rangoon. The Chinese were farther to the

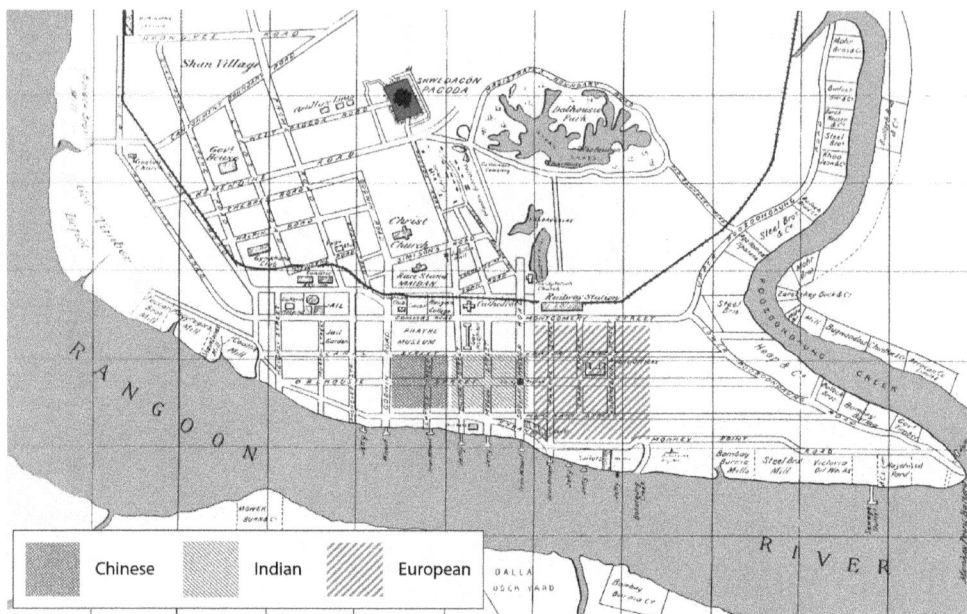

Map. 3. Spatial hierarchy in downtown Rangoon indicating spheres of influence for the European, Indian, and Chinese populations. Based on N. F. Singer, *Old Rangoon, City of the Shwedagon*, page 79.

west, one step removed from the colonial power center but still within the planned city. This placement reveals the status of the Chinese in Rangoon as people who did not have direct access to colonial trade but could indirectly gain entry, unlike the local Burmese.

In the six blocks known as the core of Tayout Tan, the Sit Tek Tong and Tse Iong Tong clan halls are but two of the numerous kinship- and place-based associations spread throughout the neighborhood. On some streets such as Sint Oh Dan or Bo Ywe, nearly every other row house is an association. For the hurried pedestrian and those who do not read Chinese characters, most of these halls blend into their context, with little to distinguish them besides a plaque with Chinese characters and sometimes the Burmese name for the association. Some associations have simply transliterated the entire name from the Hokkien pronunciation into Burmese such as Soo Tee Tong in Hokkien rendered as Suti Taung in Burmese (Fig. 1.2). Others, usually the more prominent associations, have transliterated a part of the name and appended in Burmese *boudhabadha hpayakyaung*, meaning "Buddhist temple." While these associations can be conceived of as religious because

1.2　Soo Tee Tong (clan hall), with its name in Hanzi, Burmese, and English. Photograph by the author.

ancestors are worshipped like gods and native places are always intimately bound with particular deities, the use of *Buddhist temple* in association names is a survival tactic the Sino-Burmese employ. Even secret societies such as Kien Tek and Ho Sing label themselves as Buddhist temples. After the 1967 anti-Chinese riots, the Chinese in Rangoon emphasized their worship of the Buddha and framed all associational activity around Buddhism to make themselves more Burmese, that is, more like the dominant Burman Buddhist majority.

Among Chinese societies within and outside of China, kinship (real and fictive) and native place are entwined sources for self-identification and communal belonging. As leading Chinese anthropologist Fei Xiaotong explains, traditional Chinese society was a peasant society formed through a flexible set of relationships that grew out of their ties to the land.[32] Most were farming families who remained rooted to the land of their forefathers and came to see their place of birth as integral to their identity. As families grew they formed clans, and these clans often formed villages in which the village was synonymous with the clan. However, the definition of kinship was and remains flexible. Fei likens these relationships to the ripples that appear on the surface of a lake when a rock is thrown in: "The most important relationship—kinship—is similar to the concentric circles formed when a stone is thrown into a lake. . . . [These networks] can be extended to embrace countless numbers of people—in the past, present, and future. The same meaning is implied in our saying 'Everyone has a cousin three thousand miles away,' with three thousand miles indicating the vastness of kinship networks."[33] In principle, Han culture defines kinship by patrilineal descent, and a clan would include only those who share the same surname. However, actual practice allowed various accommodations: "The aura of patrilineal orthodoxy (communal ritual centers and genealogies extending back many centuries to a notional common ancestor) could cover aggregations of non-kin to achieve a common interest. . . . In venues abroad, where intact homeland lineages were rare, willingness to form pseudo-kinship associations under a common surname was a potent adaptation for community solidarity and survival."[34] This flexible definition of family makes it possible for men with two different surnames, Chua and Ko, to belong to the same Tse Iong Tong Clan Association in Rangoon. Clan elders have generally expended some effort to explain how different surnames stem from one original ancestor, but during the colonial era, when most of these associations were established, membership rarely required historical verification.[35] The population of Chinese migrants in Rangoon remained small in number, as already noted, and male dominated because the Qin dynasty government severely restricted the emigration of women. This encouraged an inclusive approach in the clan associations, and elders saw themselves as fathers, responsible for the well-being of the young Hokkien and Cantonese men arriving in Rangoon.

Furthermore, these clan associations were often tied to particular native places. Kiu Liong Tong on Lanmadaw Street is a Lim clan hall but only for the Lims from Ankue Township in Fujian. This correlation between ancestry and place is not surprising given the ties to the land stated by Fei. "The significance of place in the Chinese cultural imagination is an important transhistorical force of geographical orientation and individual and group identity formation."[36] Within imperial China, people who sojourned from their native places to cities such as Shanghai established native place associations to help fellow villagers succeed in unfamiliar and competitive environments.[37] Outside of China, overseas populations established native place associations that were generally more inclusive, defining everyone from the same province such as Fujian, rather than from just one town, as belonging to the same place-based family. The exact requirements for membership in an association depended more on the local context than on any prescribed rules transposed from China. A critical mass had to be achieved before an organization could be formed, and finer-grained divisions into town-based associations would not be desirable unless the numbers grew too large to be manageable or conflict arose between different groups within an organization.[38] Nonetheless, native place, understood as the birthplace of one's ancestors, has remained a defining marker for Chinese families, even for the successive generations who were born outside of China. These places, such as Ankue Township for those who belong to Kiu Liong Tong, might only be known as a name or a location on a map, but even young Sino-Burmese who speak no Chinese languages are able to state that their family originated from Fujian or Guangdong.[39]

In Rangoon, clan/surname association halls became second homes for the local Chinese and recreated the extended families that sojourning young men left behind in Fujian and Guangzhou, as evidenced in the following recollection.

> When I was young, in the 1960s and 1970s, we always went to our clan association. My parents went very often for all sorts of matters. The elder of our clan solved our problems for us. We children went whenever we wanted. We were always there for Chinese New Year and on other special holidays when there were large banquets for everyone to enjoy. The hall was just a few blocks away from our house, so it was a part of our daily life. But I don't go anymore, and I don't take my children. The hall is still there, but it is very quiet.[40]

By 2006, when I first arrived in Rangoon, the doors of these association halls were closed. When I knocked on their doors, no one answered. Eventually, I learned that I could schedule visits through the executive committees of these associations but that the halls remained empty except for the elderly caretakers who lived in or near the halls. However, these buildings, usually repurposed three-story row houses, are still dutifully maintained by their executive committees and serve as historical sources of belonging. Representatives from twenty-four clan associations make up the governing body of Kheng Hock Keong (the Hokkien Kuanyin Temple), and elderly Chinese with no family support can approach associations based on their surnames to access benefits reserved for the old and poor.

In addition to these surname- and place-based associations, voluntary brotherhoods, sometimes referred to as secret societies, were also established in Rangoon in the colonial era. In particular, Kien Tek Tsonghue and Ho Sing Gongsi are still active and well known in contemporary Rangoon. Kien Tek stands prominently on Latha Street and draws attention to itself through its architecture and activities. Like the clan associations mentioned above, a prominent Chinese temple with an elaborate roof stands on top of the three-story building. Unlike the other associations, it is three bays wide, occupying the space of three row houses rather than the one or two of other associations (Fig. 1.3). The brotherhood demands an initiation and blood oath to enter the fraternity, and therefore the brothers were not willing to divulge their history to an outsider. However, many middle-aged and older men in Tayout Tan say that it was once an extremely powerful organization with a formidable martial force and has roots in Penang. Chen Yi-Sein traces Kien Tek's history back to 1868, when it was established as a branch of the Malaya Kien Tek Association.[41] Both Chen and the older men in Tayout Tan recall pitched battles between Latha and Twenty-Fourth Streets where Kien Tek brothers fought Ho Sing brothers to protect their allied businesses and territories.

Today music rather than violence is the most obvious action originating from Kien Tek. Every Sunday afternoon, amplified live music pours out of its third-story windows and fills the lower block of Latha Street. For about two hours, different singers belt out pop songs in standard Chinese and Burmese backed up by a small band playing keyboard, guitar, and drums. When I asked the first-floor attendant about the singing, I was directed to the music director, who allowed me to join their weekly practice. In addition to the exclusive brotherhood activities conducted by Kien Tek, the association supports a band that performs at Chinese weddings.[42]

Similarly, Ho Sing Brotherhood, Kien Tek's historical nemesis, no longer engages in violence even though their brothers proudly talk about

1.3   Kien Tek Association on Latha Street. Photograph by Lee Roberts, used by permission.

their martial origins, pointing to the portrait of Shaolin masters hung on a wall of their association. Ho Sing was a branch of the transnational Hong-men Hui / Tiandi Hui that was established by Ming loyalists who sought to overthrow the Manchu rulers of the Qing dynasty.[43] Two elders in the fraternity said that Ho Sing's anti-Qing sentiments led the brotherhood to support the republican revolution because Sun Yat-sen also sought to drive out the Manchu rulers. In contrast, Kien Tek was a part of the Save the Emperor Society network that sought to reform the state while keeping the Qing emperor in power. The two brotherhoods continue to see each other as competitors but have reached an agreement to respect each other. When the leader of Ho Sing passed away in 2008, the Kien Tek

1.4   Plaques of ancestors in Ningyang Huiguan, the oldest native place
       association in Rangoon. Photograph by the author.

Association sent a team of representatives and a traditional funeral wreath to honor Ho Sing Gongsi.[44]

All of the above association halls, regardless of their organizing principle, house an ancestor/deity altar in the most sacred place in the building, the uppermost level or the roof. These ritual spaces are reserved for members, but by participating in the singing rehearsals at Kien Tek, I was allowed to glance in at the sacred space. The altar on the roof of Kien Tek was a large, elaborately carved, multilayered structure painted in red and gold. There were the usual plaques with names of past leaders and a few deities, but it seemed inappropriate to ask detailed questions. In clan/surname associations, the altars are filled with plaques engraved with the names of deceased ancestors, as seen in Ningyang Huiguan, a largely abandoned surname association (Fig. 1.4). In the place-based associations, saints such as Tsing-tsui-tso-su and Matso who share a native place with their worshippers are venerated as protectors of all people from that ancestral place, regardless of location of residence.

Although Sino-Burmese Rangoonites were essentially cut off from China for two and a half decades, all of these Chinese places bear a strong resemblance to ancestral halls, native place associations, and secret societies within China. Between 1962 and 1978, the Socialist government of Burma and the Cultural Revolution in China made it extremely difficult for the Sino-Burmese in Rangoon to reconnect with their native places in Fujian and Guangzhou.[45] After the Revolutionary Council took control of Burma in 1962 and established the Burma Socialist Program Party (BSPP), it severed most connections with other nation-states, rejected international aid, and nationalized all large-scale businesses and industries, effectively closing Burma's borders. In addition, the BSPP sought to drive out all colonial and foreign influences, targeting local Indian and Chinese residents as alien populations with questionable allegiance to Burma. Concurrently, the violence and chaos of the Cultural Revolution (1966–76) made China an undesirable destination, even for those in Burma who saw themselves as exclusively Chinese. In this national and transnational context, the Sino-Burmese maintained Hokkien and Cantonese traditions to the extent possible, referring to the teaching passed down by their elders to live as people of Chinese descent in Rangoon. Indeed, contemporary Sino-Burmese state that their surname and native place associations were central to their lives during the Socialist period. Those buildings offered them a place in which to be Chinese when public display of Chineseness was not safe. Even today, when native place associations no longer serve as shelters for Chinese cultural expression, Sino-Burmese still maintain a sense of connection to these association halls and, through them, a connection to their ancestral native places.

COLONIAL CHINESE PLACES

In comparison, the eclectic Chinese mansions built during the colonial era have experienced swift and ongoing decline since the British left Burma in 1948. Although once opulent estates such as Chin Tsong Palace still stand out in Rangoon's urban landscape, they are empty relics that hold little meaning for contemporary Sino-Burmese.

Connections with Penang were often necessary for Chinese migrants to succeed in Rangoon. Those who became wealthy usually had direct business or family relations with Peranakan merchants in the Straits Settlements. Peranakan, also known as Baba-Nyonya (*Baba* for the men, *Nyonya* for the women), are descendants of Han immigrants who settled in Penang, Melaka, and Singapore from the fifteenth century onward.[46] These settlers married local women and formed hybrid families that integrated Malay culture with Chinese practices. Many served as *kapitans* (headmen) for the British and became the local elite. Their hybrid way of life and amalgamated architecture became signs of prestige that were emulated by the Chinese in Moulmein and Rangoon.

This legacy is still evident in contemporary Rangoon. A few examples are located on the upper block of Latha Street, the prime real estate in Tayout Tan. One of these residences, a three-bay-wide mansion with a symmetrical facade composed of arches framing French doors and Chinese fan-shaped vents, stands as a prime example of Pashu/Peranakan architecture (Fig. 1.5).[47] The combination of European and Chinese architectural elements suggests that this residence followed the Straits Eclectic shophouse style of the Baba-Nyonya and was likely built after Rangoon became the third-largest port in the British Empire in 1910.[48] During my fieldwork, the tenants in the house's middle unit knew neither the history of the building nor the owners, past or present. They said they were renting from a second party and guessed that the residence was *pashu,* even though they could not identify how this building differed from others in Tayout Tan. *Pashu* is the Burmese word for *Malay* or *Malayan* but among the Sino-Burmese in Rangoon often designates the Chinese from that region, or the Peranakan.

Peranakan practices were transferred to Rangoon through close connections between the Chinese in Burma and the Straits Settlements.[49] Indeed, wealthy Chinese in Lower Burma looked to Penang for ways of maintaining Hokkien traditions when travel back to Fujian was impractical or impossible. As evident in Chinese family portraits from turn-of-the-century Rangoon, successful Chinese merchants took Nyonya brides, because daughters of Straits Chinese were considered the best matches if a wife could not be summoned from Fujian.[50] Nyonya women are easily identifiable in these photographs because of the hairstyle and dress they wear—a high chignon wrapped in a crown of jewels and *kebayas* (fine embroidered blouses with a deep V-neck and swallowtail bodice), batik sarongs, and delicate beaded slippers. When successful Hokkien merchants in Rangoon needed brides for their sons, they sought out wealthy Baba-Nyonya families in Penang for suitable candidates.[51] As a poor young man, Chan Mah Phee had married a Mon woman, but once he established himself, he ran his household as a Chinese patriarch, demanding that all of his children and grandchildren speak Hokkien and that all Chinese holidays be strictly observed according to tradition. Even four generations after the his passing, his progeny identify themselves as Sino-Burmese and faithfully celebrate Chinese New Year with an appropriately set altar and all the requisite dishes of pork, chicken, and fish.[52]

1.5   Pashu/Peranakan house on Latha Street. Photograph by Lee Roberts, used by permission.

Baba-Nyonya culture was emulated by the Chinese in Rangoon not only because it provided a way to maintain their shared Hokkien heritage but also because it represented modernity in British Burma. Migrants from southeastern China were more established in Penang, Melaka, and Singapore because of their earlier arrival and larger numbers. Unlike in Rangoon, the local Chinese were the dominant foreign population and enjoyed direct access to colonial trade. In addition, the Straits Settlements, as a British Crown colony, were directly administered by the Colonial Office in London instead of the Indian government in Calcutta. This meant that Straits Chinese dealt more directly with the British government and quickly learned to champion their causes by adopting British conduct.[53] The Peranakan led the way in learning English, courting British officials, buying European luxury goods, and building eclectic villas that blended Palladian forms with traditional Chinese architecture. Numerous hybrid villas were built by successful Peranakan in Penang and Melaka, but only one hybrid estate was constructed in Rangoon.[54]

Chin Tsong Palace, named after rubber baron Lim Chin Tsong, was built between 1915 and 1919 in the gardens area north of Shwedagon Pagoda. Lim, the son of an immigrant from southern Fujian, owned an expansive business that included, among other industries, a rubber plantation, a sugar refinery, peanut oil production, minerals prospecting, and a fleet of steamships that ferried passengers and freight between southeastern China, the Straits Settlements, and Rangoon. Soon after he inherited the business from his father in 1888, he became a local agent for the Burmah Oil Company and grew his franchise exponentially. By 1910, he was recognized as the most prominent Chinese merchant in Rangoon and was featured in the volume *Twentieth Century Impressions of Burma*. However, Lim's success was meteoric, with the brilliance of his ascendance matched by the speed of his fall. He died in 1923 with much mystery surrounding his demise. Some say he committed suicide after he went bankrupt or was caught counterfeiting money. Whatever the actual circumstances, Lim and his family disappeared from Rangoon, and no Sino-Burmese in contemporary Rangoon seems to know anything about him but the few facts and speculations mentioned above.[55]

In stark contrast, Lim's Chinese-inspired octagonal tower perched on top of the symmetrical Palladian villa is known by everyone in Rangoon. Although the building stands in a state of disrepair and its once manicured grounds are overgrown with weeds, its striking blend of European and Chinese architecture draws the eye of every passerby (Fig. 1.6). It is now the State Fine Arts School. During my fieldwork, only students and faculty of the State Fine Arts School were officially allowed into the compound, but I was able to see the interior through the kindness of a painting instructor. The neoclassical vestibule and the grand staircase immediately evoke a sense of European grandeur, while the numerous Chinese details painted in gold and red express the opulence of Chinese aristocrats. Throughout the villa, *dougongs* (Chinese structural brackets) and carved screen walls were applied as decorative motifs, much like the interiors of Straits style villas in Penang and Melaka.[56] This amalgamated architecture reveals how these Chinese overseas along the Andaman Sea and Strait of Malacca endeavored to maintain their Hokkien traditions while pursuing modernity as practiced and represented by the British Empire.

1.6   Chin Tsong Palace on Kabaei Pagoda Road. Photograph by the author.

In the context of Rangoon, this immersion into the colonial world became a liability after the founding of independent Burma on January 4, 1948. Fueled by Burman nationalism, the new government, the Anti-Fascist People's Freedom League (AFPFL), sought to build a Burma for the Burmese by driving out foreign, in particular British colonial, influences. The various people residing within the nation-state boundaries of Burma were officially defined as indigenous races or foreigners, with differing access to citizenship. Anyone who was part Burmese by blood, inclusive of the officially recognized ethnicities, was granted citizenship. In addition, anyone born within the national boundaries to parents who were also born within these territories and whose ancestors had resided permanently within Burma for at least two generations was eligible for citizenship. Lastly, anyone born in British Burma who had lived in Burma for at least eight years before independence and wanted to remain in Burma permanently could apply for citizenship.[57] Given these stipulations, most of the wealthy Chinese discussed above were eligible for Burmese citizenship because their families had lived in Burma for two or more generations, and many of the men, like Chan, had married local (usually Mon) women.[58] According to the 1931 census, 56 percent of the Chinese population was born in Burma (89,600 out of 193,600), and, in 1953, the Chinese embassy estimated that 39 percent of the Chinese population was of mixed Chinese and Burmese blood and that 33 percent were born in Burma.[59] In this moderately antiforeign environment, the social life of urban hybrid Chinese changed incrementally, until General Ne Win led a coup to overthrow the AFPFL in 1962 and instigated an aggressive nationalization campaign.[60]

In comparison, their economic life was more immediately restricted because the larger-scale trade opportunities made available through the British Empire were curtailed after 1948. The economic situation between 1948 and 1962 was extremely complex, and the withdrawal of the British drained the financial support necessary for maintaining lavish mansions. Although Chinese entrepreneurs were initially able to rebuild or establish businesses at many scales and even profit from the postwar chaos, standardized operation implemented through the British pursuit of ultimate order was no longer available to facilitate transnational trade. Furthermore, the opulent European-influenced architecture of these buildings likely stood out as a symbol of the ill-gained wealth of colonial collaborators.

In contemporary Rangoon, Lim Chin Tsong and his palace seem emblematic of the ambivalence surrounding Chinese connections with the British and the riches accrued through those colonial relationships. Unlike Chan Mah Phee, who is often named as an exemplar for all Sino-Burmese and immortalized in Sino-Burmese publications, Lim is mentioned only briefly in two Chinese-language publications.[61] When I inquired about the man and his estate, everyone said that he was one of the very few people who worked with the Burmah Oil Company and that his life ended in ignominy. They noted that he was extremely wealthy but did not heap praise upon him as they did with Chan. Chan is still remembered as a self-made man who gave generously to both Chinese and Burmese organizations and whose public legacy is the Women's Hospital in Ahlone Township. Lim, however, is remembered as a man who overstepped his station. In explaining his demise, a prominent Sino-Burmese man said: "Lim Chin Tsong never should have built an octagonal tower. The octagon is a sacred and powerful symbol as seen in the *bagua* [octogram], and no average person should use that form in his house. He went bankrupt because he didn't know his place."[62]

Peranakan mansions and Lim's palace, like Grindlays Bank and other imposing imperial institutions, stand today as hollow monuments paying tribute to a bygone and extremely unequal era. The Chinese in British Burma were not the favored middlemen, but they were third in line after Indian merchants and many steps ahead of the local Burmese who were unable to compete in the international port city. The legacy of that inequality is still evident in contemporary Rangoon society despite the many twists and turns in the city's economic and social history. These colonial Chinese places figure dimly in the lives of contemporary Sino-Burmese because most people have no connection to those elite families.[63] The Sino-Burmese who live in Tayout Tan today are mostly the children of working- and middle-class Chinese. Even those who are wealthy come from families that started making money after 1948, when new business opportunities were made available through the absence of Indian merchants who were unable to return to Burma or were driven out after World War II. These colonial Chinese spaces, by being exclusive, have little or no meaning in contemporary Sino-Burmese society.

HYBRID CHINESE PLACES

In direct contrast, public spaces such as the section of Mahabandula Road between Latha and Lanmadaw Streets, known as Guangdong Dadao (usually translated as "Canton Road") to the local Sino-Burmese, remain vibrant with activity and meaning. All Sino-Burmese and other Burmese residents of Rangoon know this area as the core of Tayout Tan and as one of the best night markets in town. Many taxi drivers told me that this stretch of Mahabandula was the place to go for dinner or an evening snack because the food was good, plentiful, and cheap. In the words of one Indo-Burmese taxi driver: "You don't know about the night market in Tayout Tan? You have to go over there. Every night, half of Mahabandula Road is blocked off and that entire half is filled with vendors selling great food. You can get anything there: fried rice, Shan noodles, fritters, Burmese salads, and *lahpet-yei* [Burmese tea]. The prices are really cheap. When I drive the night shift, I take my break there."[64] Many other taxi drivers described these blocks on Mahabandula in similar terms. When I asked if there were other night markets in town, most said one could go to Dagon Center but that the food there was more expensive.

Locals from Tayout Tan and other neighborhoods crowd into this market every night because it is one of the few places that offer affordable nighttime entertainment. For those who could walk to this section of Mahabandula, this broad avenue serves as a space of leisure. In the tropical monsoon climate of Lower Burma, most people reserve their leisure activities for the cooler hours around sunrise and after sunset. In the dense living quarters of central Rangoon, residents spill out onto the streets in the evenings to escape their overheated buildings and enjoy the cool night air. A common scene on the smaller, thirty-foot-wide numbered thoroughfares such as Seventeenth, Eighteenth, and Nineteenth Streets is local residents lounging in front of their apartments on plastic chairs and bamboo recliners to chat with their neighbors or listen to the radio. After sitting a while, many people walk down streets that feed into the one hundred–foot-wide Guangdong Dadao to stroll along the six-lane boulevard. On any given night, I saw families with their children already in their pajamas ambling along, window-shopping or buying evening snacks. Although there have been periods during which governmental regulations or martial law dampened the night market's activities, contemporary Sino-Burmese say that vendors and nighttime revelers have always been present along this stretch of Guangdong Dadao.

Around the end of the nineteenth century, the Chinese in Rangoon started referring to Dalhousie Road as Guangdong Dadao because Cantonese shops lined the twelve-plus blocks from Mogul Street to Godwin Road. At least eighty Cantonese businesses sold Chinese goods such as herbal medicine, silk, Chinese food, and other sundries as well as European luxuries such as watches, suits, leather shoes, cameras, and whiskey. According to Chen Yi-Sein, these Cantonese businesses thrived until the Japanese invaded in 1942 but never recovered after World War II.[65] Although most of the Cantonese merchants did not return to reopen their shops, the name Guangdong Dadao is still widely used in Tayout Tan.

However, in contemporary Rangoon, Guangdong Dadao is much shorter, six blocks instead of the original twelve, because commerce in Burma underwent a precipitous decline after 1962. Today the street is lined with businesses selling Chinese and foreign merchandise, but Asian products have replaced British luxury goods. Next to the shop selling joss paper and incense are supermarkets selling Singaporean and Thai food and clothing stores selling Giordano and other popular Asian brands. This stretch of Mahabandula Road continues to be alive with activity because it is practical and inclusive. The street is centered on commerce and provides services that residents of Rangoon, regardless of ethnicity, find useful and affordable. There are other places in Rangoon such as the Dagon Center, Sein Gay Har, or Junction Square that sell similar wares and food, but all of them are considerably more expensive.

The vendors who sell their food and products along Guangdong Dadao are mostly working-class people of Sino-Burmese and other heritage, looking for ways to make a living. They go through the daily hassle of transporting and setting up their stalls because they have been unable to find a job or other sources of income. A young Cantonese Sino-Burmese man I met sold cold drinks at the southwest corner of Eighteenth and Mahabandula. When he was not tending his stall, which was fairly frequently, that corner was just a pile of tattered boxes, looking more like rubbish than a small business. He was not making a profit, so he was not motivated to set up anything more substantial. Similarly, when I talked with a middle-aged woman selling Shan noodles and *tohu-nwe* (warm, soft tofu), she said that she was not making a profit but there was nothing else she could do. She had moved from the Palaung area in northern Shan State to be with her grown children, but all of them were struggling financially in Rangoon. I spoke with her in a combination of standard Chinese and Burmese and found out that she was of Tayout, Wa, Palaung, and Kokang descent. Whether her situation and background are typical of the vendors on Guangdong Dadao is difficult to determine without reliable statistics. However, her struggle as a commoner with no special connections is endemic in Burma and likely widespread in Tayout Tan. The lowbrow character of the Mahabandula night market and much of Tayout Tan challenges the common perception that the Sino-Burmese have special access and are generally rich. This market is lively because it draws people from all over Rangoon who want an affordable meal and some form of leisure.

Similarly, the upper block of Nineteenth Street has become a popular destination for Rangoonites looking for a night out. It has been featured in paintings by local artists and is generally known as the place for cheap beers and tasty barbecued food. Shortly after sundown, this block becomes a continuous open-air bar and restaurant, with roadside eateries lining both sides. Young men who live in Tayout Tan told me they have been eating their dinners on this street for years, and older men said it was becoming too crowded. People seemed to come from all parts of Rangoon, even distant suburbs, to hang out on Nineteenth Street. U Moat Thone, an artist who lives an hour northeast of downtown Rangoon, said he frequents Nineteenth Street because it is one of the few places in Rangoon with nightlife and because it is a great spot for a beer. He also appreciates the raw aesthetics of the block and has produced five watercolor paintings highlighting the festive quality of the street.

Because most residents in Rangoon are still poor, Nineteenth Street and the Mahabandula night market offer a rare source of leisure, a temporary escape from the daily nuisance and surveillance in their lives. These two nightspots are a part of Tayout Tan, the Chinese neighborhood, but are open to everyone in Rangoon, regardless of ethnicity or descent. In fact, they have become public spaces within which Rangoonites could mingle with little fear of unintended consequences. Commercial consumption of this sort fell neatly into the Myanmar government's agenda to promote economic growth and was therefore unproblematic. These public spaces have not achieved the status of public realm wherein individuals act in concert to achieve shared political goals.[66] However, they have begun to create an opening in which different identities can be witnessed and negotiated in public. Some might criticize this public space for its service to the bourgeois objectives of promoting economic growth and a conflict-free public realm, but this incremental and tactical approach has been necessary under military rule.[67]

CONCLUSION

The British government may have departed Rangoon in 1948, but it left behind a rigid physical and societal infrastructure that continues to influence the lives of contemporary Rangoonites. The rational hierarchical grid of streets that was completely alien to the local residents in the twentieth century has become the mental map of every Rangoonite. Everyone knows the downtown core in terms of the upper, middle, and lower blocks that are created by the intersecting streets and understands the order of major and minor streets, often giving directions by explaining the sequence of named larger streets followed by three smaller numbered streets. Many even know the exact width of the streets and the size of property lots. In Tayout Tan, Sino-Burmese commonly refer to Latha Street as One Hundred–Foot Street and Bo Ywe Street as Fifty-Foot Street. They express pride in having such broad streets in their city because wide and straight streets are seen as signs of modern advancement. Those who live on these streets understand their address as a mark of social status. While I was chatting with a Sino-Burmese woman on Fifty-Foot Street, she said: "We used to live on one of those small numbered streets beyond Lanmadaw, but we made some money and now live on Fifty-Foot Street. It took many years, but we made it. Did you know that Rangoon was one of the first cities to have such nice broad streets?" Beyond the downtown core, the former Cantonment and European settlement are still known as the most desirable neighborhoods inhabited by the rich and powerful.[68]

This precise and value-laden comprehension of Rangoon illustrates the colonial government's success in dictating a particular world order based on British civility. The capital city as a rational and absolute space successfully supplanted the heterogeneous and dynamic marshland that was Rangoon. In that process, the colonial plan introduced a new definition of a city that determined not only movement through and behavior in the city but also perceptions of the city. Nonetheless, Rangoonites have maneuvered around these strong constraints, making a life for themselves in whatever way possible. Often the power structure embedded in the city overwhelms their temporary tactics, but sometimes they are able to create a place for themselves as seen in the native place and brotherhood associations and in the nightly re-creation of the Mahabandula night market and the Nineteenth Street eateries. Another successful spatial and social tactic, the Hokkien Kuanyin Temple, is the subject of the next chapter.

2.1   Kheng Hock Keong (Qingfu Gong), also known as Kuanyin Ting,
       Kwamyin Medaw Hpayakyaung, and the Hokkien Kuanyin Temple.
       Photograph by Lee Roberts, used by permission.

CHAPTER TWO

THE HOKKIEN KUANYIN TEMPLE AS A CENTER OF BELONGING

AMONG Chinese who have sojourned outside of China, religion, kinship, native place (the birthplace of one's ancestors), and shared dialect (Hokkien, Cantonese, and Yunnanese, among others) are core affinities that enable a group of people to self-identify as a community. Indeed, all four attributes as entwined "compatriot affinities" have consistently shaped the Chinese migrant's sense of belonging.[1] The Hokkien Kuanyin Temple, known as Kuanyin Ting in Hokkien (the language of southeastern Fujian Province) and as Tayout Hpongyi Kyaung and Kwamyin Medaw Hpayakyaung in Burmese (Chinese Temple and Guanyin Temple, respectively) and officially named Kheng Hock Keong (Qingfu Gong in standard Chinese), embodies all of these compatriot affinities (Fig. 2.1).[2]

Since its founding in 1861, it has served as a center of belonging where the local Chinese have gathered to retrieve their past through daily rituals and a place where they could reshape their communal identity. The unpredictable circumstances in Burma have at times threatened Sino-Burmese well-being, and in response they have flexibly represented themselves but have also continually returned to the Hokkien Kuanyin Temple as a manifestation of their ancestral home: southern Fujian Province. Despite numerous challenges, this place-based understanding of themselves has surpassed the ideological influence of Chinese nationalism and remained central in their self-understanding. In explaining the significance of the temple, a resident in Tayout Tan said: "When my aunt visits from the countryside, the first thing she does is go to the Kuanyin Ting. If she arrives during the day, she immediately goes to the temple to offer incense. If she arrives late at night, she will go first thing in the morning, very early, like 5:30 a.m. It is very important to her to get protection from the gods in the Kuanyin Ting.

There are many people like her. These gods are our gods from our home-town in Fujian and the gods of this place."[3]

Although Han culture gradually spread over millennia to encompass the territory we now know as the People's Republic of China, regional differences based on shared dialect and native place were the primary sources of identification that not only bound compatriots together but also engendered intercommunity rivalry. Within China, armed conflict between groups of Cantonese, Hokkien, and Hakka people arose periodically. Outside of China, these same allegiances were maintained. Shared dialect and native place were the main determinants of the destination of sojourning and eventual settlement. For example, Teochiu people from the region around Shantou largely settled in Siam (today's Thailand); Cantonese from the Pearl River Delta mostly migrated to Annam (today's Vietnam) and Cambodia; and Hokkien from Quanzhou and Zhangzhou Prefectures (also known as southern Fujian) resided in Manila and the Straits Settlements.[4] Where Hokkien and Cantonese settled in the same city in similar numbers and around the same time, dialect-based communities segregated themselves from each other in most aspects of life, thereby transposing regional particularism to areas outside of China.

At the turn of the twentieth century, calls for national unity propagated by reformists such as Liang Qichao and revolutionaries such as Sun Yat-sen roused nationalist sentiments within China and overseas, but the nationalism that had emerged by the early twentieth century was complex and ambiguous. A series of defeats by Western and Japanese military forces stirred feelings of national humiliation among many Chinese in many locales, but pan-Chinese nationalism rarely supplanted the centrality of native place loyalties. "Nationalism among the Nanyang [today's Southeast Asian] Chinese was not self-generated but rather a 'taught nationalism' borne by activities from the homeland."[5] Nationalism formed an additional layer of identification that sometimes encompassed hometown identities but was at other times rebuffed by regional loyalties. This chapter focuses on the Hokkien Kuanyin Temple (Kuanyin Ting from this point forward), where communal deities from southern Fujian have been gathered together to create a home away from an ancestral home that continues to sustain Rangoon's Sino-Burmese community.

Unlike the overseas Chinese in the Nanyang destinations mentioned above, both Cantonese and Hokkien people arrived in significant numbers in precolonial and colonial Rangoon. As populations with mutually unintelligible languages and distinct cultures, they established two separate worlds that were not only culturally segregated but also economically and physically divided. The Cantonese lived and worked on the north side of Canton Road (Mahabandula Road), and the Hokkien established themselves on the south side, dividing Tayout Tan in half.[6] Although all of the Chinese in Rangoon were relatively disadvantaged compared to the Indian and European populations, they were able to establish themselves in niche markets. In general, the Cantonese *let-to* in Rangoon were the carpenters, tradesmen, periurban produce and pig farmers, and owners of pawnshops. The Hokkien *let-shei* operated larger businesses that sourced grains and other goods from rural areas and traded with the Straits Settlements.[7] Businesses were strictly located within their dialect-based neighborhoods, with Cantonese shops on the north side of Canton Road and Hokkien shops on the south. Similarly, surname and native place associations, secret brotherhoods, schools, and temples were placed according to this spatial divide.

Kuanyin Ting is located in the Hokkien half, at the southern edge of Tayout Tan, right along the Rangoon River. Similarly, the Cantonese Guanyin Temple was placed in the northern half of Chinatown, at the corner of Guangdong Dadao and Latter (now Latha) Street. Both temples have been and continue to be anchors for their respective communities because the gods and goddesses housed within are regional deities that are believed to maintain a special place-based connection with their worshippers. Some deities are even seen as originating from the same native places as their congregations. For example, Po-sin-tai-tei (Great Emperor Who Protects Life) is worshipped in Kuanyin Ting and known as a Tsuantsiu (Quanzhou) native who was transformed into an immortal, and Tsing-tsui-tso-su (Patriarch of the Clear Stream), a native of Ankue (Anxi), is worshipped as the ultimate ancestor of Ankue's people in Tso Su Miou. On a larger geographic scale, Matso (Mazu), known as the protectress of seafarers, is a favorite among the communities of China's southeast coast and the migrants from that region. Today Matso is worshipped in both Kuanyin Ting and the Cantonese temple, but the protectress of seafarers is rarely visited in the latter.

The Cantonese Kuanyin Temple seems deserted on most days, and the mixture of Chinese- and Burmese-style Buddha figures housed within seems forlorn. The Sino-Burmese in Rangoon conjecture that the comparatively smaller population of Cantonese people in contemporary Tayout Tan has led to the dramatic decline of the Cantonese temple. Most Cantonese shop owners did not return to Burma after World War II. In addition, many left during the Socialist era when nationalization and antiforeigner policies made Burma increasingly inhospitable to Chinese people. Much more research is necessary to uncover the history of the interactions between the Cantonese and Hokkien populations in Burma, but several contemporary

Sino-Burmese espouse the view of this first-generation Sino-Burmese man: "Originally, Rangoon was the territory of the Cantonese. Then it became the territory of the Hokkien. A lot of Cantonese left in the sixties; they went to Hong Kong. Now there are more Hokkien than Cantonese people. But there are also people who are Chinese, but we don't know whether they are Hokkien or Cantonese, because they don't speak Hokkien, Cantonese, or standard Chinese. And things are changing. Rangoon is becoming the territory of the Yunnanese."[8] Within this dynamic context, Kuanyin Ting continues to be the most vibrant center of worship and daily activities in Tayout Tan, suggesting that the prominence of Hokkien culture has yet to be eclipsed by the growing Yunnanese presence.

RITUAL AND BELONGING

For people of Hokkien ancestry, Kuanyin Ting remains an enduring and powerful center of belonging. It is known as a *hiunong* (profuse incense) temple where many worshippers come to offer incense, and its resident deities are believed to be *ling* (efficacious in granting wishes and thereby worthy of devotion). From about six to nine o'clock every morning, devout worshippers arrive in a steady stream to complete their daily rituals and follow a customary procession to show proper respect to all the gods (Fig. 2.2). Traditionally, temple facades have three large red gates that lead into the temple proper from a forecourt. Facing the temple, one should enter through the gate on the left and leave through the gate on the right. The gate in the middle is reserved for the gods. After stepping, right foot first, over the oversize threshold that stretches across the bottom of traditional Chinese gates, worshippers begin their daily obeisance at the altar to Tin-gong-tso (Lord of Heaven) in the central light well. First, devotees bow three times facing the altar and then place one stick of incense into the urn. They then bow three more times to Tin-gong-tso before walking toward the back wall. In the central bay of the back wall, Kuanyin sits elevated above all the other deities and Matso sits right below her. In Chinese temple architecture, the central bay in the innermost hall of a multi-structure complex is reserved for the supreme deity who presides over the court of gods that populate a temple. Devotees bow three times to Kuanyin and offer one stick of incense and then bow three times to Matso, inserting each stick gingerly into the urns placed in front of each goddess. Next they walk to the left bay and pay respect to Po-sin-tai-tei, the god who watches over one's health, and then to the right bay to pray to Guan-tei-gun, the god of merchants, who is supposed to ensure great wealth. Finally, most worshippers end their

2.2 Altars in Kuanyin Ting. Stone columns with dragons carved in high relief, such as those pictured here, are commonly found in Hokkien temples. Photograph by the author.

daily ritual by bowing in front of Tua-pei-gong, a spirit of the earth who assures fruitful harvests. However, if a devotee is about to take an exam, he or she will offer incense to Bun-tsong-gun, who assists students in passing examinations, or if a woman wishes to have children, she prays to Tsu-tsin-niu-niu, the goddess who brings women fertility. After the worshippers complete the circuit they chat with temple attendants or friends who might have arrived, but they never dwell too long, because this worship is only the first task in their day.

This quotidian practice has continually reestablished the relationship between generations of local Hokkien Sino-Burmese and their place-based deities that simultaneously embody a spiritual home and an ancestral home. The above procession through the temple is still practiced in temples throughout southern Fujian, and most of these deities and the qualities attributed to them are specific to that region. Matso is a deified woman from Mitsui, an island off the coast of Tsuantsiu, whose devotion to her father and brother supposedly helped them survive a terrible typhoon and return safely from sea. Po-sin-tai-tei was a physician whose gift of healing and service to patients became so legendary that he was transformed into a god.[9] Guan-tei-gun, the deification of a historical figure, Guanyu, who was known for his loyalty and righteousness, is worshipped in southeastern China as the patron god of all merchants.[10] Loyalty and honor are the essential characteristics of a good merchant. The presence of these deities in a temple designates it as a house of worship particular to the Hokkien people and extends the spirit of southern Fujian to Rangoon. These regional deities represent in religious terms "the villagers' mental map of the community and its vicinity."[11] In effect, by transferring these local deities to Rangoon and enshrining them in Kuanyin Ting, early Hokkien migrants overlaid the mental maps of their home villages onto an unfamiliar city to create a sense of security for themselves. Traditionally, when Hokkien people leave their hometown, they carry with them an image of their patron god along with some incense ash taken from their family altar or community temple. This practice, called *hunhiun* (to divide the incense ash), is a means of transferring the spirit imbued in one's native place to an unknown land, to make the foreign less alien. Once the incense ash has arrived in the alien place, it is placed in an urn in front of the patron god to serve as the foundation for future ash to be generated in worship. Because traditional Chinese society is founded upon its rooted relationship to the earth, native place is a deeply felt source of identification embodying familial, communal, and religious significance.

This transference of place-based meaning is particularly evident in the worship of Tsing-tsui-tso-su, housed in the Tso Su Miou (Grand Ancestor Temple). Known also by its official name Hock Suan Si (Hock Suan Temple) and as Kokine Tayout Hpongyi Kyaung (Kokine Chinese Temple) in Burmese, Tso Su Miou is a subsidiary temple of Kuanyin Ting.[12] Each year on the sixth day of the Chinese New Year, those whose forefathers originated from Ankue Township in Tsuantsiu Prefecture gather to celebrate the birthday of the patriarch (Fig. 2.3). Most of them refer to Tsing-tsui-tso-su as Tso-su-gong, the "grand ancestor," and believe that he is the special protector of Ankue people. The annual ritual begins around five o'clock in the morning and continues into the night, ending only at the break of dawn the next morning. During the day, Ankue families crowd into Tso Su Miou to worship the patriarch, and lion dance troupes arrive one after another to pay tribute. After nightfall, Hokkien people, regardless of native town or village, arrive in carloads. Young and old know about the raucous festivities that take place on the evening of Tso-su-gong's birthday and gather at the temple to enjoy the fun. In the past, traditional Minnan opera and music

2.3   Hock Suan Si (Fushan Si), also known as Tso Su Miou and Kokine
       Tayout Hpongyi Kyaung on Kabaei Pagoda Road. Gathering to cel-
       ebrate Tso-su-gong's birthday. Photograph by the author.

were performed, but those art forms are no longer practiced in Rangoon.
Instead, the temple's executive committee hosts an annual dragon dance
competition. Troupes from all over Rangoon and Lower Burma travel to
Tso Su Miou to compete. In addition, vegetarian food is offered by the
temple to all of its guests, and vendors of all sorts sell noodles, sausages,
sticky rice dumplings, barbecue, and iced drinks. The atmosphere is carni-
valesque, with young and old enjoying the festivities into the early hours of
the morning. Hokkien Sino-Burmese believe it is good luck to stay at the
temple throughout the entire birthday celebration, and many do so to bring
themselves some good luck.

Daily and annual rituals such as those described above constitute core
practices in the Sino-Burmese way of dwelling in Rangoon, in their common
ethos, and help them to maintain a spiritual connection to their ancestral
place in southern Fujian. The rituals practiced in Kuanyin Ting have been
maintained unself-consciously, passed on from one generation to the next
in the embodied act of worship without pursuit of doctrinal or ritual purity

2.4   A father teaching his children how to worship. Photograph by the
       author.

(Fig. 2.4).[13] They are simply an aspect of Sino-Burmese life. When asked
about the way to worship, devotees and temple staff easily described the
proper progression through the temple. When questioned about the various gods, they explained the benefit of praying to each deity. And when
asked why they worship these particular gods, they simply stated that these

gods protect them and have always been the gods of Hokkien people. Even Sino-Burmese who speak no Hokkien or standard Chinese and have little understanding of Hokkien culture visit the temple. Elderly Hokkien whose forefathers arrived in Rangoon in the 1880s say that until the 1980s or 1990s, they never failed to worship at the temple after a couple was married or a baby was born and that they always went to the temple on special holidays.[14] Many Sino-Burmese who live in Tayout Tan worship at Kuanyin Ting daily, and even some who must drive in from the suburbs do so religiously. Others have an altar to their chosen patron gods within their homes and make more elaborate offerings in Kuanyin Ting and Tso Su Miou on special holidays such as Kuanyin's and Tsing-tsui-tso-su's birthdays and Chinese New Year.

The pantheon of place-specific deities in Kuanyin Ting serves as an originary source for the Hokkien, one that retrieves tradition as a fount of shared understanding, which guides, not dictates, their actions in the present and provides hope for the future. As first pondered by Heidegger and interpreted by contemporary scholars, originary is not a static point of origin but a dynamic force. It continues to open up possibilities that draw from the past while allowing for reformulations of tradition.[15] Understood through this mind-set, Matso, Po-sin-tai-tei, and Tsing-tsui-tso-su have become gods of Rangoon, connected to but no longer bound by southern Fujian. The distant connection in time and location to an ancestral place provides an ethereal but necessary foundation for the Sino-Burmese to understand themselves as belonging to a localized Hokkien community, still Hokkien but different. As revealed in the quotation at the beginning of this chapter, the gods of Kuanyin Ting are "our gods from our hometown in Fujian and the gods of this place." This place is Rangoon, Burma. The native place, Fujian, is nested within their place of residence, Rangoon, and is a source of memories that are continually retrieved and retold to consciously maintain, not manufacture, their tradition.[16] As philosopher Hans-Georg Gadamer explained: "Traditions do not persist out of sheer inertia or force themselves on us whether we will or not. Instead they are preserved. Even the most violent revolution preserves far more than it alters and the traditions so maintained are preserved not because they are overlooked in the rush of innovation but because they are remembered, affirmed, embraced and cultivated. Acts of preservation are no less free than acts of revolution, even if they are less conspicuous."[17] Acts of preservation are also flexible, guided but not predetermined by tradition. They are agile tactics that respond to the local environment to create a sense of internal continuity despite external challenges. The Chinese in Rangoon have contended with numerous political and economic difficulties threatening their survival in Burma and demanded accommodation. At the scale of the Chinese and later Sino-Burmese community, these accommodations have been supported by the practices in Kuanyin Ting, enabling the people of Chinese descent to reshape how they understand themselves and live in Rangoon without losing their connection to a shared ancestral past.

NATIVE PLACE ASSOCIATIONS AND NESTED PLACES

Kuanyin Ting is a nested place that gathers together the past and present to open up possible futures. It stands as a physical representation of a distant homeland that is much more than an imagined past. Rather, it is an active center of belonging that has provided an opening for the local Sino-Burmese to create a home for themselves.

The first Kuanyin Ting was constructed in 1861 after a group of prominent Hokkien merchants took it upon themselves to build a native place temple to serve all of their fellow migrants. Among overseas sojourners, native place was often interpreted on the largest possible scale, the province, to encompass all migrants who share a dialect and common customs. Historically, native place associations were both secular and spiritual institutions where religious rituals were a means to gather people together to address everyday concerns and an instrument to organize the local society.[18] Kuanyin Ting, the temple, and Hokkien Gongsi, the native place association, were built as one conjoined complex to provide mutual aid and organize the Hokkien population into a cohesive community.

The early history of Kuanyin Ting and Hokkien Gongsi is still unclear because most documentation has been lost through natural and man-made disasters. Elders in the temple's executive committee say that a book about the history of the temple sits on a shelf in their office, but if one opens the book, the contents will blow away, because termites have turned the pages into dust.[19] They also say that other historical records were either lost or destroyed during World War II.[20] Fortunately, some events such as the founding and rebuilding of the temple have been inscribed into stone tablets that are embedded in the temple's eastern and western walls. The founding stone in the eastern wall specifies that Kuanyin Ting was built as a commons to support all the Hokkien who had settled in Rangoon by the middle of the nineteenth century.

> Those who build abodes for the gods are the people. Those in
> whom people take refuge are the gods. . . . We merchants have
> been trading in Rangoon for many years. The sea is calm and the

river is clear. The people are healthy and the goods are plenty. These are blessings from the gods. May they always bless us. We invited upstanding men on this land and shipping families in the four directions to assist us, to collect funds, to establish joyous connections and help each other, to hire carpenters [and] begin construction of the new temple in the Xingzhou year. . . . The construction was completed in the Kuihai year [1861]. Within are honored three gods who are well versed in both the literary and martial arts. They are complete under one hall and are vested with spirit from above, rendering the temple grand and the place stable and auspicious. *Therefore, having gathered the good work of many Fujian people and organizations, Qingfu Gong is a common space.* Situated on a winning site facing the river, where the water flows smoothly and the boats sail swiftly and where the golden pagoda on the hill protects us from the back, this temple will flower like a lotus, observing the happenings of Rangoon, bringing the people of Rangoon to the gods, and sowing good deeds for all. Through the diligence of the director, there is good.[21]

Details about the people who contributed to this construction are unclear because they are not specifically named or numbered in the inscription. There were clearly enough Hokkien people, with sufficient financial success among them, to enable the building of the temple. The inscription also suggests that the wealthy families gained their riches through maritime trade.

When reconstruction of the temple was begun in 1899, the merchants who gathered to make their place of congregation more befitting of their elevated status maintained the same goals as their predecessors. They sought to create a place for worshipping their common gods, for building connections between one another, and for preserving Hokkien traditions.

Kheng Hock Keong stands on Strand Road between the streets of Sint Oh and Yin Lan with Shwedagon Pagoda in the back and the river in front. *It is the place for those from Fujian who live on this land to gather, to build neighborly connections, to celebrate, to carry out cultural activities, and to speak of faithfulness and righteousness with one another.* Since those from Tsingtsiu and Tsuantsiu constitute the majority, the province [of Fujian] is used [as the defining characteristic]. May Kuanyin bless us and prove potent.

2.5   "Foken Chinese Temple" on Strand Road. Photograph by Philip Adolphe Klier taken in 1895. Used by permission from the British Library.

The temple complex that was built in 1861 and rebuilt in 1903 included a central hall that housed the pantheon of gods, the temple proper, a western wing that housed the native place association, Hokkien Gongsi, and an eastern wing that housed the *tsi-siok* (study hall) (Fig. 2.5).[22] These institutions that addressed spiritual, practical, and educational needs were established to serve all people from Fujian, regardless of their native village or town. Although dialects of Hokkien in Tsingtsiu, Tsuantsiu, Ankue, and other townships are discernibly different, these variations could be accommodated under one umbrella organization in the diverse environment of Rangoon. Such fine-grained differences must have seemed insignificant in comparison to the Indian and British cultures and languages that dominated the city during the colonial era.

Any persons who could trace their ancestry back to southern Fujian were considered members of the regional Hokkien family network and invited to contribute to the building of Kuanyin Ting. Again from the stone tablets:

The temple was built in 1861, as recorded in the founding stone. Through time, the temple has become dilapidated and the size is too small. We gathered to discuss the repairs and jointly claim, "Expand!" Khoo Sui Hian was elected as our director, Yeoh Tin Siu as our assistant director, and Tan Yiao Hun as our financial director. Fund-raising began with Taw Ko Liong calling out for support, and many people rose to the occasion. Over [Rs] 10,000 were collected but proved insufficient, so individual clans were approached. Although the distances were great, wherever there were Minnan merchants, Chan Tsing Hong and Ko Man Bang traveled, paying their own way, to solicit funds. Several thousand contributed, and their names are listed to the left. In total, Rs 30,400 were collected.

Materials and labor were assembled and the ground was broken in 1897. After two years, construction began in 1899. Another three years later, the temple was completed in January 1903. . . . Greenish white stone was shipped from China, and the columns, lintels, walls, and surfaces were intricately carved and painted, creating a grand and beautiful space.

The temple property was insufficient for the expansion. Therefore, after a joint decision and much effort, a forty-by-five-foot piece of public land was acquired [from the government] at the cost of Rs 1,800. The temple is sited auspiciously by the geomancer Chew An Si. Those who managed the construction and solicited funds were twenty-three in number, and fifteen clans were involved. With those from within and outside putting forth exhaustive effort, the task was accomplished. Upon completion, everyone celebrated with wine. To commemorate this building, these words have been carved into stone to ensure that the deed does not wither away in time. Those who contributed are listed to the left.

As evident in these inscriptions, funds were solicited from merchants in an extensive region poetically described as the four directions. These four directions included merchant families from Rangoon, Tavoy, Mergui, and Moulmein (within British Burma) and Penang, Melaka, Semarang, Amoy (Xiamen in standard Chinese), Singapore, and Jakarta (in Nanyang / Southeast Asia). The list of contributors includes over two thousand merchants, merchant families, and organizations from Nanyang that contributed over Rs 180,000 total. The Chinese in Rangoon were clearly a part of a large network that stretched throughout Southeast Asia, and they maintained close enough ties that merchants outside of Burma felt compelled to contribute. In fact, in the extensive list of individuals, Koh Tsing Kuan of Penang donated the single largest amount at Rs 1,200.

The larger Kuanyin Ting that was completed in 1903 still stands in Tayout Tan today. The distinctive architecture of the temple, with its curved and ornamented roof, intricately carved pillars and decorations, and bright colors, is typical of the Minnan temple style. Contemporary Hokkien in Rangoon proudly point to Kuanyin Ting as an example of traditional Chinese architecture, and many know that the carved dragon columns marking the central bay of the temple came directly from Fujian. This type of stone column carved in high relief is unique to the architecture of southern Fujian and graces the temples of those whose ancestors came from that region.[23] In 1897, when the prominent merchants in Rangoon wanted to rebuild Kuanyin Ting, they sought to build something more befitting their status and modeled it after a temple in Amoy, Fujian. According to the commemorative book published for Kuanyin Ting's hundredth anniversary in 1961, the model was the Yeoh clan's Da Si Yia Temple, the grandeur of which was memorialized in song.[24]

The limited temple records do not provide additional information about this selection, but it was probably a decision based on traditional Hokkien culture and the power structure within Rangoon's Hokkien society. The Yeoh clan was one of the most prestigious families in Rangoon, as evident in the election of Yeoh Tin Siu as assistant director. In addition, Amoy was famous throughout the Nanyang. Around the turn of the twentieth century, Amoy was a major international port and the main point of exodus for Hokkien venturing overseas.[25] Furthermore, in southern Fujian, the design and craftsmanship of temples were and continue to be seen as indicators of the virtue and status of their founders. Exceptionally beautiful temples are known to people throughout the region and were often memorialized in rhyming couplets or, as in the case of the Yeoh clan's temple, in song.

Materials and craftsmen were shipped directly from Fujian at great cost to achieve the ideal southeastern Chinese temple. Chan Mah Phee paid for some of the labor and material, while Lim Chin Tsong, the major owner of the Chinese Shipping Company, transported the craftsmen and materials.[26] A traditional Chinese temple was constructed with a main hall in the north, a light well in the center, two wings to the east and west, and an open courtyard in the south. Throughout the temple, intricately carved screens depicting traditional folktales of filial piety and motifs representing diligence and perseverance were installed in the walls and windows. The structure and details of the southern Fujian temple were reproduced in Rangoon as a manifestation of tradition that would bring the local Hokkien together to maintain their shared customs.

Since the completion of the expanded Kuanyin Ting in 1903, the temple has undergone periodic maintenance, with major repairs after World War II and before the hundredth anniversary celebration in 1961. According to members of the executive committee, they have always tried to preserve the temple as it was built in 1903, but historical circumstances have sometimes prevented faithful restorations. In the 1990s, the temple committee hired an architect from Hunan to rebuild the damaged roof structure. When asked why they chose someone from Hunan instead of Fujian, committee members said that their connections at that time directed them toward the Hunan architect. Similarly, most of the paintings and carvings in the temple are now maintained by Burmese, not Sino-Burmese, artists and craftsmen. One of the artists interviewed has actually gone to China to study traditional Chinese painting, while two others learned from Chinese artisans in Rangoon. When asked about this practice, Teng Ki Hua, an executive committee member, said that very few Chinese practice these trades anymore and that Burmese artists are available to do the work.[27]

This flexible maintenance of tradition is a tactic the Chinese in Rangoon have employed in which an ideal is recognized and desired but approached with utmost practicality. Effort is put forth to live up to tradition, but if circumstances demand otherwise, good enough is accepted as a viable solution, not a failure. This tactical approach undergirds their common history and has enabled them to weather many economic and political challenges. It has also helped them maintain Kuanyin Ting in a form that looks very much like the temple of 1903, thus preserving their communal history in a physical place and connecting them through architecture and ritual to their ancestral homeland in Fujian.

THE KUANYIN TEMPLE AS COMMUNITY CENTER

For Sino-Burmese in Rangoon, this connection to their ancestral home would have likely dissipated if Kuanyin Ting had not been created as a common space for migrants to connect with one another and thereby reconnect with their native place. The temple complex, including the temple proper and Hokkien Gongsi, was not only a place of worship; it was also a resource center where fellow provincials could find a place to stay, a bite to eat, a job, and, ultimately, a place to be buried. Native place associations in China and Southeast Asia were centers of meaning that catered to the physical, emotional, and spiritual needs of migrants.[28] They were and many remain community centers that sustain the vitality and distinctiveness of resident minority populations.

Historically, Chinese overseas practiced chain migration wherein familial and regional ties connected a sending township with a recipient city. At the destination, members of the family, interpreted in the broadest sense, were expected to look after the newcomer and integrate him into the local society.[29] This type of assistance was most often provided through associations such as Hokkien Gongsi, which assumed the responsibility of organizing Rangoon's diverse Hokkien population into a cohesive community. Drawing from operational norms common in traditional Chinese associations, Hokkien Gongsi was established as an umbrella corporation composed of surname associations that shared equal responsibility in the maintenance of the temple and in serving the Hokkien population.

After the first director, Khoo Tai Kun, passed away in 1894, an executive committee composed of two representatives each from six surname associations was established.[30] Associations each held the responsibility of nominating a president from within their organizations to lead the *gongsi* for one year in rotation. As the Hokkien population in Rangoon increased, more surname associations were founded. Associations that became successful enough to buy land were invited to join the executive committee. The stated reason for this requirement was that landed merchants would not easily leave Rangoon and thus were rendered more committed to the place. However, this condition was likely influenced by the traditional practice of Chinese corporations in which members had to buy into the organization (often land) as shareholders and thereby assume financial responsibility. Except for the forty-by-five-foot piece of public land purchased for the expansion, Kuanyin Ting stands on a lot that was granted by the British government in 1853, when religious organizations (mosques, temples, and churches) were given land. Therefore, associations desiring membership could not buy into the executive committee and had to prove their financial capacity through owning other properties. Committee members were and are expected to supply the necessary funds whenever a need arises. In fact, the president and his surname organization are expected to provide the largest sum for any events and emergencies during his term. In 1935, the executive committee was expanded to include twelve surname associations and further enlarged in 1938 to encompass twenty associations. Today there are twenty-four surname associations in the Kuanyin Ting Executive Committee: Chua, Tan, Ko, Kwek, Ang, Oh, Ng, Kang, Lee, Lim, Lao, Lu, Soh, Ong, Goh, Cheah, Koh, Yeoh, Yap, Iu, Chan, Teh, Teoh, Chew, and Tseng.[31] This inclusive structure encompasses most Hokkien families in Rangoon and has been a cohesive force, in addition to native place ties and shared religious practices, that has bound the Hokkien population together.

From its earliest days, Hokkien Gongsi has ministered to the everyday needs of Rangoon's Hokkien migrants. Various committees were established to oversee specific tasks such as temple maintenance, support for the poor and ill, finance (remittances back to Fujian and local money matters), and burial. Although migrants from southeastern China often conceived of themselves as sojourners who would return to their native place after accruing great wealth, many, if not most, died overseas with no means of returning their bodies to their ancestral home. Dying in a foreign land without a proper burial is considered among traditional Chinese to be the greatest of misfortunes. A person who dies without the requisite ceremony and grave is believed to become a hungry ghost, doomed to wander aimlessly in a world between the living and the dead. This eternal suffering is dreaded by most Chinese, and Chinese overseas have expended great effort to ensure a peaceful death for their compatriots. Today Hokkien Gongsi manages the Fujian cemetery in Yay Way and hires buses on Tomb Sweeping Day (the fifteenth day from the spring equinox) to help those Hokkien without cars travel to Yay Way to pay respect to their ancestors. The executive committee also manages all aspects of the head temple, Kuanyin Ting; the subsidiary temple, Hock Suan Si; the free medical clinic on Sint Oh Dan Street; and free sutra study and standard Chinese classes.

As a part of its service to the Hokkien community, Kuanyin Ting also provides basic necessities and a stipend to all elderly destitute Hokkien without living family members. To access this service, impoverished elderly people must prove themselves to be Hokkien and can do so by approaching their particular surname associations for written certification of their membership in the Hokkien community. Many of these elders, in their seventies, eighties, and nineties, are illiterate, but if they know their names in Chinese and the surname association can trace their membership in the family, they are eligible to receive alms.

Around the fifteenth of every other month, over a hundred elderly Hokkien people shuffle into Kuanyin Ting before seven o'clock in the morning and take a seat in the central courtyard. Soon after they sit down, a temple attendant greets them and serves them a bowl of hot porridge. Most of these elderly people arrive alone and seem to be in ill health. They need assistance moving around, and when the time comes to pick up their alms, young people must prop them up by their elbows as they inch along. Throughout the year, they receive an envelope of cash, along with some basic food and

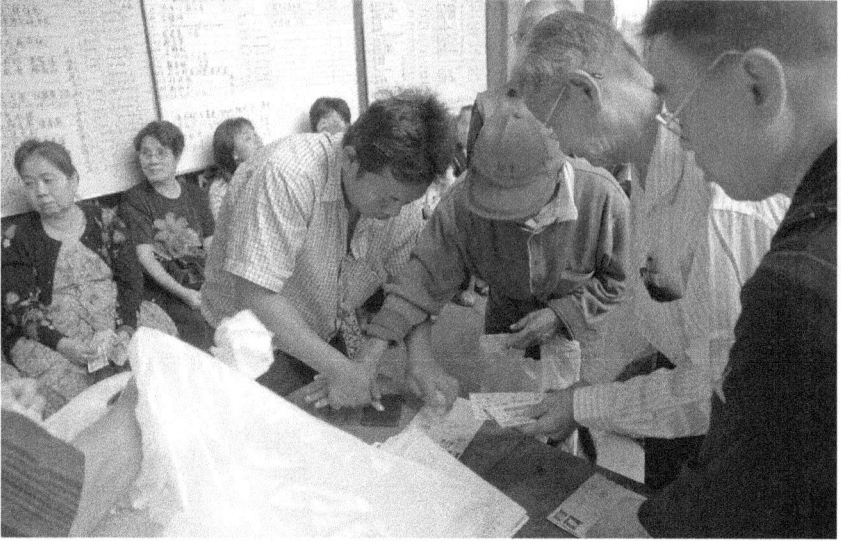

2.6
Elderly man signing with thumb print in order to receive his alms. Photograph by Lee Roberts, used by permission.

2.7
Elderly woman being assisted through the donation line. Photograph by Lee Roberts, used by permission.

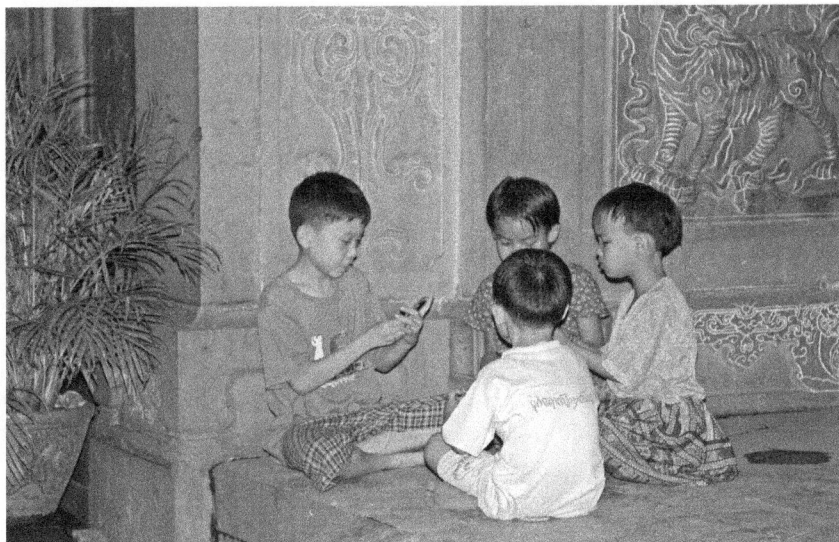

2.8   Children playing on the temple steps. Photograph by the author.

necessities. To receive these goods, they must show their identification card, which is checked against the records maintained by Kuanyin Ting, and sign their names, often with a thumbprint (Fig. 2.6). For Chinese New Year, the elderly not only receive money and the usual bag of basics from the temple, but they also are presented with red envelopes and bags of special food from the local Hokkien community. Many local Sino-Burmese know about this special day of caring for their communal elders and bring boxes of noodles, biscuits, cake, and other food to give to the elders. They line themselves up against the walls of the temple and hand out their gifts to the elderly one by one as each old person shuffles past them with a bag in hand (Fig. 2.7). By the end of their procession around the temple's central court, the elders' bags are weighted down with gifts and often need to be carried by the young people assisting them. This care for the larger Hokkien family identified through membership in surname associations reveals the influence of kinship, both actual and fictive, in generating a sense of belonging. It also speaks to the power of Kuanyin Ting as a center of meaning where elders are honored as living expressions of past wisdom and where younger generations gather together to learn about the past.

Every evening, soon after nightfall, children arrive to play in the temple. Some chase each other around the forecourt and into the temple proper, jumping over the thresholds and dodging adults who sit or stand in their way. Some sit near the thresholds playing cards and marbles, while their parents lounge on plastic chairs scattered throughout the forecourt (Fig. 2.8). The heat and humidity in Rangoon make many homes unbearably hot, so many seek cooler spaces to enjoy their evenings. The forecourt of Kuanyin Ting serves as an open-air living room for people who reside in Tayout Tan. Those who live within a couple of blocks of the temple gather in the forecourt nearly every evening, bringing their own plastic lawn chairs to sit and chat with friends before they retire for the night.

CONCLUSION

For the Hokkien in Rangoon, Kuanyin Ting is a charged place imbued with meaning. Since its founding in 1861, the temple complex has been the center where Hokkien gather to worship, interact, and remember their ancestral home, laying down meaning through 120 years of daily use. The merchants who oversaw the building of the temple sought to create for their fellow Hokkien a common space that would reside at an auspicious convergence of three important forces: blessing from the gods, collaborative effort by the Hokkien, and protective *qi* (energy) from the physical environment. These forces, when properly aligned, were seen as a manifestation of their good work and their rightful claim to inhabit that space, to belong to Rangoon. The siting of the temple with a hill in the back crowned by Shwedagon Pagoda, one of the most sacred Buddhist sites in Burma, and a river in front was and continues to be understood as a most fortunate location that ensures the safety and prosperity of all who gather at Kuanyin Ting. In their minds, the good deeds of their forefathers have continued and will continue to provide Hokkien Sino-Burmese with good fortune. It is now their responsibility to continue to maintain the temple and do good deeds so that their children might also prosper.

CHINESE SCHOOLS
AND CHINESENESS

J UST as the Hokkien Kuanyin Temple has served as a center of belonging for the Hokkien Sino-Burmese, Chinese-medium schools, whether in Hokkien, Cantonese, Yunnanese, or standard Chinese, have drawn populations of Chinese people together to form distinct but overlapping communities. The entwined compatriot affinities of shared dialect, native place, and religion were so intimately bound that all three aspects of Hokkien Chineseness were built into Kuanyin Ting.[1] The temple complex included the temple proper in the central bay flanked by the Fujian Native Place Association on the west and the *tsi-siok* (study hall) on the east. During the precolonial and colonial eras, children were gathered in the study hall to learn Chinese through classical texts verbalized in the Hokkien dialect.[2] While literacy was largely reserved for the wealthy in traditional Chinese societies, the hope of escaping humble beginnings through diligent study and then entry into a meritocratic official hierarchy was a common dream. Overseas, this traditional aspiration was maintained through institutions such as the interconnected Hokkien Gongsi, Kuanyin Ting, and study hall.[3]

Shared dialect, as one of the compatriot affinities, was often the main determinant for a sense of fellowship because Hokkien, Cantonese, and standard Chinese are mutually unintelligible, distancing those who speak different dialects.[4] Standard Chinese was a court language spoken by imperial officials that gradually spread through China via conquest and migration. Yunnanese, a variant of standard Chinese that incorporates local and non-Han words of the many ethnic minorities in southwest China, is understandable to standard Chinese speakers but incomprehensible to those who only speak Hokkien and Cantonese. All Han, regardless of regional dialect, share the same written language, but most migrants before the 1950s were illiterate peasants, forced to flee southeast China because of poverty and internecine warfare. This mostly irreconcilable diversity compelled the Chinese in Burma to establish separate schools and maintain distinct sub-Han communities that would repeatedly challenge campaigns to fabricate a unitary China and a singular Chinese identity.

The history of Chinese schools in Burma, in particular Huaqiao Zhongxue (Overseas Chinese Middle School) and Nanyang Zhongxue (South Seas Middle School), reveals the interactions between language, education, and politics that have significantly shaped the Sino-Burmese understanding of self. The standard Chinese–based education at these two institutions not only instilled the students with a sense of Chinese pride through explicit nationalistic propaganda in the 1950s and 1960s; it also has continued to influence how the standard Chinese–speaking Sino-Burmese position themselves in contemporary Burmese society. Although both schools were closed in 1965, they remain powerfully present in contemporary Sino-Burmese society. The sub-Han groups of Chinese in Rangoon began their settlement as mutually exclusive populations on opposite sides of Canton Road, the section of Mahabandula Road within Tayout Tan. However, their shared experience of living as a minority foreign population buffeted by national and international politics has encouraged them to place practicality above historical concerns and to adopt trans-regional practices of Chineseness, especially the modern national language of China—standard Chinese—as a way of being Chinese in Burma.

LANGUAGE, EDUCATION, AND POLITICS

During the earliest times of settlement in Rangoon, wealthy merchants hired private tutors from southern Fujian to teach their children in the temple's study hall and in their private homes. According to Huang Chouqing, a respected chronicler of Sino-Burmese history, both the Hokkien and Cantonese Kuanyin Temples had established study halls in the eastern wings of those temples by 1887.[5] A separate Chinese school was not founded until 1903, when prominent Hokkien merchants from the Tan, Tseng, Koh, and Lim families and hybrid Chinese such as Taw Sein Ko established Tionghua Kihak (Zhonghua Righteousness School), a boys' school renamed Tionghua Outeng (Zhonghua Study Hall) in 1905.[6] Within the following decade, approximately ten Chinese schools were established in Rangoon, catering to the different populations (Hokkien and Cantonese, girls and boys) and teaching in different languages (Hokkien, Cantonese, and English). Leaders in the Hokkien community sometimes disagreed on the principles and purpose of the schools, resulting in competition for students and fissures. For example, Tionghua Righteousness School, which began as a Chinese-medium school and introduced English instruction in 1905, was split into two schools by 1906. Lim Chin Tsong, who was a board member, founded a separate English-medium school, Lim Chin Tsong Tiongse Ingbun Hakhao (Lim Chin Tsong Chinese and Western English School). Wealthy merchants such as Lim who were more acculturated to Rangoon's cosmopolitan culture promoted English-medium education to increase the competitiveness of Hokkien Chinese in a British-ruled Burma. Others such as elders in the Koh and Tan families advocated a Hokkien-based education that would maintain Hokkien traditions.[7] Concurrently, Kisiong Yiahak (Kisiong Night School) was established by yet another group of Chinese to disseminate revolutionary ideology as championed by the Tongmenghui (Chinese Revolutionary Alliance) founded by Sun Yat-sen and others, which divided the Hokkien community along political lines.

Around the turn of the twentieth century, the call for a unitary China influenced conceptions of Chineseness, but that Chinese nationalism was complex and ambiguous within and beyond China. Reform and revolutionary leaders traveled to places such as Manila, Singapore, and Melaka to rally support for their causes and solicit funds. Kang Youwei, a classical Chinese scholar and reformer who endeavored to improve the imperial government through modernizing the Qing court, traveled throughout Nanyang to give talks and organized Baohuangpai (Save the Emperor Societies). Sun Yat-sen and his fellow revolutionaries also journeyed to different overseas Chinese communities to solicit support for overthrowing the Qing court and established the Chinese Revolutionary Alliance. Both parties found followers in Nanyang. Within Rangoon, antagonistic organizations arose that vied for support within the larger Chinese population. Members of the Kien Tek Association endeavored to save the emperor, while brothers of the Ho Sing Brotherhood, their historical nemesis, aligned themselves with the republican revolution.

Ironically, while a broader trans-native place identity began to form as a result of the reformist and revolutionary campaigns, the ideological differences between these two parties cleaved a new divide. Cantonese and Hokkien began to conceive of themselves as belonging to the whole of China, not just particular villages, towns, and provinces; however, what that China should be—a reformed monarchy or a republic—became a point of contention that divided Rangoon's Chinese society further, into not only language-based but also political camps. Later, the political divide would be drawn along the ideological lines of Nationalist versus Communist China.

There have been periods of greater cohesion between the Hokkien and Cantonese in Rangoon, but, as detailed below, an enduring sense of solidarity was elusive. Occasionally, a more unified national sense of Chinese identity was catalyzed by crises in China and Burma or was tactically deployed to capitalize on changing economic and political circumstances. However, a cultural, pragmatic, and flexible sense of Chineseness has been the centripetal force that has brought various groups of Chinese people together. The two competing political conceptions of China—Nationalist versus Communist—were championed by different groups from about 1919 onward, but those narrow ideological formulations would prove untenable in Rangoon and Burma as a whole.

After Sun Yat-sen and his fellow revolutionaries successfully deposed the last Qing emperor in 1911, Chinese populations in countries such as Burma found a new sense of pride and began to promote cultural institutions such as schools, newspapers, and national (as opposed to regional) Chinese associations. Between 1911 and about 1935, 299 new Chinese associations and 347 Chinese schools were established throughout Burma, but they remained divided along linguistic lines.[8] There was so little cohesion or collaboration that even in towns where the Chinese population numbered only one to two hundred, two or three schools were established to serve the separate Hokkien, Cantonese, and Yunnanese communities. In this kind of divided environment it was difficult for teachers to create a standard pan-Chinese curriculum or promote a shared national Chinese identity. Secondary education in the five middle and high schools was conducted in standard Chinese, mostly by teachers who spoke standard Chinese as a second language, while primary education in the 339 elementary schools was still in native place languages.[9] In fact, although the post-1911 government, the Republic of China, expended significant effort to identify and codify a national language (*guoyu*), the Beijing dialect of standard Chinese was not designated as the official tongue until 1932. In dynastic China, this dialect was the language of government, of mandarin officials, and its adoption as the language of a modern China was seen as unjustly exclusive of non-standard Chinese speakers and counterrevolutionary. Even after the national language was codified, China's language problem remained a political battleground between the Left (Communists) and the Right (Nationalists) and was not resolved until the People's Republic of China issued an official language policy, specifying standard Chinese as the one and only common language (*putonghua*) in 1956.[10] Therefore, the diversity of languages employed in the Chinese schools within Burma was reflective of the general disarray in a period of transition from an expansive cultural China to a unitary national China.

CHAPTER THREE

During the first four decades of the twentieth century, the rise of nationalism was not unique to China or the Chinese. Rapacious colonial practices at the hands of various imperial powers incited revolutionary action in Asia. In Burma, Aung San and other nationalists formed organizations such as Dobama Asiayone (Our Burma Union) and eventually gained independence from the British in 1948.[11] Throughout Southeast Asia, leaders such as José Rizal of the Philippines and Pridi Banomyong of Thailand were able to oppose colonial encroachment, creating modern national identities that encompassed traditional place-based loyalties.[12] Among the Chinese overseas, a national Chinese identity was propagated through associations, newspapers, and schools that encouraged identification with China and discouraged participation in the politics of their country of residence. Chinese nationalism, one might even say Chinese chauvinism, was explicitly exported by the Nationalist and Communist parties. More research is necessary to uncover the extent of participation among the Chinese in Burman nationalist movements such as Dobama Asiayone, but it would seem that Chinese people in Rangoon mostly avoided politics or focused on the politics in China.

However, there is some evidence that the Chinese in Rangoon contributed to Burma's fight for independence. In March 1940, when Bo Aung San and Bo Yan Aung were evading arrest by the British government, Li Boon Tin in Tayout Tan facilitated their escape by arranging their passage aboard the *M. V. Haili Rangoon* sailing for Amoy (Xiamen).[13] Furthermore, in 1944, members of the Huaqiao Lianhehui (Overseas Chinese Allied Association) donated money to Aung San to support the fight for Burmese independence.[14] Many contemporary Sino-Burmese cite these stories as evidence of the close relationship between the Chinese and Burman populations, but the veracity of these incidents requires further examination.

In this context of emerging nationalistic sentiments throughout Asia, the newly formulated Chinese nationalism was still evolving. For overseas Chinese, loyalty to the Republic of China had to be weighed against the political, economic, and social realities of living in a British colony and, later, a fledgling independent nation-state. Hokkien Sino-Burmese comment that they have had no *kosuan* (powerful defender) because the governments in China either were too weak to come to their rescue, as during the waning years of the Qing dynasty, or were unconcerned about their welfare, as seen in many periods of imperial and modern Chinese history. For example, when the Revolutionary Council (the Socialist government of Burma) nationalized six thousand seven hundred Chinese stores, two Chinese banks, and all Chinese schools and newspapers between 1964 and 1965, "China completely disregarded the interests and discontent of the Overseas Chinese in Burma and, instead, took a supportive attitude toward Burmese fundamental domestic and foreign policies."[15] In this environment, political activism has been a risky venture tempered by immediate and pragmatic concerns. As a whole, the exigencies of living as a foreign population in an unstable or oppressed Burma have compelled the Sino-Burmese to retreat toward the older and more intimate ties of native place and shared dialect, thereby discouraging public participation in the national politics of Burma and China.

Nonetheless, newfound pride in a modernizing China encouraged Chinese leaders in Rangoon to establish new schools, the largest of which became sources of individual and communal identification. Unlike the study halls in the temples and various Hokkien, Cantonese, and Yunnanese schools of earlier times, schools established after 1911 were often driven by nationalistic ideologies that sought to produce new Chinese citizens who would sacrifice their own well-being for the creation of a stronger, unified China. Standard Chinese would be deployed as a hegemonic force to create a national cultural unity. These ideologies were exported to communities of overseas Chinese through nationalistic curricula delivered in standard Chinese by teachers trained in China. However, broad-reaching standards would not be codified until the 1950s. Internecine warfare in China and World War II prevented faster progress.

Standardized education through an official language has been employed by many states to prescribe a national culture and create a desired citizenry. It is an apparatus of control well practiced in countries such as Thailand, where standard Thai, as first promoted during King Chulalongkorn's reign (1868–1910), has transformed the diverse cultural and linguistic populations within the territory now known as Thailand into proper subjects of the Thai state.[16] The national Thai language and a standardized curriculum enforced through six years of mandatory schooling have oriented every person born within the country toward the three pillars of national identity—the Buddhist religion, the kingship, and the Thai nation.[17]

In Burma/Myanmar, the making of Myanmars is still under way, with ethnic minorities in the former Frontier Areas still resisting the imposition of the state.[18] Under colonial rule, the territory now known as Burma was administered as two separate regions: the Frontier Areas and Ministerial Burma. The Frontier Areas were composed of ethnic minority principalities such as Shan and Kachin that had agreed to cooperate with the British in exchange for considerable autonomy. Ministerial Burma, where the Burman majority and others such as the Mon, Chinese, and Indians resided, was directly ruled by the British. Although the newly independent Union of

Burma began to standardize the Burmese language and establish a national curriculum in the 1950s, nationwide efforts failed to make much progress until the 1960s when General Ne Win and his Revolutionary Council nationalized all schools, banning instruction in all foreign languages such as English and Chinese. But even during Ne Win's Socialist period (1962–88), schooling in Burma was inconsistent and compulsory education was not declared until 1974.[19] Growing insurgency in the former Frontier Areas meant that children in the least stable areas had little access to schooling of any kind. Within central and Lower Burma, the Burman-dominated area that coincides with the former Ministerial Burma, Burmese language and culture have become the accepted norm that dictates membership in the national Burmese/Myanmar society.[20] For the Sino-Burmese in Rangoon, Burmanization or Myanmafication has been a gradual process. At times, the Burmese language and ethos have been internalized unconsciously through daily interactions, public education, and intermarriage. At other times, the Burman way of being has been resisted through the conscious establishment of institutions such as Chinese schools.

HUAQIAO AND NANYANG MIDDLE SCHOOLS

Chinese schools established in the first two decades of the twentieth century were usually housed in existing organizations or buildings. In January 1921, the first specifically built Chinese middle school, Huaqiao Zhongxue, commonly referred to as Huazhong or Hwachong, opened its doors to male and female teenagers.[21] Many of its students would come to consider the campus their second home and even forty years after the closing of the school belt out the school anthem with great joy and vigor.[22] As one of the five schools in Burma offering middle (three years) and high (three years) school education in Chinese, Huazhong was a residential and day school that provided dormitories for students from distant towns and villages. The students' experiences studying and living at the school left an indelible mark as to what it means to be a Chinese person in Burma and instilled a sense of responsibility about preserving Chinese culture. Although Huazhong was nationalized by the Revolutionary Council and ceased to exist as a Chinese school in 1965, its alumni remain active members of the Sino-Burmese community who support their local Chinese traditions and spearhead efforts to reestablish Chinese-language education. Between 2007 and 2009, the Rangoon Huaqiao Zhongxue Tongxuehui (Overseas Chinese Middle School Alumni Association) organized annual banquets to commemorate the founding of the school and, in 2013, celebrated the ninetieth anniversary with a large banquet of over four hundred guests. Even alumni who have migrated to other countries have formed branch offices of Huaqiao Middle School alumni associations such as those in Hong Kong, Los Angeles, and New York. These distant alumni regularly contribute to fund-raising efforts, and some even fly back to Rangoon to participate in celebrations.

Contemporary Sino-Burmese date the founding of Huaqiao Middle School as December 21, 1919, when leaders in the Hokkien community began fund-raising to build a Chinese middle school. Several secondary Chinese sources document the establishment of the school, but all of them focus on the key figures and necessary finances without discussing their mission.[23] The need for Chinese schools is presented as self-evident, requiring little explanation except when ideological differences result in political battles within or between different campuses. Since Huazhong was a standard Chinese–medium school established after the founding of the Republic of China, it is safe to assume that the founders subscribed to the national-ist rhetoric of the time, even if primary sources have yet to be uncovered. For those who attended Huazhong, the school is mostly remembered as an idyllic campus in Kemmendine (now Kymyindaing) Township, a northwest-ern suburb of Rangoon, marked by the grand clock tower that serves as the school's emblem. It is also known as the premier Chinese school before 1965.

Huazhong was built on an eleven-acre estate donated by Chan Mah Phee (Zeng Guangbi in standard Chinese), whose family had used the grounds and Western-style villa as a holiday home.[24] When the school opened its doors in 1921, additional construction had not been completed, but the existing villa, along with some teachers' dormitories, was sufficient for operation. The villa would be named the Guangbi Building to memorialize the school's generous benefactor.[25] Between 1921 and 1942, as World War II encroached on Burma, the school encountered many political and eco-nomic challenges that resulted in numerous changes in leadership, a two-year closure in 1922 and a temporary closure in 1930. During the war, the entire campus was bombed, leaving only a roofless Guangbi Building, but two years after the war, in June 1947, Hokkien leaders raised sufficient funds to rebuild and reopened the school.

In the late 1940s, the political struggles between the Nationalists and the Communists within China were explicitly exported to Burma, caus-ing heated confrontations and violence between pro-Nationalist and pro-Communist factions in Rangoon. The two opposing camps fought for control over Huazhong, which resulted in the closure of the school in March 1948. Nationalist officials stationed in Rangoon dismissed all pro-Communist teachers from Huazhong, which led those teachers to establish an alternative middle school named Nanyang Zhongxue, commonly referred to as Nanzhong. Their plan was to transfer all the students from Huazhong into the new school and build an even larger student body by recruiting so-called progressive students.[26] Ultimately, the Nationalists lost control of Huazhong, and both of the above schools became pro-Communist in 1948. Half of the existing student body was sent to the new Nanyang Middle School while the remainder continued on at Huazhong. According to texts produced by Sino-Burmese who now reside in Hong Kong, Macao, and China, the self-sacrificing efforts of the progressive teachers led to a flowering of Chinese education in Burma. Teachers such as Li Guohua not only introduced high school–level education to both Huazhong and Nanzhong but also produced high-caliber graduates who tested into Rangoon University, the premier university in Burma.[27] As represented in the texts produced by the Nationalist government in Taiwan, the above teachers, especially Li Guohua, were Communist stooges who destroyed Chinese education by indoctrinating their students into Communism.[28] Whatever the political rhetoric, the pro-Nationalist faction could not compete in Burma. "After China was lost to the Communists [in 1949], overseas Chinese schools were controlled by the Communists. After the [Nationalist] Chinese Education Promotion Association of Burma was established in 1951, things began to turn around."[29] However, in 1962 there were twice as many pro-Communist schools in Rangoon, numbering sixty, as pro-Nationalist schools, numbering twenty-seven.[30]

For the teachers who founded Nanzhong in May 1948, their success in fighting off the Nationalist faction was nothing short of a revolutionary triumph. In their recollections, despite insurmountable odds and little financial support, they managed to create a new school within two months through sheer determination.[31] In their narrative, they managed to obtain a piece of land in Bahan Township and transformed that property into a cohesive, collaborative school, which would produce outstanding students in its short seventeen-year history. Their narrative implies that whereas the Overseas Chinese Middle School was blessed with wealthy benefactors such as Chan Mah Phee, Nanyang Middle School was purely the product of the people's labor. Whether the students of Nanzhong hold similar beliefs about their school is difficult to determine. They have not spoken publicly about the ideological aspects of their schooling. Discussions about Communism and Chinese politics have been unwise since 1965, when the Revolutionary Council nationalized all schools, and especially since 1967, when overt political action by young students sparked the anti-Chinese riots of June 26, 1967. However, like those from the Overseas Chinese Middle School, Nanzhong graduates maintain an active alumni association that holds annual banquets and seeks to promote Chinese-language education. Successful alumni donate funds to the various Chinese schools in Rangoon. Their association also has branch offices in other cities such as Hong Kong, Macao, and Los Angeles. Graduates from both institutions speak of their school days with great fondness and recount their campus life in vivid detail.[32] As one graduate recalled: "I remember the clear sound of the school bell—'Dang, dang, dang!'—hurrying me into class. I remember my teacher Mr. Zhu Zaowo's singsong Hakka-accented standard Chinese teaching us geography. . . . Halfway up the hill at the palm leaf–covered stall, we ate our lunches. . . . My first year in middle school was spent at the bottom half of the hill. As I moved up in grades, my classroom also moved up the hill. By the time I graduated from middle school, my classroom was already at the very top."[33] In 2009, as a part of Nanzhong's sixty-first anniversary celebration, a busload of alumni visited their old campus in Bahan Township. Although nothing remained of their old school, the men and women, chatting in a combination of Burmese and standard Chinese, easily identified to one another the locations of their classrooms and dormitories and spoke nostalgically about where they used to buy barbecued snacks, the paths they took to their classrooms, and where they took their daily baths.[34]

Huazhong and Nanzhong were formative places where their students transitioned into early adulthood and did so during a turbulent time in both Burma's and China's history. The Union of Burma was a highly unstable nation-state during the 1950s and 1960s, as it contended with internal ethnic conflicts and external security threats from countries such as the People's Republic of China. In the 1950s, thousands of Nationalist troops and their US "advisers" were on Burmese soil. After being defeated by the People's Liberation Army in 1949, Nationalist forces initially tried to retake China from Shan State in northeastern Burma but, after two failures, occupied territories around the Salween River as if they were intending to stay. The newly independent government of Burma was afraid that the presence of armed Nationalist troops within its national boundaries would provoke the Chinese Communists into annexing the entire country. Despite repeated appeals to the United Nations for assistance, the government of Burma was not able to remove the Nationalist occupiers until 1961.[35] During my fieldwork, these events in northern Burma were only mentioned by one Sino-Burmese Rangoonite who had served as an interpreter in Shan State.[36] However, this silence likely speaks to their reluctance to be involved in politics or to discuss politics with strangers. The Nationalist occupation in Upper Burma must have affected the lives of the Sino-Burmese in Lower Burma, because the ideological battles conducted by Communist China were certainly felt in Rangoon. During this period, the newly founded People's Republic of China endured a series of intensifying radical movements that culminated in the Cultural Revolution (1966–76), and these movements were not contained within China's national territory. In this context, most Sino-Burmese stayed clear of politics, focusing on the increasing business opportunities in the 1950s and early 1960s, but some, particularly teachers and students, were caught up in Red Guard mania.

THE ANTI-CHINESE RIOTS OF JUNE 26, 1967

Although all Chinese schools in central and Lower Burma were national-ized in May 1965, private tutorials of twenty or fewer students were allowed to continue. Many teachers dismissed from Chinese schools continued to teach in their homes and Chinese associations. Analysis to date suggests that pro-Communist teachers were particularly active in maintaining Chinese education.[37] This education was heavily influenced by Maoist propaganda that targeted schoolchildren through texts such as *The Little Red Book* (quo-tations from Mao Zedong) and extracurricular activities such as the perfor-mance of model plays (*yangban xi*) and model music (*yangban yinyue*). In organizations such as the Irrawaddy Choir (Yijiang Hechangtuan), students performed pieces such as *The East Is Red* (Dongfanghong) and *Legend of the Red Lantern* (Hongdengji).[38] Those who underwent this pervasive indoctri-nation remember their teenage years as full of righteous passion and dedi-cation toward New China, the term used by patriotic Chinese to refer to the newly founded People's Republic of China. They defended their China against "Nationalist capitalist lackeys" by sabotaging Nationalist events and fighting students identified as pro-Nationalist.[39] Sino-Burmese now in their fifties and sixties say that street fights between pro-Communist and pro-Nationalist youth were common. A woman who now lives in Taiwan recalls: "When we were little we lived on a street where we, the Nationalists, were on one side and the Communists were on the other. We would sit at our windows and throw rocks against the Communists, and they would throw rocks back at us."[40] There was no middle ground between the two factions, and they were not afraid to reveal their animosity publicly. Some Chinese youth from Burma even returned to China to join the Red Guards.[41]

In this climate, Chinese students defiantly wore Mao badges to school despite government regulations forbidding the wearing of any insignia other than the emblem of Burma and the image of Aung San on school grounds. Activities outside of school were not regulated. On June 22, 1967, a brawl occurred at Rangoon National Elementary School No. 3 (formerly the Chinese Girls Middle School) when teachers confronted students wearing forbidden Mao badges. Although the brawl was settled on that day, Chinese students continued to defy the government's ban and continued wearing Mao badges. On June 24, the Burmese government closed Rangoon National Elementary School No. 3. In addition, it replaced the principals at the former Overseas Chinese Middle School and Nanyang Middle School with soldiers and demanded that each student sign an agreement to abide by school regulations before entering the campus.

On June 26, spurred on by the Burma Overseas Chinese Teachers' Union and the Chinese embassy in Rangoon, Chinese students again wore their Mao badges to school. A large quantity of Mao badges and copies of *The Little Red Book* had been air-freighted to Rangoon, and the teachers' union distributed this propaganda freely.[42] Students at the former Overseas Chinese Middle School were asked to sign the mandate to obey school regulations but refused. Parents of the students were called in, but the tension increased, causing school officials to close their front gates and lock in the students. In response, the students chanted Chinese slogans and read aloud from *The Little Red Book*. At that time, a mob of Burmese people was already making its way to Kemmendine. When the mob arrived at the school, they attacked the parents and anyone wearing a Mao badge. That afternoon, another Burmese mob struck the Chinese embassy and then shops and organizations in Tayout Tan, in particular the Burma Overseas Chinese Teachers' Union and Irrawaddy Choir.[43] On July 1 and 2, 1967, the PRC newspaper *People's Daily* reported that thirty-one Chinese people were killed, numerous people were injured, over ten organizations were vandalized, and Tayout Tan as a whole was pillaged and burned.[44]

On June 29, the government of Burma enforced martial law in Tayout Tan and the neighborhood around the Chinese embassy, effectively containing the violence. However, China's barely veiled efforts to extend Mao Zedong Thought and the Cultural Revolution to Burma had severely strained Sino-Burmese relations. Each government withdrew its respective ambassador in 1967 and sent strongly worded communiqués through their chargés d'affaires. Diplomatic relations were not restored until 1971 and remained poor until China withdrew its support for the Burma Communist Party in 1986.[45] The government of Burma had been frustrated by PRC-supported Communist activity within Burma but dared not confront China directly until June 1967. Under the rhetoric of maintaining separate party-to-party versus government-to-government relations, the Chinese Communist Party was directly supporting the Burma Communist Party despite protestations from the

Union of Burma.[46] The anti-Chinese riots forced the Communism issue to the foreground and placed Maoists in Burma under considerable threat.

The brutality of the riots shook the Chinese community to the core. In people's own retelling, no one realized they were so vulnerable. Their collective experience under U Nu's Parliamentary government (1948–62) suggested that they would be able to live much as they pleased. The new Union of Burma introduced regulations to Burmanize the country but was unable to enforce the new laws. Therefore, in the 1950s, Chinese people found themselves with greater opportunities in education, business, and other aspects of life than they had experienced under the British. They assumed that Ne Win's Revolutionary Council would offer similar freedoms through its inability to implement new policies and took little notice until the violence landed on their doorsteps.

Furthermore, those Chinese who had imbibed Mao Zedong Thought fully believed New China would come to their rescue. After all, they were only answering the chairman's call to action. Zeng Xiuying, who had been detained during the riots and now resides in Yunnan, China, recalled, "When we heard the roar of airplane engines, we sang revolutionary songs because we thought that Chairman Mao had sent the airplanes to call for us."[47] Unfortunately, the Chinese government had no effective strategy to assist the Maoists in Burma despite the fact that it was the People's Republic of China's blatant export of Maoism that had placed these revolutionaries in a bind. "In such troubled times, the Chinese in Burma, and especially the Maoists, 'complained that Beijing was inept and could not handle the trouble and crises.' Some Chinese even charged that 'Mao-thought harmed us and we were scapegoats.' As a result, some Overseas Chinese either shifted their support to the Kuomintang (KMT) or alienated themselves from the CCP [Chinese Communist Party] altogether."[48]

Contemporary Sino-Burmese living in Rangoon avoid the topic of the anti-Chinese riots and brush the event aside with comments such as "That is the past, things are better now," "It is better not to talk about such things," or "It was not Burmese people who carried out the rioting."[49] They say that many Burmese sheltered Chinese people during the riots and emphasize the brotherly (*pauk-hpaw*) relationship between the two communities. They also say that the mobs were soldiers in civilian dress sent by the Revolutionary Council and were not disgruntled Burmese.[50] Indeed, the tendency to skip over that period of history is so prevalent among contemporary Sino-Burmese that organizations such as the Myanmar Chinese Chamber of Commerce celebrated its hundredth anniversary and the Chinese Rotary Club celebrated its eightieth anniversary, both in 2009, dismissing the fact that their organizations were closed for twenty-odd years after the riots. The 1967 anti-Chinese riots were a pivotal but sublimated event in Sino-Burmese history that has since reshaped the Sino-Burmese community and how it understands itself.

DISAPPEARANCE OF STANDARD CHINESE AND CHINESENESS

Whereas private Chinese tutorials continued after the nationalization of schools in 1965, all education in standard Chinese stopped after the anti-Chinese riots. No one in Rangoon would dare open a Chinese school until the 1990s. Like Hokkien and Cantonese, which had retreated into the private realm after the establishment of standard Chinese schools in the 1920s, standard Chinese became a private language, seldom spoken even in the safety of one's home. For Hokkien and Cantonese people, standard Chinese was a language of the state, disseminated by the Nationalist Party and the People's Republic of China in its campaign to promote Chinese nationalism. The languages of the home were Hokkien and Cantonese and gradually included Burmese. After the spoken language of standard Chinese was excised from schools, a public realm, there was no place for it to go. In contemporary Rangoon, most Sino-Burmese under age forty-five cannot speak standard Chinese, a situation that can be partly attributed to the riots.[51]

Although standard Chinese–medium education privileged state-dominated Chinese culture, the closing of Chinese schools effectively removed all Chinese culture from Rangoon, both public and private. Sino-Burmese could no longer read the Chinese classics that had been the main transmitters of literate Chinese culture for millennia. Most Sino-Burmese, especially those who graduated from Huazhong and Nanzhong, say that they lost a generation of Chinese during the Socialist period because they lost the language. Anthropologist G. William Skinner in his assessment of Chinese society in Thailand in the 1950s wrote, "Without a Chinese education grandchildren of Chinese immigrants at the present time become Thai."[52] For the Sino-Burmese, the banning of Chinese education from 1964 onward initiated a similar trend, but that trend was not irreversible.

The unexpected violence of the riots forced people to reevaluate their position in Burmese society and replace their former complacency with wariness and cautious modulation of self-expression. Pro-PRC Chinese were disappointed by China's inaction and pro-Nationalist Chinese felt unjustly entangled in an ideological struggle they despised. Both camps feared continued violence, leading thousands of overseas Chinese to leave Burma. Clear data are not available, but contemporary Sino-Burmese say that the richest overseas Chinese emigrated to Hong Kong and the United States, those with fewer resources went to Macao and Taiwan, and the Maoists returned to China. Those who could not leave or elected to remain intentionally adopted Burmese names and dress and emphasized cultural similarities such as the worship of the Buddha and respect for all elders. Some even began to conceal their identity, denying their Chinese heritage and claimed to be Shan or ethnic minorities.[53]

The anti-Chinese riots fundamentally altered how the Chinese in Rangoon conceived of themselves. Before 1967, most thought of themselves as fundamentally Chinese, whether that was Hokkien or Cantonese inflected, pro-Communist or pro-Nationalist. After 1967, they transformed themselves into a hybrid people originating from China but living in and belonging to Burma. They became Sino-Burmese. Those in Rangoon not only altered their public self-representations by adopting Burmese names and dress but also applied for Burmese citizenship, which was once deemed unnecessary and undesirable. They endeavored to keep a low profile and withdrew from political participation, choosing to focus on commerce and other practical necessities.

The period between 1967 and 1988 is shrouded in mystery because the Sino-Burmese in Rangoon have selectively erased that segment of their collective history and the Sino-Burmese who left Burma lack firsthand knowledge of that time. Sino-Burmese living within and outside of Burma have published several books in Chinese such as the *Myanmar Chinese Chamber of Commerce One Hundredth Anniversary Special Edition, One Hundred Years of Myanmar Chinese History, Pauk-hpaw Feelings*, and *Analysis of Myanmar Chinese Society*. All of these books were published after 1990, but none of them include the period between 1967 and 1988. Most end their records and stories in 1967. Some Mainland Chinese scholars with greater access than researchers from other countries have investigated this period but have mostly focused on Mandalay and the northeastern border regions and have yet to publish a cohesive history. Given the extent to which the Ne Win regime closed off the country, this state of research is not surprising, but the lack of information also speaks to the suppression of Chineseness during the Socialist period.

THE AUGUST 8, 1988, UPRISING

The Socialist government's attempt to free itself from regional and Cold War politics as well as global economic constraints through the Burmese Way to Socialism turned out to be an utter failure. By 1987, Burma was listed by the United Nations as one of the world's least developed countries, a distinction that coincided with a host of problems that would push the populace toward a popular uprising. Pressure had been building for many years as the Ne Win regime crushed student protests in 1962 and 1974, incurring the ire of Burmese youth, and demonetized the kyat in 1964, 1985, and 1987, robbing the savings of Burmese people. Sparked by the clumsy handling of a brawl between college students and out-of-school youths that led to the inadvertent death of one student, the protests escalated into a mass pro-democracy movement that spread from Rangoon throughout the entire country. On August 8, 1988, thousands of students, teachers, monks, professionals, and farmers held a peaceful general strike across Burma but were met with military gunfire that killed thousands. During this time, former political and military leaders such as U Nu and Aung Gyi reemerged to push for a new government and Aung San Suu Kyi, daughter of Burma's founding father, General Aung San, entered the political arena after returning to her birthplace to care for her ailing mother. Shifts within the military power structure, including the resignation of Ne Win, suggested movement toward a civilian government, but the generals in power were not ready to relinquish control. Ultimately, battle-tested soldiers from insurgent areas (former Frontier Areas) were deployed to crack down on protesters, and military rule was reinstated on September 18, 1988, under the guise of the State Law and Order Restoration Council (SLORC). However, an ember of hope remained as the SLORC promised and delivered a multiparty election in May 1990. Political parties such as the National League for Democracy (NLD) led by Aung San Suu Kyi were formed in the aftermath of the uprising, and their candidates campaigned for office against military candidates. Much to the generals' surprise, the NLD won by a landslide, winning 392 out of 492 seats, but those elected were barred from taking office through a series of delays and excuses put forth by the SLORC.

This pivotal event in Burmese history shapes the lives of all Burmese people, including the Sino-Burmese. Whereas the 1967 anti-Chinese riots laid bare the cost of participating in PRC politics, the 1988 uprising underscored the danger of contributing to a Burmese cause. Self-preservation for the Sino-Burmese would seem to dictate exclusive focus on practical concerns such as making money in order to create a safety net.

STANDARD CHINESE REEMERGING AS A MARKET LANGUAGE

After 1988, economic and political developments in Myanmar and the Asia region have increased the utility of standard Chinese and elevated its status to that of a desirable market language. Within the framework of this book, market language is defined as a transnational language of commerce that sometimes provides access to other avenues of power. During the colonial era, the market languages in Rangoon were Hindi and English. Indian merchants had dominated medium and large enterprises, while British colonialists monopolized the most lucrative sectors of international trade. In independent Burma, English remained the language for advancement until Ne Win's regime officially rejected all foreign influences in the 1960s. After the government of Myanmar reopened its borders to international trade in the 1990s, standard Chinese became a marketable asset that increased job and business opportunities. Studies regarding national education in Thailand show that mandatory schooling in standard Thai gave villagers greater access to the market economy, enabling them to assume roles in the capitalist sector.[54] In a similar fashion, standard Chinese fluency has become a desirable skill that has enabled growing numbers of people to reach beyond the local market into transnational trade and services. This occurred in tandem with the resurgence of English when young Burmese strove for high levels of English literacy in order to obtain jobs with international organizations such as the United Nations or work in tourism.[55]

Although the failing Socialist regime began to open up Burma's economy in 1987, it was the SLORC (later renamed the State Peace and Development Council [SPDC]) that actively sought foreign direct investment from 1988 onward. Large corporations were interested in Myanmar's potential oil and gas reserves and established joint ventures with government ministries and organizations. Smaller-scale enterprises and individual investors were also attracted to the country by the low cost of labor and other commercial opportunities. These investors often arrived through unofficial channels and were willing to gamble on short-term profits.

From the perspective of the Sino-Burmese, many standard Chinese–speaking businesspeople landed in Rangoon hoping to capitalize on a virgin market. As one businessperson stated: "In the 1990s, all of these foreigners came with their language and wanted to start new businesses. We had no work before they came. Only when they came from Singapore, Taiwan, and Hong Kong did we have jobs. We didn't speak standard Chinese very well before they came, so lots of people started studying standard Chinese. It was good for business. . . . Then Burmans, not just Sino-Burmese, started studying standard Chinese."[56] Those who could speak standard Chinese when these foreign businesspeople first arrived profited immediately. They served as interpreters, intermediaries, and partners in establishing new restaurants, karaoke bars, factories, and export businesses. Many Sino-Burmese who now own large companies such as supermarket chains and hotels remember the 1990s as a volatile but profitable period, which sowed the seeds for their current wealth. Some landed jobs as managers of these new establishments, while others had to work from the ground up because they had minimal standard Chinese–language skills. However, many people also found themselves out of work in a year or two because the market was unstable and at times exploitative. In Rangoon, full-time employment has been elusive in recent decades, compelling job seekers to make compromises. Some young women found themselves to be the objects of unsolicited sexual attention in karaoke bars but had little recourse besides quitting.[57] Many of these Chinese foreign investors were driven out of Myanmar by the fickle policies of the military junta, but businesses from Mainland China came soon on their heels, maintaining the market advantage of being able to speak standard Chinese. The general perception is that fluency in standard Chinese is a valuable asset in the Burmese and regional markets and, like English, provides access to the world outside of Myanmar.[58]

The demands of the market have increased the utility and attractiveness of standard Chinese, rendering the language less problematic. In contemporary Rangoon it is now possible for the Sino-Burmese to approach standard Chinese as a practical foreign language as well as a carrier of Chinese culture. Elders in the Sino-Burmese community have capitalized on this transformation and opened schools such as the Eastern Language and Business Center in Ahlone, the largest Chinese school in Rangoon, and Fuxing Technology Center, which offers classes for learning Chinese and English and enhancing computer skills, subjects they see as essential for the future.[59] The founders and executives of these schools are alumni of the Overseas Chinese Middle School and the Nanyang Middle School who not only manage these new institutions but also donate money to cover operational costs and periodic upgrades. They foreground the pragmatic use of Chinese in the names and functions of these schools, not as an unthinking, utilitarian application of the language but as a tactical maneuver to promote Chinese literacy, not Chinese patriotism, without drawing unnecessary attention. A similar tactic was employed in the 1980s when these same elders organized *sutta* (the Pali equivalent of *sutra*, Buddhist scripture) study classes in the various temples in order to maintain Chinese literacy. Studying Chinese in the name of Buddhism is safe because Burmese people revere the teachings of the Buddha and because Buddhism is nearly a state religion. Although the Sino-Burmese have conscientiously integrated themselves into Rangoon society since 1967, they are still somehow other, and this difference could brand them as targets for resentment and racism. Therefore, pride in their cultural heritage must be balanced with the political, economic, and social realities of their environment. They must find a way of being both Chinese and Burmese.

The number of Chinese-language schools in Rangoon has increased significantly since the mid-1990s, but no reliable statistics are available. Foreign-language-medium schools are officially prohibited, meaning that nongovernment schools operate through an implicit understanding (*nalehmu* in Burmese) struck between schools and local officials. Chinese sources state that more than ten new schools have opened since 1996, but the figure must be higher since advertisements for Chinese classes are posted in many neighborhoods. In February 2009, buses that routed through Sanchaung Township, a transportation hub for Rangoon, had ads that read in English: "To Be Smart, Be Learned Chinese [*sic*]." As unofficial institutions, these schools are more like part-time tutorial centers where students study Chinese for one to two hours before or after school and on weekends.

CONCLUSION

The Sino-Burmese youth in these recently founded schools, like their Burman, Indian, Indo-Burmese, and other classmates, are learning Chinese as a second language.[60] Their parents neither speak standard Chinese nor read Chinese. Scholars in the field of Sinophone studies have called for a reframing in the study of the Chinese because ethnicity is not synonymous with identity and nationality and because the study of the Sinophone is the "study of Sinitic-language cultures and communities on the margins of China and Chineseness."[61] For the Sino-Burmese in Rangoon, Chineseness is more appropriately labeled Tayout-ness since their dynamic practices of self-understanding have not adhered to a single conception of China or demanded absolute authenticity. Rather, they have become Tayout—local Chinese—who often discover or recover Chineseness along with their Burmese neighbors.

Many Sino-Burmese only learned about Chinese culture through television series such as *Pauk Chin* (the Burmese transliteration of *Bao Qingtian*), which aired nationally in the mid-1990s. *Pauk Chin* depicted the life of the legendary Judge Bao of the Song dynasty, whose indomitable application of justice made him respected by the masses and feared by the corrupt elite. This righteous figure was so well liked that neighbors gathered to watch the show at the homes of those with televisions, and children followed the story with such fervor that they adopted the morals from this traditional

Chinese lore. Without naming Pauk Chin, children who wanted to admonish one another against doing bad deeds would say, "Your head will be cut off by the *kwe yout, kya yout,* or *naga yout* if you do this bad deed."[62] These three *yout* are the Burmese names for the dog head, tiger head, and snake/dragon head guillotines that were used to behead people of different social status: the dog head guillotine for the masses, the tiger head for government officials, and the dragon head for royalty. Pauk Chin's fearless application of justice and his ability to punish everyone, even those in power, must have been attractive to the Burmese audience who suffered under an unjust government.[63] This series, like other shows from Taiwan, Hong Kong, and now Korea, was in its original language (standard Chinese) with Burmese subtitles. The positive image of Chinese culture projected through shows such as *Pauk Chin* and the utility of Chinese as a market language have made it possible for Sino-Burmese to study the language without fear of political or societal repercussions. In fact, Chinese classes in Rangoon cater to young and old, with Sino-Burmese in their twenties and thirties attending class in the evenings to reexamine what it means to be Chinese in their being Sino-Burmese.

In postindependence Burma where differences in ethnicity, religion, and language have been construed as potential threats to national unity, the resurgence of Chinese-language education after 1990 must be understood as a side effect of the SLORC/SPDC push for economic modernization and growth.[64] The space for the Chinese language and Chineseness is the marketplace. Although the Socialist government had defined the Chinese language as a foreign imposition and excised it from public education, its utility in regional trade has rendered it once again permissible. Furthermore, the political ideologies once entangled with Chinese-language education have been explicitly removed by the Sino-Burmese and their PRC sponsor, Hanban (the Chinese National Office for Teaching Chinese as a Foreign Language). Throughout Rangoon and most of Myanmar, Chinese schools highlight the employment opportunities made possible through fluency in standard Chinese and Chinese is taught as a second language to students unfamiliar with Chinese culture. As with the maintenance of the Hokkien Kuanyin Temple and other Sino-Burmese places, the Sino-Burmese of Rangoon are fundamentally practical in their preservation of Chinese culture.

CHAPTER FOUR

SINO-BURMESE COMMERCE
AND CITY MART

I N the relatively more open market of post-1990 Myanmar, Sino-Burmese merchants, like their predecessors during the colonial era, were able to succeed in the interstices, by filling small- and medium-scale market niches. As characterized by Eng Tsing Yian, a respected Hokkien merchant, the Sino-Burmese have made the best of leftovers: "Really, we must smile secretly to ourselves. If the Myanmar government had not cast aside so many small businesses, we would not have been able to succeed. Today all Sino-Burmese businesses are found businesses. It is like we picked them off the street."[1] Indeed, in the opaque and unpredictable economic environment of Myanmar, Sino-Burmese merchants have maintained a reactive, wait-and-see attitude, taking calculated risks to capitalize on last-minute opportunities. In the history of the Sino-Burmese in Rangoon, financial success has generally been transitory, and wealth has not been shared by all people of Chinese descent. As already noted in the discussion about *let-to* and *let-shei* Chinese, there were and continue to be merchant- and working-class Sino-Burmese. There are also destitute Sino-Burmese who must rely on the assistance of organizations such as the Kuanyin Ting to provide for their daily needs and families living in Dala, North Okkalapa, and other more remote townships who manage to survive just beyond subsistence farming.

These different classes exist within the various Burmese and hybrid Burmese populations of Rangoon. However, this reality is often superseded by ethnic categorizations that define Chinese and Indian people as rich and likely rapacious foreigners and Burmese as poor disenfranchised natives. During my fieldwork, Burmese and Sino-Burmese Rangoonites used this well-known adage to characterize the three main populations in the city: "Work like the Chinese. Save money like the Indians. Don't throw away money like the Burmese" (*Tayout lo lout. Kala lo su. Bama lo ma hpyoun ne*).[2] This shorthand notion remains pervasive in Rangoon, despite the fact that all of my informants named friends who were Chinese but not greedy, Indian but not miserly, and Burman but not poor.

Rangoon was explicitly designed to serve the needs of the colonial state: to encourage trade in order to accrue profit for the empire and to instigate order in a newly conquered territory. In that process, the highest common factor became the economic imperative and commerce became the ethos of Rangoon. John Sydendam Furnivall, a British civil service officer turned colonial critic, observed that British rule in Burma created a *plural society* in which individuals met, but only in the marketplace, and were unable to come together to form a common social will. Without the mediating influence of a common social will, the unfettered capitalism unleashed by the colonial government promoted "materialism, rationalism, individualism, and a concentration on economic ends far more complete and absolute than in homogenous western lands."[3] The ethnic divisions outlined by Furnivall appear to be an enduring colonial legacy that continues to influence contemporary society in Rangoon.

In this milieu, the Sino-Burmese pursuit of wealth is not only the manifestation of a so-called Chinese characteristic but also a logical response to a colonial environment and its lingering effects. For them, merchant culture is understood as a culture of individual and group empowerment. Defined as foreigners in the nation-state of Burma/Myanmar, they view financial success as a way to protect themselves and exercise some control over their lives. As they witnessed in the history of the Muslim Indo-Burmese, the most direct targets of Burmese nationalism, political activism has not led to sustained and enhanced well-being. Some Sino-Burmese Rangoonites commented that although Indians participated directly in government during the Parliamentary era, their political activity ultimately achieved little, because they remain outsiders whose outspokenness labels them as demanding and un-Burmese.[4] The "Chinese love of money" might be problematic, but it has also been a real means for Chinese to integrate themselves into Burmese society. Again, reliable statistics are required for valid analysis, but among Burmese Rangoonites, Tayout are considered to be good candidates for marriage because Tayout men are not only hardworking but also able to keep their wealth for multiple generations.[5]

City Mart, the most successful supermarket chain in Myanmar, stands as an example of how Sino-Burmese merchants have both sustained practices common in the Chinese diaspora and integrated themselves into the local society, despite political, economic, and social constraints.

For the Sino-Burmese and overseas Chinese originating from southeastern China, making money has been one of the few means of establishing a sense of security. Historically, they were neither supported by the imperial or modern governments of China nor treated as equals by colonial rulers. Driven out of China by poverty and internecine warfare, Hokkien and Cantonese migrants were officially seen as fugitives by the Chinese state until their riches became desirable assets for bolstering the failing Qing court. Private foreign trade was banned for two hundred years, from the fifteenth to the seventeenth centuries, and overseas travel was banned until 1893.[6] Furthermore, the Confucian political and social order of dynastic China placed merchants at the bottom of a four-tier hierarchy, beneath the literati, peasant, and artisan classes. Historically, successful Chinese merchants overcame their social inferiority to some extent, but higher status was attained by rejecting their merchant origins and identifying with the elite culture of the literati.[7]

Beyond China, Chinese merchants were generally valued as industrious intermediaries—*kapitans* and *compradors*—who could serve colonial states by facilitating trade between indigenous populations and European companies.[8] However, the Chinese who settled in Rangoon were not the chosen middlemen of the British colonialists—that lucrative position was occupied by Indian entrepreneurs. As third-tier foreigners, placed below the Europeans and Indians, Chinese merchants were unable to compete with Indian businesses, until a series of anti-Indian policies drove thousands of Indians out of Burma after World War II.[9]

Nonetheless, like other overseas Chinese in Southeast Asia, the Chinese and later Sino-Burmese in Burma practiced the merchant culture of their native provinces. Chinese merchant culture (*huashang wenhua*) arose despite prejudices and constraints imposed by mandarin officials and the literati. Merchants had to operate in the most difficult conditions of any group in traditional China and formulated an eclectic blend that incorporated Confucian values shared by all Chinese people and commerce-specific practices such as profit seeking, risk taking, coalition building, and philanthropy. As in the literati, peasant, and artisan classes, Chinese merchants employed the Confucian patriarchal family structure as the ordering principle for all social interactions, and thrift, honesty, trust, loyalty, and industriousness were prized as virtues. Therefore, family became the primary body of trade, and the characteristics listed above were integrated into a set of values that has been termed the "will to profit."[10] The will to profit directs thrift, honesty, trust, loyalty, and industriousness toward profit seeking and the risks inherent in pursuing high returns. It also assists merchants in building reliable connections with one another in order to establish mutually beneficial associations. Lastly, philanthropy was most systematically developed among successful merchants even though it was a practice encouraged in all Chinese. As people from a class with low social status, merchants used their wealth as an instrument for gaining respectability and upward social mobility.[11]

Outside of China, where mandarin officials no longer dominated society, this set of values and practices enabled overseas Chinese to capitalize on the maritime trade in Southeast Asia and to play key roles in major trading ports as middlemen to the Portuguese, Spanish, Dutch, and English. However, freedom from mandarin control did not remove all constraints. The various colonial governments of Southeast Asia explicitly promoted international trade and established rule of law, but those laws were not consistently enforced across the different populations. Racial discrimination reared its ugly head on multiple occasions. When overseas Chinese merchants were treated unfairly by colonial governments, China provided no official protection whatsoever.[12] While in various colonial cities many of these merchants rose to the class of local bourgeois, such as the Baba-Nyonya and Peranakan, their relationship to the state always involved conflicts and contradictions.

Western officials and traders recognized Chinese merchants as the most enterprising and dynamic group in the region but also saw them as potential threats to colonial order and profit. In port cities such as Batavia, Singapore, and Rangoon, Chinese merchants organized themselves into native place, surname, and trade associations to provide mutual aid and to represent merchant interests before officialdom. Often housed within temples, as seen in the Fujian Native Place Association (Hokkien Gongsi) that occupies the western wing of the Hokkien Kuanyin Temple, these organizations were sometimes able to argue for the rights of overseas Chinese but usually subverted colonial control through hidden alliances that forged alternative networks of power. In Singapore and Penang, battles between secret societies such as Ghee Hin and Kien Tek were so disruptive that the police instigated the Dangerous Societies Ordinances of 1869, 1882, and 1885 to register and regulate these societies.[13] In Rangoon, although the Kien Tek Association was established as a branch of Penang's Kien Tek Society and Ho Sing Brotherhood was an offshoot of Penang's Ghee Hin Society, Chinese organizations in Burma never troubled the colonial government to the extent of requiring direct intervention. The much larger Indian population required more policing and interacted more directly with the state.

For the Chinese in Lower Burma, financial success has relied on the *intimate economy*, wherein family is inextricably intertwined with work and profit seeking.[14] Although global capitalism has tended to make business external and impersonal, at the scale of specific places, capitalism is a social and cultural practice that is mediated by and affects intimate relationships. Whereas the Peranakan of Indonesia, Baba of the Straits Settlements, Sino-Thai, and others gradually rose above the status of mere merchants to become capitalists, the Chinese in Rangoon have remained small and medium enterprise operators. Situated in a colonial outpost that was the port of last hope for Chinese migrants who had failed in other Southeast Asian cities and located in a secondary port that traded more with Calcutta than with the maritime hubs of Southeast Asia, the Chinese in Rangoon lived on the periphery of British India and the Straits Settlements. Their marginality within the overseas Chinese network and their third-class foreigner status within Rangoon society limited their access to business opportunities. For the Chinese in Rangoon operating within these constraints, personal connections coupled with an intimate understanding of their local society would become the only means by which they could make a profit.

Although all overseas Chinese have learned from long experience to expect little of governments, the Chinese in Rangoon, as a doubly marginalized population, have been particularly reliant on personal, nonstate connections. Some merchant families such as the Chan, Khoo, Lim, and Yeoh managed to accumulate sufficient wealth to mimic the Baba-Nyonya lifestyle in the Straits Settlements, but none became powerful enough to be known throughout the overseas Chinese network.[15] Rangoon was a product of colonial-driven capitalism, and everyone in the city was subjected to the risks of a globalizing market, but the Chinese could not profit directly from international trade. Their merchant community was dependent on the connections in Penang, and their sphere of influence remained limited. As such, they focused on the domestic market and contended with the effects of colonial and later global capitalism through multiple and intimate economies.

These negotiations that interweave public and private life have affected how migrant populations understand and represent themselves in general. In the case of the Sino-Burmese in Rangoon, the economic environment has been the dominant but not the exclusive factor in encouraging or discouraging expressions of Chineseness and Chinese merchant culture. The chronicle of the Sino-Burmese in Rangoon can be conceived of as a history of successive tactics in which the economic imperative superseded less immediate concerns.

Tactics in this analysis of Sino-Burmese commerce are the calculated risks undertaken to temporarily subvert or benefit from the actions of government. In the contexts of colonial and independent Burma where political participation was difficult, if not impossible, for the Sino-Burmese, commerce was the only realm through which they could exert some control over their lives. Money gave them more choices, and their business acumen rendered them valuable assets to the various governments. Although they were not the chosen middlemen for British colonialists, they were still recognized as an enterprising group of people who contributed to the economic growth of British Burma. Chinese merchants focused on the domestic and smaller-scale businesses during the colonial era and accumulated sufficient wealth to build association halls and create a place for themselves in the neighborhood of Tayout Tan. Unlike the Indians in Rangoon or the Baba-Nyonya in Penang, the Chinese did not become the local bourgeois class but were nonetheless secure enough in their investments and properties that they returned to the city after World War II.

When the Japanese army descended on Burma in 1942, about half of the two hundred thousand Chinese living in Burma fled to China, but China itself was war-torn, fragmented, and fighting Japanese forces.[16] In Rangoon's Tayout Tan, approximately nine out of ten homes and shops were empty, but soon after the Japanese troops left in 1945 Chinese immigrants returned in large numbers.[17] The civil war between the Nationalists and the Communists made life difficult in their native places and the weakness of the imperial and republican governments impressed upon many overseas Chinese that their fatherland was not their *kosuan*, a powerful entity they could depend on for their personal security.[18]

The diverse Indian population in Burma also fled in 1942. About half of the one million Indians escaped overland to Assam, largely on foot, and thousands died along the way. Only a small portion of those who fled returned after the war, so that by 1947–48 the Indian population was reduced to about seven hundred thousand.[19] After 1947, Indians were no longer able to move between South Asia and Burma as residents moving from one district to another. In June 1947, the returned British government promulgated the Burma Immigration (Emergency Provisions) Act requiring visas for entry into Burma, effectively halting large-scale Indian immigration into the country.

This act coupled with the mass exodus of the British and other communities most dependent upon the colonial state significantly altered the ethnic composition and socioeconomic structure of Rangoon.[20] In this changed landscape, the Chinese in Rangoon were able to capture the lucrative trade opportunities such as rice milling and international trade that were once monopolized by European and Indian companies.[21] This trend that began during the interregnum of 1945–48 continued into the Parliamentary period (1948–62) of independent Burma despite governmental regulations.

PROFIT SEEKING IN THE PARLIAMENTARY PERIOD

The new Union of Burma led by U Nu and the ruling coalition, the Anti-Fascist People's Freedom League (AFPFL), was a fervently nationalistic government, and its leaders, mainly of Burman descent, wanted to build a Burma for the Burmese. Under colonial rule, the native Burman population had to watch as the British and their collaborators stripped their country of its natural resources and promoted foreigners and certain indigenous ethnicities to positions of relative power.[22] To remedy this unequal status, the fledgling government implemented policies to regain political and economic control. One such policy was the Citizenship Act of 1948, which defined citizenship by blood and restricted national belonging to the "indigenous races of Burma" that had settled in the union before 1823.[23] Through these definitions, foreigners were officially excluded as interlopers with no place in Burma. In actual practice, the 1948 act was not systematically implemented and provided other conditions for acquiring citizenship, making it possible for Chinese people to continue living in Burma with few impediments.[24]

The Union of Burma also forbade noncitizens from owning property or operating large-scale enterprises. Importing and exporting, arguably the most lucrative businesses, were regulated through licenses allocated to Burmans alone. Unfortunately, most Burmans had little or no experience with large-scale international trade and covertly sold their licenses to Chinese merchants who operated businesses under the names of Burman owners but exercised complete control.[25] Chinese merchants accepted the risks of these technically illegal actions because they produced significant profits and also because postwar Burma was in a state of chaos, with opportunities opening up at the fringes of government control.

In a period of fervent nationalism, the status of the Chinese as nonnationals could have been an absolute liability, but their commercial acumen was a much-needed skill for postwar reconstruction. They were the remaining population with expertise in international commerce.[26] Furthermore, the AFPFL was inundated on multiple fronts after achieving independence. World War II had ravaged the country, and the formation of the union from historically separate ethnic sovereignties was politically precarious. Different ethnic groups such as the Kachin and Karen were fighting for self-rule, and the Burmese Communist Party periodically attacked the central government, threatening to topple the fragile inchoate nation. Under these circumstances, the government was often unable to enforce its new laws and turned a blind eye to the manipulation of economic policies that were intended to return power to the Burmese.[27]

In addition, the departure of the British left Burma to supply itself with basic necessities such as cooking oil, soap, and hardware for reconstruction. Under colonial rule, these goods were largely imported. The role of Burma had been to supply cheap natural resources in exchange for manufactured goods from England. Therefore, independent Burma lacked the industrial and entrepreneurial infrastructure to rebuild its war-torn economy. To encourage private investment, U Nu said to a gathering of industrialists in 1958: "In developing our industry, the government cannot undertake all of the work and we have not managed some projects well. Therefore, we need to give some of this work to private industries."[28] Under these circumstances, the Chinese in Burma were able to build factories such as the Reizhi (Shwedi) Soap Company and the Reiman (Shweman) Oil Company in the 1950s.

As remembered by the Sino-Burmese, the period under U Nu was a golden era in which official policies were flexibly enforced, leaving an open market for profit seeking in the many areas that the government could not manage.[29] During the Parliamentary era, the bulk of trade that was once dominated by Indian and European businesses was handed over to Chinese merchants by default. Despite the AFPFL's reluctance in divesting its hard-won power to yet another foreign population, it had to utilize whatever means possible to rebuild its devastated country.

RELYING ON TRUST IN THE SOCIALIST PERIOD

Although the Chinese in Rangoon experienced life under the AFPFL as a golden era, that era was short-lived. In 1958, when AFPFL infighting threatened to escalate ongoing civil wars, General Ne Win instigated emergency military rule. Under this caretaker government, a superficial order was reestablished, and an election was held that reinstated U Nu in 1960. However, in 1962 the military once again instigated a coup d'état, and a military Socialist government was established that would reign until 1988. Between 1962 and 1988, Burma was ruled first by the Revolutionary Council and then by a military-backed single party, the Burma Socialist Program Party

(BSPP), both dominated by General Ne Win. Foremost in the policies of this government was the pursuit of the Burmese Way to Socialism, which sought to nationalize most sectors of society (business, media, production) and to drive out unwanted foreign influence and resident aliens, once and for all.

British enterprises had mostly been expelled from Burma after independence, but English-language education still remained and Indians were still a significant portion of Rangoon's professional and commercial class. On June 1 1963, as a part of the Burmese Way to Socialism, the Enterprise Nationalization Law nationalized all major industries including import-export trade, rice milling, banking, mining, and teak and rubber manufacturing. The objective of this law was to return all commercial assets to the hands of the Burmese in order to break the monopoly of foreign firms on the Burmese economy. Beginning in 1964, under orders from Ne Win, about three hundred thousand Indians, men, women, and children, were expelled from Burma and sent to India and Pakistan.[30] All of them were stripped of their homes, property, and businesses, and those who remained suffered similar injustices. Many Indians who were not expatriated had their properties and assets, both commercial and private, confiscated.[31]

Like the Indians, Chinese merchants also lost their properties, but their losses were limited to commercial assets as stipulated by law. Along with Chinese schools and newspapers, six thousand seven hundred Chinese stores and two of Beijing's banks were nationalized. This was a tremendous blow to the Chinese community and was made worse by the political machinations of the People's Republic of China. In the name of promoting Communism, China disregarded overseas Chinese discontent and supported Burma's Socialist policies.[32] Despite this double bind, the Chinese escaped the crueler racial discrimination endured by the Indians because they were less wealthy and more able to blend into the local Buddhist society. The dramatic economic success of Indians in the colonial Burmese market rendered them more visibly alien, and their professions as colonial clerks, soldiers, and police officers defined them as collaborators explicitly involved in the oppression of the Burmese. The relative leniency shown to the Chinese enabled many to keep their private property. Even the wealthiest Chinese families such as the descendants of Chan Mah Phee were able to maintain ownership of their multiple estates.[33] A notable exception was Lim Chin Tsong, whose hybrid Sino-Palladian villa was expropriated by the Socialist regime.

In this constricted economic environment, trust and personal connections became more important than ever for commerce. The BSPP had declared all private business illegal, forcing the market to go underground.

Trade had to be conducted within an intimate network wherein trust between associates safeguarded the livelihood of all involved. In theory, the nationalized economy was supposed to supply all daily necessities through the People's Stores that were established in every neighborhood. In reality, the BSPP was not able to manage the national economy or deliver basic goods. To compensate for the shortfall in essentials such as rice, cooking oil, and vegetables, alternative, barter-based markets developed throughout the country. One such market flowed along the Irrawaddy River, which traverses the entire span of Burma from north to south. The Irrawaddy was known as "the bank," with a network of traders who relied on personal relationships and trust in shipping goods up and down the river.[34] Through private channels, people involved in this network knew exactly where and when the boats would dock and which products would be delivered. According to Sino-Burmese men in their fifties and sixties, there was great excitement along the river in Tayout Tan whenever a shipment was about to arrive. They watched men rush to the Rangoon train station to take orders for the incoming products and then load the products for delivery as soon as the ferries arrived. Other forms of commerce such as black market trade across the Thailand-Burma border also increased. By necessity, these risky entrepreneurial networks strengthened personal connections between merchants, enabling those involved not only to profit but also to build relationships that would be tapped in the post-1988 liberalized economy.

Concurrent with the pursuit of the Burmese Way to Socialism, the BSPP further restricted Burmese citizenship, marking some such as the Rohingya, Indians, and Chinese as ineligible for citizenship or as lesser citizens.[35] Efforts to Burmanize all of Burma were more persistent under Ne Win than under U Nu, and by 1982 the new citizenship law declared three classes of citizens: (1) full citizens—those descended from residents who lived in Burma prior to 1823 or those born to parents who were citizens at the time of birth; (2) associate citizens—those who acquired citizenship through the 1948 Union Citizenship Act; and (3) naturalized citizens—those who lived in Burma before January 4, 1948, and applied for citizenship after 1982. Chinese and Indians who had obtained full citizenship under the 1948 law were demoted to associate citizens and lost their official positions in government as well as access to the most prestigious majors in universities: medicine and engineering.[36] However, according to contemporary Sino-Burmese, the 1982 law was taken in stride because it was never fully implemented and because by that time most Chinese had already become Sino-Burmese, both culturally and legally.[37] The trauma of the 1967 anti-Chinese riots forced them to reevaluate their place in Burmese society and compelled them to take both legal and illegal measures to gain citizenship. While most Sino-Burmese fell in the category of associate citizens, it was not difficult for them to bribe officials to register as full citizens.[38]

During the Socialist period, Sino-Burmese business acumen was no longer an asset desired by the government, but as long as the Sino-Burmese towed the Socialist line, they were not targeted as aliens. Indeed, contemporary Sino-Burmese who lived through that period said that the anti-Chinese riots were instigated by the government due to tensions between the People's Republic of China and Burma, not as an expression of social discontent. They also stated that after 1967–68, everyone had to endure the pervasive poverty. Similarly, Rangoonites, regardless of ethnicity, said all people suffered equally during the Socialist era, so it did not matter if you were Burman, Chinese, or Indian. No one was immune to the economic roulette of the BSPP, and everyone survived as best they could.

In particular, the demonetizations of 1964, 1985, and 1987 robbed most people of their savings and shattered the Burmese economy. The demonetization of various kyat notes in these three years was ostensibly undertaken to curtail black marketeering, although other explanations such as Ne Win's predilection for numerology have been cited as the underlying cause. Whatever the motivation, the people of Burma suffered real losses as a result of these government actions. In 1985, the K 25, K 50, and K 100 notes were demonetized without warning, although the public was allowed to exchange a limited amount of the old notes for new ones. In 1987, the government demonetized the K 25, K 35, and K 75 notes without warning or compensation, rendering some 75 percent of the country's currency worthless. These sudden and ill-considered actions were particularly harmful because many people did not trust the government-run banking system and kept their cash savings at home. The resultant economic fallout would become one of the precipitating factors for the people's uprising on August 8, 1988.

Ne Win and the BSPP eventually recognized their failure and began to move the country away from Socialism by liberalizing the economy. In 1987, farmers were permitted to sell grains and rice in the open market, and overland trade was legalized in 1988.[39] However, years of economic and governmental ineptitude had greatly tested the populace, and when rice prices rose after the third demonetization in September 1987, widespread dissatisfaction was evident. On August 8, 1988, thousands of everyday Burmese held a peaceful general strike across Burma but were met with military gunfire that killed thousands. The Tatmadaw (Myanmar's armed forces) believed that the nation was once again devolving into chaos and saw itself as the only body capable of reinstating order. Ultimately, the generals cracked down on protesters and military rule was reinstated on September 18, 1988, under the guise of the State Law and Order Restoration Council (SLORC), renamed the State Peace and Development Council (SPDC) in 1997.

The SLORC/SPDC's strategy seemed similar to that of China's—open up the economy to lift the country out of poverty but suppress all political activity. The steps away from the Socialist economy that were haltingly implemented in 1987 picked up some momentum in the 1990s. Foreign investors entered Burma to tap the abundant natural resources (natural gas, oil, and teak, among others) and eager labor force. One of the first actions undertaken by the SLORC was the publication of the Foreign Investment Law in 1989 to entice international companies with the promise of profits and long-term financial security. Myanmar was desperate for financing and saw foreign direct investment as the means out of its economic troubles. Although the most lucrative investments were reserved for the junta in projects such as the Yadana pipeline, which delivers natural gas from the Andaman Sea to Thailand and generated billions of dollars each year for the generals, smaller-scale investments were also available.

From 1987 through the 1990s, Sino-Burmese merchants seized all the opportunities available to them. Some took advantage of the officially open border between China and Burma to import household products, snacks, and small goods not produced in Burma. Others connected with Japanese investors, establishing textile factories and pulse-export businesses that continue to be profitable. Yet others with less access to established networks grasped whatever business was available, setting up highly flexible, time-sensitive, and opportunistic trade that waxed and waned on a daily basis. In the early to mid-1990s, some Chinese who had left Burma in the 1960s and 1970s returned to capitalize on the open market and others tried to make a profit from afar via old merchant family networks.

Around that time, large Burmese tiger prawns became a sought-after delicacy in Hong Kong. Restaurants were willing to pay top dollar for live prawns caught and shipped within twenty-four hours to Hong Kong. Sino-Burmese who learned of this opportunity immediately set up ad hoc businesses by locating shrimp fishermen along the coast of Lower Burma, hiring trucks to carry the shrimp north to Rangoon, and establishing connections with people working in Rangoon's Mingaladon airport in order to send live freight whenever necessary via whichever airplane was departing. The typical transaction went as follows: Sometime in the early morning, if restaurants in Hong Kong wanted Burmese prawns, a phone call would come to a Sino-Burmese merchant in the network. The merchant would then call shrimp fishermen in Lower Burma, placing an order for a certain number of prawns. Those prawns would be caught alive and quickly loaded onto trucks to make their half-day journey to Rangoon. Upon arrival on the tarmac of the Mingaladon airport, many of the prawns would have died due to the heat in the trucks, but the 50 percent or more remaining would be packed in dry ice, temporarily freezing them for their flight to Hong Kong. However many arrived alive in Hong Kong would earn top dollars for the Sino-Burmese merchant, making the loss of prawns on the trucks or airplanes more than worthwhile. Although business was unpredictable, with little regularity or longevity in demand, Sino-Burmese engaged in this trade because they could operate without investing in an infrastructure or dealing officially with the government. There was no need for an office, just a phone and connections to the various subcontractors along the way. A man who made his initial wealth in selling prawns conducted most of his business on the tarmac where he received the prawns and packed them into airplanes. Every morning he waited for a call from Hong Kong, and if a call came through, he switched himself and his subcontractors into high gear to get the prawns out that same day. Although business was stop-and-go, he made enough money to purchase properties in the urban periphery just as the real estate market was exploding and has used those assets to bankroll more investments. Today he is one of the wealthiest Sino-Burmese and owns City Mart, the largest and most successful chain of supermarkets in Burma.

This story of success is not unique. Wealthy Sino-Burmese merchants all tell a similar tale in which their willingness to seize every single business opportunity, however small or troublesome, led to financial success. The chairman of the Myanmar Chinese Chamber of Commerce said: "In some ways, we have to be grateful to this country and this government. We pick up the leftover business opportunities that the generals do not want. If they didn't throw us this bone, we couldn't succeed."[40] Another Sino-Burmese entrepreneur said: "The military government made it so difficult for foreign companies that almost all of them lost money and left. If the government had not driven them out, we local businessmen could not compete. . . . They had to come and then leave before we could succeed."[41]

Despite the promising policies outlined in the Foreign Investment Law, the actual and inconsistent practices of the SLORC made operating foreign-owned businesses difficult and unprofitable. Many Singaporean, Japanese, and Taiwanese companies that had established large hotels, restaurants, and supermarkets in Rangoon were driven to bankruptcy, and most abandoned their businesses by about 1997. The 1997 Asian financial crisis was certainly a contributing factor, but their expectations for a stable market with consistent import and export regulations were not met, and their standardized international business practices proved impractical in the volatile Myanmar economy.

The failure of large Singaporean and other international companies reminded the Sino-Burmese that one must take calculated short-term risks and that being too obviously successful could draw unwanted attention. Several Sino-Burmese merchants point to the closure of two successful private banks in 2003 as a cautionary tale. In their interpretation, the junta sabotaged Mayflower Bank and Asia Wealth Bank, owned by a Chinese and a self-claimed "Shan" person, respectively, because the generals became jealous of the modernity and the financial success of these two institutions.[42] Analysis by Sean Turnell, economist and Burma watcher, indicates that the national Myanmar banking system was improperly regulated, leading to a liquidity problem that ultimately forced the closure of nonstate banks.[43] However, Sino-Burmese businesspeople believe there was governmental malice in the closing of the above two banks and operate their businesses as quietly as possible to stay under the radar. They walk a fine line between seizing the opportunities made available by the government and evading its attention.

This maneuvering within a shifting, unclear zone is partly facilitated by the fact that the largest, most lucrative industries such as airlines and natural gas are beyond the reach of the Sino-Burmese. Those opportunities are given to people with direct connections to the generals. Some people of Chinese descent have access to the inner circle, but those Chinese are not considered to be a part of the Sino-Burmese community in Rangoon and do not participate in Chinese events or associations. As defined by the Sino-Burmese, the few Chinese who are directly doing business with the junta are (1) Yunnanese who are new guests in Rangoon and (2) Burmanized Chinese who have some Chinese blood but no longer maintain Chinese customs.[44] Contemporary Sino-Burmese are careful to distinguish these people as neither Hokkien nor Cantonese and emphasize that they are not long-term residents of Rangoon. They define the Sino-Burmese community of Rangoon as old Hokkien and Cantonese families that have lived in the city for several generations and have maintained Chinese practices. The owner of a pharmaceutical company said: "We (the Sino-Burmese) are careful not to break the law. We work within the law to make money. We are not like the Yunnanese. They take big risks. But in Myanmar, the law is applied differently at different times."[45]

CHAPTER FOUR

Given their experiences in the anti-Chinese riots, the three demonetizations, and shifting relations between China and Burma, the Hokkien and Cantonese of Rangoon are afraid to break the law, but they must bend the law to do business. The legality of their actions is certainly questionable, but, as understood by them, this tactic is a reasonable reaction to the whims of the military government. In explaining their actions, a successful Sino-Burmese merchant stated: "In our business of exporting beans and pulses, we have to have a very good relationship with the export permit office. Sometimes, you will get a permit to export the beans in the morning, but when you go back in the afternoon with all of the beans, the permit will have been revoked. So we have to act quickly and send out our goods on the spot, as soon as we get a permit. We also have to make sure the people giving and checking permits are 'sympathetic.'"[46] This businessman has likely lined the pockets of some export permit officials, but given the circumstances, his business tactics are understandable. In fact, this mode of operation is common among all businesspeople in Rangoon, regardless of ethnic background. When I inquired about shipping goods from Burma, a Burman shipping agent said the company could not state an exact shipment date because things change so often in the export permit office. But agents also assured me that they could ship products out of Burma because they have some contacts.[47] During my fieldwork, everyone, not only merchants, complained about the capriciousness of the Myanmar government and the ubiquity of bribery. There was a shared understanding that the most powerful generals took bribes as a matter of course and that lower-level officials were forced to seek inducements because they were not being paid a living wage. This sympathy toward fellow sufferers rendered the act no less onerous, but no one felt empowered to challenge or change the system. Everyone, even merchants with more money to curry favor, had to make do.

CITY MART: A BURMESE SUCCESS STORY

As if repeating the history from the Parliamentary era, the government of Myanmar needed commercial expertise in rebuilding the national economy, and the departure of better-financed and more connected competitors opened up the market for Sino-Burmese merchants. Before the mass exodus of foreign companies in the mid-1990s, local entrepreneurs were not able to compete in terms of capital, scale, or standardization. Once the better-financed foreign companies vacated the scene, local startups could infiltrate the market through their understanding of the local culture and through immense flexibility. As stated by U Kyaw (Tan Tai Mo), one of the owners of City Mart: "Singaporean companies do not understand Burma or the Burmese. There is a Burmese way of doing business, and only we, the locals, know how this works. The Singaporean supermarkets sold things that nobody could afford, so they lost money. We know what to sell. But if they had not left, we probably couldn't have opened our supermarkets."[48]

With fourteen supermarkets and a host of other businesses including pharmacies, bakeries, bookstores, and shopping centers, City Mart Holdings is not only the premier supermarket chain in Myanmar; it is also the largest retail company.[49] Its success has drawn international attention since the initiation of reforms in 2011, and Daw Win Win Tint, U Kyaw's daughter and the managing director of City Mart Holdings, was dubbed "Myanmar's supermarket queen" by CNBC's business news channel in June 2013.[50] However, the company began its life as a small family-based operation that had to endure the various challenges of working in an unpredictable economic environment. As told by the parents, U Kyaw and Daw Tin Tin (Tan Tsi Tsing), and affirmed by their daughter, local knowledge and perseverance combined with the right set of circumstances enabled their family to build a profitable business. Like other Sino-Burmese merchants who have experienced the boom and bust of the Burmese economy, the Tan family recognizes luck and force majeure as real players in business. They understand their success not only as intimately bound to everyday Burmese society but also in Burmese Buddhist terms.

When Daw Win Win Tint decided to open the first City Mart in 1996, supermarkets were a rarity in Rangoon and were unable to attract customers. Most residents were accustomed to shopping in the traditional wet markets that were available in every township. Even wealthy Sino-Burmese such as the matriarch of City Mart, Daw Tin Tin, bought her fish and produce from the wet market on Seventeenth Street in Tayout Tan.[51] By 2000, the idea of shopping in supermarkets had begun to catch on with Rangoon's upper and middle classes. However, since City Mart was a retailer of basic necessities such as rice, oil, and produce, its business could not be divorced from the reality of daily life in Burma. Unlike those who opened hotels or export companies that target an international clientele, City Mart's focus, by the very nature of its business, has been local residents: expatriates; returned Burmese from overseas; and upper-, middle-, and even some working-class Burmese. In addition, City Mart's location within Burma, a country with deficient electrical, transportation, and financial infrastructure, has meant that little of its operational costs are externalized. It has been forced to supply its own electricity with generators, purchase and maintain its own fleet of trucks in order to ship goods on the poorly maintained roads, and finance its operations through multiple avenues rather than rely on standard banking. It has also had to dedicate significant resources to train its employees because education in Myanmar has been at a standstill for five decades.

As with any business, City Mart's objective is to make a profit. However, its profit seeking is still guided by personal relationships rather than by purely abstract calculations or the capitalistic drive. At a New Year's Eve party on December 31, 2008, Daw Tin Tin said offhandedly: "I think we are so successful because we are doing *kudho* [performing good deeds]. We sell products like Ensure that help people take care of their aging parents. Some people have even called me a *kyezushin* [benefactor] because our stores provide the things they need for their families."[52] Daw Tin Tin's understanding of her family's success is framed by the Buddhist principle of *kamma/karma* (cause and effect). In the same conversation, she said that her family has been *kan kaunde*, or "has had good luck," noting that many people, including some of her distant relatives, cannot afford to eat meat or buy cooking oil. *Kan*, often translated as "luck," is a manifestation of *kamma* and is central in the Burmese understanding of life.[53] She has clearly internalized some Burmese beliefs and perceives life in Buddhist terms.[54]

Similarly, the parents in the Tan family see their numerous City Mart employees as integral, even family-like, members of their company. Overseas Chinese merchants see family as the primary body of trade and utilize the family structure in organizing their businesses. U Kyaw and Daw Tin Tin own the enterprise and their children oversee the operations, with their eldest, daughter Daw Win Win Tint, as the general manager and their three sons managing specific sections such as product sourcing and marketing.[55] In 2009, the Tans invited me to the City Mart family Chinese New Year's Eve party held in their home. The entire family of two parents, one daughter, three sons, a son-in-law, and two grandchildren lived in the same house. The party was held in their front yard, where they served a mixture of traditional Hokkien dishes such as *lunpian* (bean sprouts, tofu, bean sauce, and peanut powder wrapped in a spongy crepe) and Burmese favorites such as *mohinga* (fish soup with rice noodles).[56] According to Chinese custom, the duty of the host is to welcome the guests and to *king-tsiu* (invite each guest to drink at least one cup of wine). The Tans not only welcomed their guests; they stood behind the buffet line serving up bowls of *mohinga* and even delivered plates of food to guests. When one of their employees said in Burmese that she felt *anadei* (as if she could not possibly be served by the owner of the company), U Kyaw said, "You've been working hard serving our company all year long, it is only right that I serve you now."[57] When I overheard this statement, it sounded unrehearsed. U Kyaw stood there for most of the night serving *mohinga* and seemed unself-conscious in his actions.

One could categorize the two events above as performance. There was certainly an element of spectacle in the Western and Chinese New Year's Eve parties. However, even if the actions of the Tans were a performance, it was a performance based on the understanding that their lives and fortunes are directly connected to the lives of their employees and Burmese people in general. For them, as it is for all of the Sino-Burmese merchants I interviewed, business is personal even at the societal scale. Unlike the Yunnanese businesspeople they criticized, the Sino-Burmese feel a greater sense of responsibility toward their fellow residents because they are Rangoonites with personal connections throughout the city. They are a people of the place—Rangoon—and endure similar hardships. Furthermore, as people who have consciously adopted Burmese culture and the teachings of Theravada Buddhism, they have been rendered more wary of ill-gained wealth. As one Sino-Burmese merchant stated: "In my business, I sell incense for worshipping the Buddha. I am doing good business, so I have little to worry about."[58] They seek profits but moral profits, partly because they are more sensitized to the mutual interconnections between people, but also because they are afraid of the consequences of immoral action.

CONCLUSION

Contemporary Sino-Burmese see themselves as underdogs, resourceful and industrious entrepreneurs who have overcome significant odds. In their words: "We worm our way through the small cracks to find business opportunities. The opportunities are small, but we still make a lot of money."[59] In general, they are content to occupy this sector of the market and will maneuver within the system to make a profit. Before 2011, more lucrative businesses meant more entanglement with the military government and, in their minds, posed an unnecessary risk. They still hold out hope for reconnecting with the overseas Chinese business network after three decades of isolation, but large enterprises within that network have little incentive to work with Burmese businesses. The failure of foreign investors in the late 1990s along with the unstable and immature economic environment makes investment too risky. Members of the Myanmar Chinese Chamber of Commerce attended the World Chinese Entrepreneurs Convention in Osaka, Manila, and other cities but were not able to draw major players to their hundredth anniversary celebration between December 31, 2008, and January 2, 2009.[60] Despite the chamber of commerce's generosity in paying for accommodations at the Sedona Hotel, one of the premium hotels in pre-2011 Rangoon, guests mainly came from less developed markets such as Yunnan Province.[61]

The reforms initiated by President Thein Sein are dramatically altering the market in Myanmar. Whether local Myanmar companies, including those owned by the Sino-Burmese, will be able to compete with international corporations remains to be seen. Economic regulations to date remain unclear and changeable, thereby giving Sino-Burmese merchants the local advantage. However, in the regional and international markets, Sino-Burmese are lagging behind. By the time they began reconnecting with the overseas Chinese network in the 1990s, Malaysian-Chinese, Sino-Thai, and other hybrid Chinese companies were already billion-dollar enterprises that operated across national borders in and through Hong Kong, Indonesia, Malaysia, the Philippines, Singapore, Taiwan, and Thailand. These other Chinese had already transformed themselves into capitalists, while the Sino-Burmese remained merchants struggling for social status and political recognition.

Nevertheless, it is the smaller-scale, more intimate operations of Sino-Burmese businesses that might safeguard Myanmar as the country pursues economic development and national growth. The incremental and locally inflected modernization that has transpired in the development of businesses such as City Mart has gradually introduced Burmese people to the forces of globalization. During fieldwork, I noticed that shoppers in City Mart rarely rushed through the aisles but instead meandered leisurely, picking up various items and studying the packaging. When I bumped into my landlady in the Myaynighone City Mart and asked her what she was shopping for, she said that City Mart products were mostly too expensive for her to purchase but that she enjoyed walking through the orderly aisles in the cool air-conditioned space. Other women I came to know commented that supermarkets and shopping malls were places where they could gain general knowledge (*bahuthuta*) and that Burmese people, given the state of their education and society, lacked general knowledge. Even Burmese women who had some experience traveling overseas or who worked for international organizations such as United Nations agencies said that frequenting City Mart and shopping centers enabled local people to gather new information and learn new behavior. They learned what kind of products foreigners used, how to use those products through explanations provided by the in-store salespeople, and how to line up and behave oneself in a "modern" store. These places of commerce have served as intermediaries in Burma's interaction with the world beyond its borders and will continue to transform Rangoon's urban culture. The SLORC/SPDC's pursuit of economic growth has rendered the market once again unproblematic, opening up a space of greater freedom for Rangoon residents to gather and experiment. Increasing wealth has not only made it possible for merchants such as the Tan family to build more supermarkets in which more Burmese can shop in a "modern" fashion; it has also made it possible for other Sino-Burmese to finance public celebrations that take Chinese New Year out into the open.

CHAPTER FIVE

CHINESE NEW YEAR
AND PUBLIC SPACE

O F all of the holidays in Chinese culture, Lunar New Year (Chun-jie) is the most important. The cyclical transition from winter to spring around February of each year brings Chinese communities together to celebrate a common tradition, reaffirming the participants as Chinese. For Chinese overseas, the annual enactment of New Year customs offers an opportunity to gather together as a common people living in a particular place outside of China, helping them to maintain their shared and yet changing cultural heritage. As Hans-Georg Gadamer stated, "Tradition is not simply a precondition into which we come, but we produce it ourselves, inasmuch as we understand, participate in the evolution of tradition and hence further determine it ourselves."[1] Tradition is a continual effort to discern a proper placement for oneself in the complex fabric of the present by retrieving what remains meaningful from the past while creating the conditions for the best possible future.

Regardless of place of origin or location of residence, Chinese overseas who maintain traditional customs gather together on New Year's eve to pray to the gods, pay respect to their ancestors, and have a large family meal. In the following ten to fifteen days, specific activities are carried out on specific days, such as visiting one's maternal family on the second day of the first lunar month, welcoming the Kitchen God back from heaven on the fifth day, and eating sweet rice dumplings on the fifteenth day. Throughout this period, Chinese people don new clothes and visit relatives and friends to wish them a fruitful new year. Those receiving guests prepare sweets to welcome the well-wishers and to wish them a sweet new year in return. In exchange for these good wishes, older family members and friends give younger members red envelopes (*angbao* in Hokkien) stuffed with red bills to wish them good luck. No negative sentiments should be expressed during this period because everyone wants to begin their new year on a good note. These practices are consistent across the various Chinese subgroups and constitute the core of Chinese tradition surrounding Chinese New Year.

In the city of Rangoon, the above family-based and private practices have been supplemented with public celebration. Like many Chinese overseas who do not live near extended family or friends, the Sino-Burmese have created alternative festivities to occupy the ten to fifteen days of the holiday. Native place and surname associations, acting as large families, organize banquets to wish all members a happy new year and to create the festive atmosphere that is expected during this time. In addition, cultural performances such as lion dancing are staged not only for entertainment but also to affirm and preserve their common tradition. As remembered by contemporary Sino-Burmese, Chinese New Year banquets have always been held in one form or another and people have always worshipped at their native-place temples—Kuanyin Ting or the Cantonese Kuanyin Temple—to ring in the New Year.

Customary practices during Chinese New Year in Rangoon exemplify how, from the 1950s to the present, Chinese tradition has been and continues to be reformulated by the Sino-Burmese. From the height of Chinese prosperity in the 1950s and early 1960s to the suppression of Chinese businesses and culture in the late 1960s to 1970s and culminating in the resurgence of Chineseness from the 1980s to the present, Sino-Burmese in Rangoon have been able to sustain and even promote Chinese tradition despite precarious circumstances. This is not the invention of tradition deployed by a ruling elite to dictate a national culture and identity.[2] Rather, it has been the temporary and tactical occupation of public spaces to celebrate hybrid Chineseness. Their collective effort, both jointly organized and individually initiated, discloses how tradition can be practiced flexibly and expressed more or less publicly according to the political, economic, and social environment. This waxing and waning of cultural practices reveals how the local Chinese community has defined itself within Rangoon, in relationship with multiple groups of people: other Sino-Burmese, other Chinese overseas, Chinese people within China, the Burmese, and other residents of the city.

Tradition as practiced by the Sino-Burmese continually refers to the past to make sense of the present. Juxtaposition of contemporary practices with older ways of celebrating Chinese New Year allows for an understanding of how history influences the present. As with everything else in this retelling of the life and the history of the Sino-Burmese, the people involved have

5.1   Chinese New Year banners sponsored by Myanmar Beer on Nineteenth
Street, also known as Barbecue Street. Photograph by the author.

tactically retrieved dimensions of their common tradition to make the best
of their situation. This process was not always conscious and rarely tidy but
incrementally laced together a communal history of the Sino-Burmese.

CHINESE NEW YEAR IN CONTEMPORARY RANGOON

In contemporary Rangoon, signs of the arrival of Chinese New Year first appear
in the marketplace. In supermarkets, red and gold *duilian* (rhyming couplets
wishing everyone a prosperous new year), sparkly Chinese zodiac decorations, red envelopes, and prepackaged traditional sweets such as candied
peanuts and sesame puffs are placed on shelves near the cashiers, announc-
ing the holiday to Chinese and non-Chinese alike. Soon after, a temporary
Chinese-style gate is erected at the mouth of Nineteenth Street, also known
as Barbecue Street, where local Sino-Burmese and Burmese often gather to
drink beer and enjoy the evening. Along this stretch of Nineteenth, bold red
banners sponsored by Myanmar Beer are hung along the entire block, creating a colorful canopy that adds an extra festive feeling to the street (Fig. 5.1).

5.2
Numbered lots
for the Chinese
New Year market.
Photograph by
the author.

About four to five days before the Lunar New Year, the annual Chinese New Year market begins to materialize on Mahabandula Road between Latha and Lanmadaw Streets. At first, three rows of white rectangles are painted on the asphalt along the north side of the road. From Lanmadaw westward to Latha, half of the broad six-lane boulevard is divided into orderly three-foot-by-five-foot spaces that are numbered from one to over one hundred. These numbered boxes appear like ghosts in the middle of the night, transforming a road into a market, altering the way people move through that space even before the vendors arrive. Many people avoid the would-be stalls marked by the white squares, unconsciously walking or riding in the passageways in between the rows rather than crossing the lines that demarcate the small lots (Fig. 5.2).

Four days before Chinese New Year, vendors arrive in droves and begin to construct their temporary stalls. In 2009, city officials decided that the market would run for only three days to minimize traffic congestion on a

5.3   Requisite goods such as mandarin oranges for sale at the Chinese
       New Year market. Photograph by the author.

major thoroughfare.[3] However, some vendors did not know or disregarded
the official decision and set up their stalls early in the hopes of making extra
income. With cardboard boxes, planks of wood, bamboo mats, and large,
worn umbrellas, they create temporary structures that are good not only for
displaying their merchandise above but also for sleeping underneath. For
three to four consecutive days, these vendors sell their goods from about
five o'clock in the morning to midnight and camp out under or next to their
merchandise overnight. They stock special products and produce such as
ang-gu-ge (red turtle-shaped pastry), *tin-ge* (sweet rice cake), mandarin
oranges, stalks of sugarcane, dragon fruit, and pussy willow (Fig. 5.3). My
informants said that most of the vendors are not Sino-Burmese but have
learned what the Sino-Burmese community wants during this special holiday. They also know that those who celebrate Chinese New Year are willing
to pay a premium for rare and higher-quality goods.[4]

For three days before Chinese New Year, the north side of Mahabandula
Road is a sea of people creeping between and around the numerous stands.
Everyone who celebrates Chinese New Year comes out to the market to see

if there are special products, because the gods who must be honored during this holiday should be offered exceptional food. The crowds are largest during the cooler hours, between five and ten o'clock in the morning and after four o'clock in the afternoon. When night falls, bare fluorescent tubes strung loosely across makeshift bamboo structures cast a pale blue glow on the fruits, vegetables, and other merchandise, guiding nighttime shoppers and revelers through the semidarkness of the market. They inch forward shopping and enjoying the spectacle, making the best use of the rare opportunity to celebrate in public.

After the 1988 people's uprising, the military government imposed strict regulations on public assembly, defining gatherings of five or more people as illegal, and discouraged traditional Burmese nighttime festivals such as Thadingyut (Festival of Lights) and Tazaundaing (the end of Buddhist Lent). According to Rangoonites, Burmese festivals in years past were much more lively because the government did not censor performances or public expression. Local artists remember a time when they could display cartoons critical of the government and everyday residents could enjoy plays that made fun of officials.[5] Although Chinese New Year celebrations carry no political message, the Sino-Burmese community still treads lightly, carefully tracking political and social shifts to avoid drawing unwanted attention. To date, the Chinese New Year market, as a commercial event in support of a cultural practice, has escaped governmental pressure except in the form of fees extracted by neighborhood officials.[6] Vendors must pay for their stalls, and neighborhood officials monitor the market to ensure proper payment. Commerce, as the ethos of the city, and economic development, as the explicit goal of the military junta, have created a buffer, sheltering this tradition from excessive regulations.

In the collective memory of the Sino-Burmese, this market has taken place every year without fail, but there have been times in which the market was more subdued. According to the local Sino-Burmese, the New Year's market used to run all night, with crowds coursing through the street. Now the five blocks between Lanmadaw and Latha are quiet by eleven o'clock at night, with vendors curled up under their fruits and vegetables and a few stragglers roaming the street. No one is sure when the nighttime festivities tapered off, but everyone remembers a time when the Chinese New Year market and Chinese New Year in general were more *laole* ("festive" or "lively"). Some attribute the decline to the depressed national economy, while others say that the local Sino-Burmese have lost their Chinese culture. However, to an outside observer, the celebrations in Rangoon do not indicate a culture in decline.

5.4   Lion dance troupe walking through downtown Rangoon. Photograph
       by the author.

In addition to the bustling market, traditional Chinese practices are abundantly evident on the day before Chinese New Year begins. Along every single street in Tayout Tan and in many streets in townships such as Dagon and Kamayut, families set out temporary altars in front of their homes to pay respect to their ancestors and regional gods. On little fold-out card tables, they set out large red candles, an incense urn, and a variety of dishes that ideally include a whole chicken, duck, fish, fruit, and the traditional New Year cakes bought at the market. With incense in hand, everyone in the family worships in front of these temporary altars and then burns *kim-zua* (ghost money) for the gods. According to custom, this ritual must be performed in the morning. By afternoon, all that remains are little mounds of ash and burned paper dotting the two sides of each street.

Beginning the next day, the first day of the Lunar New Year, and continuing for ten consecutive days, lion and dragon dance troupes appear on the streets (Fig. 5.4), not only in Tayout Tan but throughout much of Rangoon, drumming, dancing, and marching from one location to the next to wish people a happy new year. They grace the homes and businesses of those who have invited them to perform and in exchange for their acrobatics, which are believed to bring good luck, receive red envelopes stuffed with cash. If the troupes need to travel longer distances, they hire open-bed trucks to transport the lion and dragon dancers, drums, and other equipment. En route, the head of the lion or dragon is displayed prominently on top of the cab, while musicians standing on the truck bed periodically bang out riotous rhythms that echo through many blocks. Typically, as they approach each destination, the percussionists play more vigorously to drive out the bad spirits and announce their arrival. In Chinese culture, celebrations must be loud and festive, or they are seen as lacking in energy and thereby unsuccessful. Abiding by this cultural principle, lion and dragon dance troupes must gather as much energy as possible by performing exuberantly to draw in crowds. This requirement would seem to cause problems for the troupes in Rangoon, where the Myanmar government could clamp down on any public activity at any time. However, the Sino-Burmese have been able to test the boundaries of acceptable public behavior, gradually increasing their visibility without incurring obvious government ire or public enmity.[7]

THE WAXING AND WANING OF CHINESE NEW YEAR

Contemporary Sino-Burmese cannot recall how Chinese New Year was celebrated before World War II. They are certain that Chinese families gathered to share a meal on New Year's Eve and their gods were properly honored in Kuanyin Ting, but details beyond these traditional practices have been forgotten. Their collective memory offers more clarity for the periods after the independence of Burma in 1948 and reveals how the Chinese in Rangoon have preserved their traditions in response to various challenges within and outside of the Chinese community: different kinds of Chinese in Burma, intra-Chinese tensions and conflicts, Burmese governmental and economic policies, and China-Burma diplomatic relations.

Taking the New Year into the Open

As with other aspects of Chinese society, the periods under Parliamentary and early Socialist rule (1950–64) are seen as a golden era for Chinese cultural practices. The ineffective rule of the AFPFL along with the prosperity of Chinese merchants created a free and fertile environment in which the Chinese residents of Rangoon could focus on their own needs and aspirations with little concern for tensions building in Burmese national politics. Many aligned themselves with Communist China and the Nationalist

Party rather than with the independent government of Burma and waged a pitched battle among themselves in their efforts to support their different visions of a modern China.

In this context, those loyal to the People's Republic of China organized the Wenyu Guangchang (literally Culture and Entertainment Plaza, which can be rendered as Culture and Entertainment Festival) to celebrate Chinese New Year. Inspired by the founding of New China, pro-Communist Chinese in Rangoon wanted to glorify the strength of a unified country and proclaim the wonder of Chinese culture.[8] From 1951 to 1964, they held an annual festival that offered traditional Chinese opera and music, traditional competitions such as Chinese chess and lantern riddles, basketball tournaments, Chinese films, Chinese food, and goods manufactured by Chinese industrialists as well as those imported from China. This way of celebrating Chinese New Year was completely new. Indeed, there was so little connection to tradition that even the name of the festival made no mention of Chunjie (Spring Festival) or *xinnian* (the new year). However, the mélange of activities seemed natural to the organizers because they saw New Year as an opportunity to commemorate the founding of New China and a means to form a new breed of Chinese people who not only maintained all that was worthwhile in Chinese tradition but also pursued modernity and national unity. Therefore, goods produced by Chinese people, whether within or beyond China, were a sign of industrial strength; contemporary films were the medium through which revolutionary thought was propagated; basketball displayed the newly cultivated physical prowess of the Chinese people; and the traditional arts and games provided a link to the past that defined these people as Chinese. The inclusion of old world, traditional opera and music to celebrate the birth of a revolutionary nation did not trouble the organizers because, at that time in China, embracing the new order did not demand absolute rejection of all tradition (that would come later in the Cultural Revolution).[9] If traditional cultural performances were still acceptable within China, it was even less problematic for the Chinese in Burma, who were thousands of miles removed from Beijing.

This festival lasted from the first to the seventh day of the Lunar New Year and drew crowds not only from the Chinese community but also from the Burmese population. By one estimate, a third of the one hundred thousand people in attendance were Burmese.[10] This public display of Chinese tradition to people beyond the Chinese community is significant given the insularity among the Chinese at that time. Since most Chinese Rangoonites had made little effort to integrate themselves into the local Burmese society before 1967, this annual festival not only proclaimed a distinct Chinese identity to non-Chinese people but also made no effort to veil their devotion to Communist China. The organizers put on the same revolutionary plays that were performed in China and espoused the same sort of patriotic fervor that could be heard north of the China-Burma border. In a national environment where the Burmese government perceived Communist China as a threat, this bold celebration reflects the sense of security and complacency among the pro-Communist Chinese in Rangoon in the 1950s and early 1960s.

However, all was not well among all of the Chinese. Intra-Chinese tensions rode high for many years and divided the community into staunchly pro-Communist and pro-Nationalist factions. Although the Culture and Entertainment Festival is remembered fondly by some Sino-Burmese, pro-Nationalist people did not participate because they could not identify with that vision of China. Instead, they sent thugs to the festival to sabotage the event. Pro-Communist organizers were well aware of the threat posed by their political opposition and stationed security personnel not only at the festival site at Huaqiao Middle School but also throughout Tayout Tan.[11]

New Year Celebrations Retreat into the Private Realm

The political fanaticism fomenting in the Sino-Burmese community finally reached a boiling point when pro-Communist Chinese students sparked the anti-Chinese riots in June 1967. The violence of the riots and the apparent callousness of the Socialist government forced the Sino-Burmese to take their New Year celebration back behind closed doors.

After the Socialist government nationalized all schools in April 1965, it was no longer possible to hold the Culture and Entertainment Festival at Huaqiao Middle School, bringing an end to this very public celebration. However, the Hongmen Youth Association, Kien Tek Association, and Ho Sing Brotherhood continued to send their Western music bands on decorated floats out into the streets to celebrate Chinese New Year. The floats drove around Rangoon during the ten or so evenings of the holiday and stopped in front of different associations and homes to perform for specific recipients as well as all Chinese people.[12] This kind of performance continued into 1968, despite the 1967 anti-Chinese riots, because some Chinese wanted to show the Burmese government that they were not afraid.[13] Sino-Burmese of all ages, from toddlers to aging grandmothers, followed the floats around Tayout Tan, gathering in front of different associations to watch the performances, some as an unself-conscious practice of tradition and some as a form of protest.[14] However, the pressure exerted by the Socialist government proved to be too much, and Chinese New Year celebrations completely retreated indoors in 1968, not to reemerge until 1981.

During this period, Rangoon's Sino-Burmese people organized private banquets in their association halls and staged cultural events such as fan dances or Chinese song performances to maintain their tradition. No Sino-Burmese seems to have a clear memory of these annual celebrations, but all are certain that these banquets continued throughout the years.

Stepping out Again into the Public

Although the Socialist period did not end until 1988, improved relations between China and Burma from 1978 onward emboldened the Sino-Burmese to once again express their culture more publicly. This was especially true after Deng Xiaoping officially renounced China's support of the Burma Communist Party, thereby resolving the central conflict between the two governments and enabling trade to flow more freely between the two countries.[15] Sino-Burmese businesses that once operated in the black market gradually came out into the open, and this freer market facilitated the flow of both basic necessities and nonessential items. Holiday-specific products and Chinese popular media trickled into Burma and began to reinvigorate traditional Chinese practices.

On December 6, 1980, sixteen members of the Burma Chinese Chamber of Commerce gathered for a meeting and decided that they should send out a New Year greetings float, just as the Kien Tek and Ho Sing brotherhoods had done in the past. Although some people felt that using Western music to celebrate Chinese New Year was an anomaly and questioned the wisdom of following in the footsteps of secret brotherhoods, the organizing committee ultimately decided that using a float was a good way to welcome the New Year.[16] It had been many years since any public celebrations were organized, and many felt that the festive spirit of Chinese New Year had faded significantly. Their objective was to revive Chinese New Year and unify the Sino-Burmese community. Factional divisions were a fact of life within the Sino-Burmese population, and few groups reached across brotherhood, language, or place-based ties to cooperate with each other. However, the chamber of commerce had successfully bridged some of these gaps in the past and sought to reconnect the larger community again.[17]

Much to everyone's surprise, in 1981 the first Overseas Chinese New Year Greetings Float was very popular and received over K 10,000 in red envelopes.[18] After this successful trial, a subcommittee, the Overseas Chinese New Year Greetings Group, with its own rock music band, was organized. From 1981 to 1988, the troupe paraded in the streets each year. For nine straight evenings, the decorated float along with lion dance teams (with forty to fifty performers in total) performed in Tayout Tan, with droves of Sino-Burmese following the traveling show. The Socialist period was one of suppression, but people in Burma could still gather in large numbers without political consequences. The organizers had to apply for permission from the township office and clear the streets to make room for the large float's passage, but the government permitted this type of mass celebration on the street.[19]

While the organizers were willing to include rock music as an acceptable part of the New Year celebrations, they were concerned about the dilution or muddling of Chinese tradition. In their effort to preserve tradition, they decorated their float with Chinese motifs and improved on the design each year. Part of the motivation was to improve the acoustics, because using a large truck as the float's foundation meant that the truck's cab blocked the sound from the large speakers. However, equally significant was the expression of Chinese tradition in the design of the float. By 1988, two Chinese dragons, icons of Chinese culture, swam along the two sides of the float and red lanterns, rather than fluorescent tubes, were installed as lighting.[20]

Apparently no one questioned the use of the floats themselves to celebrate Chinese New Year. The New Year Greetings Group was following the precedent set by the Kien Tek, Ho Sing, and Hongmen associations and thereby continuing tradition of a sort, but one with a very short history and non-Chinese origins. In fact, decorated floats are a traditional part of Thingyan, the Burmese New Year, also known as the Water Festival in English. According to custom, groups of people organize and decorate floats to participate in annual Thingyan competitions. These floats, with performers riding on top, used to drive around Rangoon and stop at designated sites to compete for prizes such as best decoration, best costumes, and best performance. Having watched and participated in these Water Festival competitions in the 1950s and 1960s, the Sino-Burmese unself-consciously absorbed these practices and naturally integrated them into their own New Year tradition.

Moving Back Indoors

After the pro-democracy uprising was subdued, martial law was imposed from 1988 to 1992. Among many other restrictions, assembly of five or more people was not permitted unless officially sanctioned. Therefore, in addition to other hardships endured by the people of Burma, no outdoor, public celebrations for any holiday could continue without drawing unnecessary attention. Burmese would have to forgo the lively festivals for Tazaungdaing

Labyeinei (the full moon day around November), and Sino-Burmese would once again have to celebrate their New Year discreetly. From 1988 to 2005, Chinese New Year parties reverted back to the indoor banquets of 1968–81.

However, the period under martial law was also one of opening toward international trade. Although the military dictatorship wanted to exert absolute control over the entire country, it also sought to rebuild the economy and courted foreign direct investments. In the 1990s, overseas Chinese from Singapore, Hong Kong, and Taiwan arrived in large numbers. They brought with them not only capital but also an affirmation of Chinese heritage and their own renditions of Chinese tradition. From the 1990s to today, Sino-Burmese have been sifting through the various influences flowing in from the south via Chinese overseas and streaming down from the north from Yunnan and in so doing have formulated a modern Chinese tradition. Although a "modern tradition" seems to be an oxymoron, it is exactly this straddling of apparent opposites that the Sino-Burmese are undertaking.[21] It is a practice of drawing from the past while trying to catch up to the future and of keeping an eye on one's ancestral homeland while planting a foot in one's adopted country. Through this process, Sino-Burmese have taken up old customs that had lain dormant for two decades and married them with new traditions practiced by other Chinese in Southeast Asia, not Mainland China.

Leaping out Again into the Public with a Reformed Tradition

The liberalized economic environment revitalized the Sino-Burmese community, gradually enabling Sino-Burmese people to rediscover their cultural heritage and take Chinese New Year celebrations back out into the streets. After the Myanmar government opened its doors to the world in 1990, Sino-Burmese businesspeople ventured out to neighboring Southeast Asian countries to seek business opportunities and young Sino-Burmese left to study overseas. While abroad, they saw the boisterous lion dance competitions in Singapore and Malaysia and brought home video clips to share with their families and friends. Some enterprising Sino-Burmese filmed these competitions and manufactured video compact discs (VCDs) to sell in the Burmese market. These VCDs became very popular among young Sino-Burmese men. Soon lion dance teams began to mimic the Singaporean and Malaysian lion dance movements and new lion dance teams were organized.

From about 2005 to 2007, at least six lion dance teams were formed, both within existing organizations and through the independent initiative of young men.[22] Transformed or newly formed, lion dancers and their coaches carefully studied the routines and techniques in the VCDs and copied aspects they found desirable. Since the tradition of lion dances had been maintained throughout the years, the new enthusiasts were not starting from zero. Coaches from the Kien Tek and Hongmen associations taught novice lion dancers the basic steps and helped them figure out the new advanced movements.[23] Until the late 1990s, lion dance troupes performed on the ground or, for special effect, on fifteen-foot poles (Fig. 5.5). VCDs from Singapore and Malaysia introduced lion dancing that is performed on a series of posts, in which the two people who compose the lion must step or leap from one post to the next (Fig. 5.6).[24] This newer form of lion dance is much more difficult and dangerous, and the thrill of achieving such physical skill has been very alluring for young men throughout Rangoon.

Traditionally, lion dances were performed by martial artists to showcase their skills.[25] Although the young men in these new teams rarely undergo martial arts training, they conceive of the strength and dexterity necessary to perform lion dances as a form of kung fu (martial art) and name their teams kung fu clubs (e.g., Last Don Kung Fu Club and Black Pearl Kung Fu Club).[26] This connection to martial arts provides lion dancing with an additional allure because popular media in contemporary Myanmar portrays kung fu as a special and often magical skill among the Chinese. Along with other influences that have entered Myanmar after the opening of the economy, popular culture from neighboring countries have inundated the country, bringing movies, television, music, and fashion from all over Asia. In particular, television series from Taiwan and Hong Kong featuring spectacular martial arts have been broadcast on Myanmar television, drawing a wide audience that has come to associate Chinese culture with martial expertise. Young Sino-Burmese with little or no exposure to Chinese culture have developed a sense of pride about being Chinese, making comments such as "Chinese martial arts are the best, better than Burmese and Korean martial arts."[27] Similarly, non-Chinese audiences have transposed the fiction on television into real life, making comments such as "Chinese are good at martial arts" even if they have never seen an actual Chinese person doing kung fu.[28]

Spurred on by these various incentives, those without associational support have sought out coaches and sponsors to obtain the necessary teaching, equipment, space, and funding to learn, perform, and compete in the new lion dances. In the past, lion dance teams were part of martial arts schools. Those schools belonged to different secret brotherhoods and were the training grounds for developing the physical prowess necessary to defend one brotherhood against another. Loyalty was the main tenet of these organiza-

5.5
Lion dancers balanced on a pole while performing *caiqing* ("retrieving lettuce"; greens symbolize good fortune). Photograph by Lee Roberts, used by permission.

5.6
Lion dancers performing new style of lion dance on posts. Their team members brace the posts. Photograph by the author.

tions, and no one crossed party lines to associate with non-brothers. During the colonial era and into the early part of independent Burma, secret brotherhoods such as Ho Sing and Kien Tek saw each other as archenemies and deployed armed squads to brutalize anyone who infringed upon their territories. The associations trained their brothers in martial arts and used lion dances as a way to assert their dominance. Therefore, when Chinese New Year arrived, lion dance teams visited only those who were affiliated with their specific brotherhoods or were neutral parties. When opposing teams met each other on the street, violent battles ensued.[29]

The new lion dance teams that arose in the late 1990s did not adhere to those old factional ties. Young men who wanted to try the new style of lion dancing did not care about old brotherhood rivalries. Lion dancers now in their thirties remember a time when different troupes would fight each other on the street but say that the spirit of the lion has come to represent connections rather than divisions. Ko Myo, captain of the Red Ruby Kung Fu Club, explained that once the young men started practicing the new form of lion dance from Malaysia and Singapore, everyone, regardless of membership in particular teams, became close friends: "We all know each other and help each other. I have taught many people in many teams how to do the lion dance. And we have all belonged to different teams. For example, I used to be in Dragon Head, but now I'm in Red Ruby."[30] Ko Japan, who now serves as a judge in lion dance competitions, provided a similar assessment: "They all flow back and forth between the teams. They are all great friends. No one fights anymore."[31]

The above changes in the form and culture of lion dancing are excellent examples of how Chinese tradition has been simultaneously maintained and altered. These lion dancers are in the process of preserving aspects that remain meaningful to them and are putting into practice facets that enable them to progress toward something new, at once reconnecting themselves to their historical cultural heritage while changing that tradition to become something attractive in the present. Although none of the young men interviewed can speak any of the Chinese languages, they call their captain *dailou* ("older brother" in Cantonese) and shout out *hoya*, a Cantonese term for "excellent," whenever lion dancers do something well.[32] This straddling of past and future is their stance in the present, a flexible, modulated positioning that has brought lion dancing out into the city of Rangoon, beyond the confines of Tayout Tan.[33]

Lion dancing in Rangoon has transformed significantly since the 1990s. It has become a cultural practice that Sino-Burmese readily and very publicly share with other residents in the entire city. In 2006, to celebrate Chinese

5.7
Headquarters of the Sint Oh Dan Lion Dance Competition. Photograph by the author.

New Year, several men who live on the upper block of Sint Oh Dan Street organized the first-ever lion dance competition (Fig. 5.7). Their goal was to enliven the celebration of Chinese New Year, to make it festive again, and to showcase a cultural practice that all of the organizers had enjoyed in their youth. Most of these men had practiced martial arts and performed lion dances when they were young. They were also inspired by the lion dance competitions held in Singapore and Malaysia and adopted that overseas Chinese practice to revitalize Chinese New Year in Rangoon. Every year since 2006, the organizers have transformed the upper block of Sint Oh Dan Street into an open-air theater by putting out hundreds of plastic chairs and a projection screen. They open the competition with great ceremony and invite anyone and everyone to attend, as if inviting guests to their living room. In 2007, 2008, and 2009, the organizers distributed water, juice bottles, and pastries because they were afraid their guests had become thirsty and hungry. The competition tended to run over three hours, and the audience in the center was always hemmed in by large crowds, making it nearly impossible to retreat for refreshments.

Since 2006, the "Latha Township Upper Sint Oh Dan [Street] Family Traditional Chinese Lion Dance and Dragon Exhibition and Competition" (Sint Oh Dan Lion Dance Competition from this point forward), has taken place and grown in scale each year.[34] In 2006, four teams competed over two nights, with an awards ceremony on the third night. By 2009, nine teams competed over four nights, and part of the competition was featured on national television. The organizers were initially concerned about such extensive exposure but ultimately allowed the television station Myawaddy to film during one night of the competition and broadcast it publicly. Such visibility in Myanmar is potentially dangerous, but the organizers decided that this was an opportunity to share Sino-Burmese culture with all of Myanmar and that lion dancing would not be perceived as a threat.[35]

Indeed, this cultural art form is now practiced by hundreds of young men, regardless of ethnicity.[36] Sino-Burmese, Burmese, and Indo-Burmese youth have joined lion dance teams and practice for about two months before Chinese New Year to prepare for the festivities and lion dance competition (Fig. 5.8). Although the lion dance is clearly Chinese in origin and culture, young men who practice the dance have no qualms about including non-Chinese members or about joining something that is not from their ancestral culture. Part of the reason is practical. The two leading lion dancers and their two understudies need about sixty people to transport, set up, and, most importantly, stabilize the posts. Without this large team of people, the posts would be too shaky for the performers to stand on, much less jump around on. Therefore, these teams recruit from wherever necessary and provide food and money to those who are willing to put in the long hours and back-breaking work.

All of the young men in these seasonal teams were poor and usually unemployed. Whether of Chinese, hybrid or other descent, they came from the impoverished classes. They viewed Chinese New Year as an opportunity to earn some much-needed, if insufficient, income. The prize money for the first-, second-, and third-place teams in the Sint Oh Dan Lion Dance Competition in 2009 was K 800,000, K 600,000, and K 300,000 (approximately US$800, $600, and $300), respectively, which served as a major incentive for the formation of new teams. In addition, each business or family that invited a team to perform provided a red envelope containing anywhere from ten to a few hundred thousand kyat (approximately ten to a few hundred US dollars), depending on the reputation and performance of the team. The total income for the traditional performance period of eight to nine

5.8
Lion dancers practicing in a friend's backyard. It was very difficult for lion dancers to find a space to practice. This location required a forty-five-minute bus ride for the lion dancers. Photograph by the author.

days can reach thousands of US dollars, to be distributed among the team sponsor, the lion dancers, and the support crew.[37]

However, practical necessities do not fully explain the degree of openness in this rendition of Chinese tradition. As already seen above with the New Year greetings floats, the Sino-Burmese have been gradually and largely unconsciously folding Burmese traditions into their own practices. Their long residence in Rangoon and the common suffering they have experienced with their neighbors have made the Chinese in Rangoon not just Chinese but both Chinese and Burmese. The young Sino-Burmese men who join the lion dance teams are nearly indistinguishable from the other residents of Rangoon. They converse with one another in Burmese, not standard Chinese, Hokkien, or Cantonese; they hang out with friends who are a mix of Sino-Burmese, Burmese, and Indo-Burmese and find it only natural that they would recruit friends to join the lion dance teams.[38] The Sino-Burmese express pride in the lion dances, but this pride is mostly based on the physi-

5.9
The Legend of Chinese New Year Traditional Culture VCD produced by the Kamayut Kien Tek Association.

cal prowess necessary to perform the movements and the association with the martial arts as shown in popular TV programs. They are only vaguely aware of the history and meaning of the lion dance and find it sufficient to know that the lion is a symbol of good luck.

Although some Sino-Burmese today are concerned about the loss of Chinese tradition within their community, they do not insist on a pure Chinese culture. Rather, they seek to formulate a way of living in Rangoon that is appropriately Chinese while recognizing and adapting to the local Burmese context. Their experience in the late 1960s taught them that despite their pride in Chinese culture, they are living in Burma. They began to consciously adapt to the local culture, seeking aspects they could incorporate to create a sustainable home for themselves. Along these lines, they began to adopt more Burmese practices such as giving donations to monks and organizing donation festivals and also sought to make themselves better known to the Burmese. These efforts were subtle at first but have become more explicit, with Sino-Burmese people actively explaining their position to other Burmese and displaying their culture for all to see. For example, the Kamayut Kien Tek Association produced two sets of VCDs in 2008 and 2009, titled *The Legend of Chinese New Year Traditional Culture* (Fig. 5.9). The narration for these VCDs is in Burmese with English subtitles and explains the origins of the lion and dragon dances. The VCDs are of higher quality than many shows and movies produced in Burma, indicative of the effort and cost put forth by the producers to inform the public and create a good impression of Chinese culture. Furthermore, the fact that the VCDs are in Burmese with English subtitles means that the intended audiences are non-Chinese speakers such as second- or third-generation Sino-Burmese and non-Chinese residents of Rangoon.[39]

Both the producers of the VCDs and the organizers of the Sint Oh Dan Lion Dance Competition state that their objective is to preserve Chinese tradition. However, the tradition that they seek to preserve is not some pure custom that has been passed down through the centuries unchanged. Rather, they seek to maintain the aspects of tradition that they find valuable and continually improve upon it by drawing from multiple sources. Si Kim Hua, an elderly lion dance coach at the Kien Tek Association headquarters, said that the new lion dancing on posts is good because it helps create a festive atmosphere for Chinese New Year by drawing in large crowds. He has no issue with the changes because Sino-Burmese youth are improving on old ways. As Si explained, "The videos from Singapore and Malaysia show more exciting and attractive movements so of course the young men in Rangoon wanted to follow their lead."[40] In his opinion, Chinese tradition is still being preserved, because the lion dance is still Chinese and more people are interested in the practice.

CONCLUSION

Through reformulated traditions such as lion dancing on posts and the Sint Oh Dan Lion Dance Competition, contemporary Sino-Burmese are revitalizing Chinese culture, shaping it to fit the local context and making Chinese customs more approachable for everyone in Rangoon, not just the Sino-Burmese.[41]

In 2009, Capital Hypermart in Thaketa Township hosted a four-night lion dance competition that was attended by over one thousand local people on each night.[42] Thaketa was built between 1958 and 1960 in the northwestern periphery of Rangoon and is generally known as a Burman neighborhood. When I casually asked members of the audience if they had seen lion dancing before, all of them said no but that they had come because "it is good to watch [kyilo kaunde]." Chairs were set out for some special guests, but most people had to stand, and they stood for two to three hours at a stretch to watch the various teams perform. A couple of newspaper reporters who were present said the lion dance was something new and interesting. Whether these comments represent a general Rangoonite perception is hard to say.[43] The acrobatics of the lion dancers is impressive and makes

5.10   Ad hoc children's lion dance troupe. Photograph by the author.

for a great spectacle. In both the Capital Hypermart and Sint Oh Dan Lion Dance competitions, everyone in the audience looked enthralled.

When lion dance troupes travel around the city banging their drums or when they enter specific businesses to perform, I have observed both curiosity and disinterest. While eating lunch in a Shan noodle shop in Dagon Township, I asked the customers what they thought when a few lion dance groups came in to perform. They said it is very common for lion dance groups to perform during Chinese New Year and seemed neither impressed nor annoyed. In contemporary Rangoon, lion dancing is performed by a variety of people, regardless of ethnicity, and they exhibit a wide range of skill levels. Some are children who, having learned that lion dancers earn money for performing during Chinese New Year, organize their own impromptu troupes to earn extra cash (Fig. 5.10). When I asked a team of them in Burmese if they are Tayout, they said no, that they had learned the lion dance by watching other people and copying their movements and drumming (Fig. 5.11). No one has tried to police lion dancing, and it remains a tradition that is Chinese but open, allowing for different representations. In addition to the children, some performers are young men between the

5.11   Burmese boys performing lion dances in Dagon Township. Photograph by Lee Roberts, used by permission.

ages of twenty and thirty who enjoy the athleticism of lion dancing and dedicate themselves to it like an extreme sport. These are the men in the competitions. Others are members of martial arts schools who diligently study
kung fu and practice lion dancing as part of their training, performing lion
dances during Chinese New Year but not participating in the competitions.
Among the Rangoon lion dancing community, it is understood that official
organizations do not participate because it would be too embarrassing if
their teams lost. The organizers of the Sint Oh Dan Lion Dance Competition
explained that it was natural for these various types of lion dancers to exist
because the people in Rangoon have grown up with lion dancing in their
neighborhoods.

Celebrations of Chinese New Year, the most important ritual practice
that defines a person as Sino-Burmese and binds together the Sino-Burmese
community, are undergoing changes based on local conditions and influences from other overseas Chinese communities. In this process, China is
not the center that determines Chineseness for the diaspora in the periphery.[44] China remains a historical reference and wields significant power
through global economics, but it is not the source for modern Chineseness.

Rather, under the pressing need to reconcile Chineseness with modernity in contemporary Rangoon, Malaysia, Singapore, Hong Kong, and Taiwan are the exemplars. For lion dance enthusiasts, it has meant the careful tracking of new techniques and routines and participation in the Genting World Lion Dance Championship in Malaysia and the International Lion Dance Competition in Singapore.[45] Through these practices of Chineseness that are not constrained by nation-state boundaries, they are becoming modern Sino-Burmese. Like their neighbors, Sino-Burmese Rangoonites are embarrassed by their country's backwardness and are desperate to catch up. They look to Chinese people in more developed countries to formulate the kind of Chinese they want to become. While the People's Republic of China might serve as a source for market success and some are courting municipal governments in Yunnan to access business opportunities, Singapore and Malaysia are the main points of reference for ways of being Chinese in the twenty-first century.

CONCLUSION

Ghosts and Uncertainties

F OR the Sino-Burmese in Rangoon, being both Chinese and Burmese
has required continual negotiation with multiple forces at multiple
scales. Some of those forces are local such as the interactions between
the Hokkien, Cantonese, and Yunnanese communities and their relationships with the diverse peoples of Burma. Other forces are national and
international such as national politics in Myanmar and China and China-
Myanmar diplomatic relations. Still others are forces that have rendered the
Sino-Burmese and all Burmese people powerless such as floods, fires, and
governments that can bring devastation through temperamental changes.[1]
Like everyone else in the country, the Sino-Burmese live in the midst of
palpable uncertainty and do everything they can to improve their odds.
They appease government officials whenever necessary and ask for protection from deities such as Kuanyin and from the Buddha. They also conduct
an elaborate ceremony on Poto (usually translated as Hungry Ghost Day)
to placate wandering ghosts. For ghosts, like the post-1962 governments of
Burma, are elusive, unpredictable, and potentially malevolent. They must be
dealt with properly to ensure the best possible future.

PLACATING GHOSTS

On August 27, 2007, about one month before two thousand monks marched
through the streets of Rangoon in public protest, the Teng clan proceeded
with the rituals for Hungry Ghost Day despite concerns about eliciting
unwanted attention. This ritual to maintain harmony between the living
and the dead has been faithfully carried out by the Sino-Burmese since their
earliest settlement. The Teng clan responsible for the ceremony in 2007 did

C.1
Offerings for ancestors
and ghosts prepared by
the Teng clan. Photograph
by the author.

not want to anger the ghosts or bring bad luck on the entire Sino-Burmese community by performing the ritual incorrectly. According to tradition, on the fifteenth day of the seventh lunar month, Chinese families and communities must honor their ancestors and guide all wandering ghosts to their final resting places. Chinese everywhere offer food and papier-mâché representations of houses, clothing, money, and other necessities to their ancestors and to ghosts who have no family to honor them (Fig. c.1). On Hungry Ghost Day, lonely ghosts lost among the living can finally cross over into the afterlife. All ghosts are conceptually included in this offering, and their successful journey onto the other shore is the ultimate goal that ensures harmony between the living and the dead.

In places such as Singapore, Taiwan, and southern Fujian, this holiday is enacted very publicly with parades of spirits through the streets, performances in public plazas (*kotai*), and communal feasts under the stars. Ancestors and ghosts must be made to understand how much effort is put forth on their behalf, and the generosity of the living is believed to safeguard them from evil spirits in the forthcoming year. In Rangoon, prominent displays in public spaces have faded with time. Political pressure has compelled the Sino-Burmese to become more attuned to local practices and to modulate how they represent themselves in public. By 2007, the outdoor stage shows that once blocked off Strand Road, a major thoroughfare, no longer occurred. Instead, all ritual proceedings were confined within the Hokkien Kuanyin Temple. But even within the compound, the burning of the fifteen-foot-tall effigy of Tai Su Yah, commonly known as the Lord of Hades, was visible for several blocks.[2]

The organizers were concerned about such high visibility during a time when rising costs were placing significant strains on Burmese people and dissatisfaction toward the government was once again mounting. On August 15, 2007, the SPDC suddenly removed fuel subsidies, precipitating a dramatic increase in fuel and food prices and making it even more difficult for the poor to bus into the city for work and pay for basic necessities. In response, activists began to protest on August 19, but the demonstrations were small and quickly subdued. By August 27, Hungry Ghost Day, there was little indication that the demonstrations would escalate into a mass antigovernment protest, but members of the Teng clan were on alert. Before August 27, the organizers discussed the risk of performing a public ritual during a time of political tension. In their minds, the elaborate ritual with mountains of food and a bonfire adjacent to a major thoroughfare could be misinterpreted as a blatant disregard for the suffering of those affected by the rise in fuel and food prices.

However, the organizers also felt obliged to maintain their tradition and feared the repercussions of offending ghosts. The effigy of Tai Su Yah had always been burned at night to create a beacon to guide wandering ghosts to the other shore, but the organizers considered conducting the ritual before dark in order to draw less attention. Burning the effigy in the light of day could confuse and anger the ghosts, so explicit permission had to be granted before the organizers dared alter tradition. After proper obeisance, the organizers obtained permission from the ghosts to perform the last step before sunset. At five thirty in the afternoon under the guidance of a Mahayana Buddhist monk, the twenty elders of the Teng clan walked solemnly into the forecourt of the Kuanyin Temple to offer *kim-zua* (ritual or ghost money) to Tai Su Yah and two flanking ghosts that had been set up on a pyre (Fig. c.2). Each clan elder bowed three times to the ghosts, lit the *kim-zua* in his hand, and then placed the burning *kim-zua* gingerly on the pyre to send all ghosts to their final resting place. The entirety of the ritual concluded

C.2   Paying respect to Tai Su Yah before the final burning ceremony. Photograph by Lee Roberts, used by permission.

before nightfall, and the forecourt was washed with water to extinguish any embers, leaving only puddles of water where a burning pyre once blazed. Neither unwelcomed guests nor government officials interrupted the ceremony. Hungry Ghost Day concluded quietly and therefore successfully.

The events of this day, with its absence of rational order, subtle sense of tension, and uncertainty of success, encapsulate the Sino-Burmese way of living in Rangoon. For the twenty elders in the Teng clan, the day had begun around eight o'clock in the morning. They had to first set up the rooms of offerings, listen devoutly as Chinese monks chanted Mahayana sutras, and complete a multistep ambulatory obeisance. At the start of the day, none of them knew exactly how Hungry Ghost Day would unfold. Other than following the instructions of the head monk and a ritual expert, they waited. Around two thirty in the afternoon, word spread that they had received permission from the ghosts to conclude the rituals early. Although powerful forces in the form of ghosts and the Myanmar government loomed large on their horizon, Teng clan elders took the risk of publicly expressing Chinese culture because they valued Hokkien tradition and because breaking tradition could make Rangoon less habitable. Unseen forces are still very real to the Sino-Burmese, and the ire of hungry ghosts could cast a pall over their upcoming year, dooming business ventures and destroying family harmony. They also took the risk of drawing unwanted attention because their marginal status as alien residents in an unstable country has always required tactical risks. The construction of a national identity remains highly contested in Burma/Myanmar, and existing formulations of national culture explicitly exclude immigrant populations, making it difficult, if not impossible, for Chinese practices to be included in the official conception of the nation-state. Therefore, Sino-Burmese culture can only remain on the periphery or seek apolitical, popular approval through spectacle and other nonthreatening means. As a people who largely landed in Rangoon by default, not by design, and were compelled to remain through the "haphazard conflicts" of history, the Sino-Burmese have had to make do with their circumstances and gamble on their present in the hopes of securing a better future.[3]

BEING LOCAL ENOUGH

Sino-Burmese continue to occupy an in-between zone. Although they have stressed the similarities between Mahayana and Theravada Buddhism since at least the 1960s, they remain other in a most fundamental way of being Burmese: being Buddhist. A common Burmese adage states, *Tayout ka hpaya ma shi, taya ma shi* (The Chinese have no Buddha and no law). When I asked Huang Aihui, a second-generation Sino-Burmese woman, about her reaction to this saying, she was visibly saddened. Huang said that she did not know what to say because she is a devout Buddhist and Vipassana meditator.[4] She saw herself as Buddhist, Burmese, and Chinese but recognized that previous generations were more narrowly focused on Chinese culture and deities.[5] Huang was not alone in her effort to be a hybrid Chinese person who belongs in Burma. Most have naturally adopted local Buddhist practices and speak Burmese as their preferred language. For example, families generally participate in the morning alms for monks and many young people donate money and necessities to the less fortunate. Several Sino-Burmese men and women between the ages of eighteen and thirty-five told me that they regularly provide food and medicine for patients in the Rangoon General Hospital because those patients generally cannot afford to buy their own medications. During the period of my fieldwork, Ko Japan, the lion dance judge, visited a patient every week.[6] Others organize meals in Buddhist nunneries or purchase basic necessities for students at Rangoon's School for the Deaf.[7] These acts of kindness have been described by some as a superficial performance by wealthy Chinese to avoid resentment from the local society. Even the Sino-Burmese said that some recent Chinese migrants donate money as a performance to improve their public relations. However, the Sino-Burmese in Rangoon do not have the luxury of passing judgment on these new arrivals, because the latter are generally wealthier and better connected.

BEING CHINESE ENOUGH

Indeed, the multiplicity of Chinese in Rangoon and Burma as a whole is a source of concern for Sino-Burmese Rangoonites. To what extent are they Chinese, and how Chinese do they have to be to access the increasing opportunities made available through the overseas Chinese network and the Chinese government? In contemporary China, religious rituals such as Poto are seen as superstitions that require official control and other customs based on tradition are rarely practiced, rendering Sino-Burmese ways quaintly old-fashioned. Although the Sino-Burmese have tended to distrust the state and endeavored to stay clear of politics, politics have directly impinged on their lives. Like their fellow residents, Sino-Burmese Rangoonites have had to endure the temperamental actions of the Socialist and SLORC/SPDC governments, wherein opaque policy changes threatened their economic and social well-being. In addition, they have had to contend with the looming influence of China. As people of Chinese descent, they have been trapped by their inability to sever the automatic associations between China and all Chinese people while simultaneously desiring the relationships and potential benefits of being a part of the overseas Chinese network. They remain perpetually other, not only in their adopted home of Rangoon but also among other Chinese populations.

When the economic, political, and social conditions in Rangoon became too oppressive in the 1960s and 1970s, many Chinese sought harbor in their ancestral land, China, or tried to find refuge in countries where fellow Chinese lived and governed: Hong Kong, Taiwan, and Macao. Under the native-place conception of family, all people from a particular region such as southern Fujian are defined as belonging to one large family despite distance in time and location. However, in China, Hong Kong, Taiwan, and Macao, the Chinese from Rangoon were not welcomed home as they had expected but were treated as uninvited guests of the wrong class. In China, they were seen as bourgeois and sent down to rural areas for reeducation through hard labor. They had the misfortune of arriving during the chaos of the Cultural Revolution. In Hong Kong, they were noticeably disadvantaged in the island's growing economy and found it difficult to compete. Those who could not survive in Hong Kong migrated to Macao, as did the people who managed to escape the cruelty of the Cultural Revolution.[8] In Taiwan, they were compelled to settle in Zhonghe, at that time an industrial periphery of Taipei, and left to fend for themselves. They had been promised subsidies by the Nationalist government but received meager amounts that barely covered their needs, forcing them to take factory jobs that were often below their status in Burma.[9] Sino-Burmese in Taiwan were treated as outsiders who had to be educated in proper standard Chinese (to overcome their accents) and learn real Chinese ways, despite their long-standing loyalty to the Nationalist-led Republic of China.[10] These people who sought the security of a Chinese space felt like outcasts. Stories of their suffering quickly traveled back to Burma, making the Sino-Burmese in Rangoon realize that, despite the numerous challenges, Burma was their only home.

This sort of double alienation wherein overseas Chinese return to their supposed homeland to find themselves not at home has greatly influenced the self-identification of contemporary Sino-Burmese within Burma and beyond. Sino-Burmese populations in Hong Kong, Taiwan, Macao, and the United States have established Burmese institutions such as *hpoungyi kyaungs* (Theravada Buddhist monasteries) and Sino-Burmese associations such as the Zhonghua Middle School Alumni Association. All of them put forth great effort to celebrate Thingyan, Burmese New Year, and distinguish themselves as a separate population of hybrid Chinese under the umbrella conception of Han Chinese.[11] Within Burma, the Sino-Burmese have developed a sense of pride for their adopted home. Without fail, every Sino-Burmese person I spoke with expressed pride in the Shwedagon Pagoda. Like all Burmese, they see the Shwedagon as a sacred place and the emblem of Burma. Daw Tin Tin, a second-generation Sino-Burmese, said: "We are the Chinese people who come from Burma. We live in a backward country and we don't have much to show off, but we have the Shwedagon. You might say that we are a poor country, but we have a beautiful stupa covered in gold."[12] Like everyone else from Burma, the Sino-Burmese have suffered the anonymity and lowly image of their country and developed a sense of indignation about their marginal status. When I saw the leader of the Teng clan at Yangon's international airport, he complained: "We flew to Bangkok on our way to Taiwan but had to come back to Rangoon. Our tour guide said that we would get our visas to enter Taiwan while we were in Bangkok, but the government of Taiwan would not give us any visas. So all twenty of us had to fly back. We spent a few days touring Bangkok, but we had all been there before. It is very inconvenient to hold a Myanmar passport."[13] The supposed access the Sino-Burmese have to the larger Chinese world has been a mixed blessing and a source of disappointment. Even Chinese governments will not recognize their Chineseness.

Indeed, the Sino-Burmese claim to Chineseness is not a simple one. From the intra-Chinese factions based on native place, language, and political ideology to the more cohesive national Chinese identity that connected different groups of Chinese in the 1950s and early 1960s, further to the highly pragmatic approach toward Chinese culture today, Sino-Burmese Rangoonites have evolved their self-understanding through relationships. Identity is activated when one interacts with others, when one is in relationship with other people in a place, a shared public realm.[14] For the Sino-Burmese, this community of others has included not only a multiplicity of Chinese but also a diversity of fellow residents: Indian, British, Burmese, and Burmese ethnic minorities. Their process of becoming at home in Burma has been a complex and selective weaving of historical, traditional, political, and economic forces that is intended to provide them with more security and opportunities. Their attachments to traditional Chinese culture are always judged against its utility in the present. Even native-place languages (Hokkien, Cantonese) that were once the bedrock of belonging are now seen as an unnecessary weight in the march toward a brighter future. In discussing Chinese-language education, Eng Tsing Yian, a leader in the Sino-Burmese community, stated: "We need to get rid of Cantonese and Hokkien as a whole, everywhere. All Chinese should just use standard Mandarin Chinese. Otherwise, it will be bad for us. When we [Sino-Burmese] go overseas, they look at our Myanmar passports and then look at us with suspicion. In 1991, I went to Hong Kong. At the airport, they spoke to me in English. I said that I don't speak English. I speak standard Mandarin Chinese. He only spoke Cantonese so he wasn't very receptive. We couldn't talk to each other."[15] In their effort to catch up with the world and reestablish themselves in the overseas Chinese network, the Sino-Burmese in Rangoon are extremely practical. Eng and other leaders in the Sino-Burmese community stated that they want to cultivate *sanyu rencai* (trilingual talent) who are fluent in Burmese, standard Chinese, and English. They see these languages as key assets that will enable their children to compete in the local and global markets, improve Myanmar's economy, promote regional interactions, and help Sino-Burmese become leaders in the Southeast Asian region.[16] Chineseness is a part of this equation but is subordinate to pragmatic concerns.

In their own estimation, the Sino-Burmese in Rangoon have succeeded because they are hardworking and resilient. They talk about the numerous obstacles in their collective history: the unfair advantage enjoyed by the Indians, the devastation of the Japanese invasion, the empty rhetoric of the Nationalist and Communist governments, and the oppressive rule of Burmese regimes. They see themselves as underdogs able to make the best of difficult circumstances. This self-assessment is in fact an oft-uttered leitmotif among all overseas Chinese and other successful migrant populations. What stands out in the context of Burma is the Sino-Burmese willingness to take risks even after five decades of oppression. The risk-taking spirit that enabled their predecessors to leave a familiar homeland for an unknown country seems to have been passed down through the generations. This aspect of Chinese merchant culture has endured.

TAKING TACTICAL RISKS

The status of the Sino-Burmese as foreigners and resident aliens has likely freed them to take more risks. Unlike that of the officially classified ethnic nationalities, Sino-Burmese identity does not coincide with a recognized territory. Sino-Burmese people cannot claim autochthonous rule and thereby threaten the territorial integrity of Burma. Furthermore, as foreigners, they could be expelled from the country, as the Indian and Rohingya populations have experienced. They might have had fewer rights than the dominant Burmans, but their marginal status gave them more room to maneuver, to tactically create opportunities in the interstices.

During my fieldwork, many educated Burmese characterized Burmese people as passive and fatalistic, incapable of pulling themselves out of poverty, fighting for a more just society, or challenging military rule. In this self-critique of Burmese society, they often uttered the adage "Work like the Chinese. Save money like the Indians. Don't throw away money like the Burmese" (*Tayout lo lout. Kala lo su. Bama lo ma hpyoun ne*) to contrast Chinese industriousness with Burmese inaction. Events in Myanmar since 2011 would refute the validity of this assessment. Local civil society has successfully suspended the construction of the Myitsone dam, and the new president, Thein Sein, has been more responsive and open to reform than any leader since the 1960s. However, there is still a sense that the Sino-Burmese have been more daring because their liminal position between Myanmar and China demands a more foolhardy stance.[17]

In the words of Lai Yansong, a leading Sino-Burmese merchant: "I have two fathers, one in Myanmar and one in China. I have to take care of both if I want to survive and succeed."[18] The father metaphor is revealing because it depicts the relationship between the Sino-Burmese and the governments of Myanmar and China as that of a powerless child against a powerful father.

Considered within the Confucian worldview in which the father exercises absolute control, Lai's reference to himself as a son is revealing of the disempowered and uncertain status of the Sino-Burmese. Although they have tried to incorporate themselves into Burma by defining themselves as one of the ethnic nationalities and most have acquired National Registration Cards, or NRCs (official proof of citizenship), they remain foreign in the eyes of the state and somehow other in the eyes of everyday people. Even though they have made a place for themselves in Rangoon, they could be targeted as scapegoats and driven from their adopted home if they somehow antagonize the Myanmar government. In Burma, ethnicity has been inextricably bound with state violence, and there is still "a great deal of work to do to *decouple* ethnicity, as it functions in the dominant discourse, from its equivalence with nationalism, imperialism, racism and the state."[19]

On December 4, 2013, a government task force from the Ministry of Commerce raided the Premium Food Service Products warehouse in Thaketa Township and seized ninety thousand bottles of wine as well as tons of imported luxury food.[20] Premium is a distribution company owned by the Tan family of City Mart. Soon after the raid, retailers, including Daw Win Win Tint, spoke up against the sudden crackdown on luxury imports: "There has been no transparency in the retail sector since we started in 1996."[21] Premium also defended its business practices by emphasizing that it sources its alcohol from importers belonging to the Htoo Group, owned by the crony tycoon Tay Za, and the ACE Group, owned by Phyo Ko Ko Tint San, son of Tint San, the sports minister. Rather than investigating major importers with close connections to the generals, the Ministry of Commerce was instead clamping down on retailers who purchased from the importers.[22] Many Burmese people have commented on the obvious corruption in this case, summarizing government action as going after the small fish when only the big fish could have imported so much wine. If City Mart, the largest and most successful retail chain in Burma, cannot escape the unpredictable actions of the government, then there is little hope for smaller businesses. With no *kosuan* (powerful person or entity) in Burma or China to depend on, they must keep one eye on Burma and one eye overseas, wagering for a better future based on changing circumstances.

Although all of my informants held NRCs, their citizenship in a barely functional state has not been a guarantee of rights. They, like everyone else in Myanmar, bear the NRC as an imposed necessity that protects them from the more extreme abuses experienced by people such as the Rohingya who are ineligible for citizenship. However, citizenship in Myanmar has been and could once again be redefined or revoked. The Sino-Burmese must have an exit strategy because they could be driven out of Burma. But as all of my informants stated, they hope that day will never come. They have made a home for themselves in Burma and see their future as intimately bound to the fortunes of the country. As Taw Tsi Ming stated: "If the economy of Myanmar is weak, there is no way we can make a lot of money. If the education system in Myanmar is bad, there is no way our children can get a good education without sending them overseas. Myanmar has to become stronger if our lives are to improve."[23]

Although the political and economic reforms initiated in 2011 suggest a transition to a more representative government, caution is still the order of the day. During my visits in Rangoon in 2012, 2013, and 2014, Sino-Burmese informants and friends discussed the likelihood of reforms being rescinded and the future status of Myanmar-China relations should Aung San Suu Kyi gain more official power. Furthermore, the sudden removal of Thura Shwe Mann as the chairman of the ruling political party, the Union Solidarity and Development Council, in August 2015 indicates the perpetuation of undemocratic practices. Nothing is for certain, and business continues much as before, when the generals had yet to put on civilian dress. The elections in November 2015 could be a turning point in Myanmar politics and society. However, given the continual flux and the rise of ultranationalistic rhetoric centered around Buddhism, the people of Myanmar, regardless of ethnicity or descent, will likely maintain the covert and temporary tactics that have enabled them to survive the various regimes in Burma/Myanmar. Their well-being remains under threat.

NOTES

PREFACE

1   Aung San Suu Kyi, *Freedom from Fear, and Other Writings*, 181.
2   Burmese themselves tend to render Burmese words according to their understanding of English spelling, which often leads to ambiguity and confusion. In consultation with Patrick McCormick, I use a system that provides enough information for the reader to recognize and, I hope, recreate the Burmese. This system is not fully phonetic (I do not indicate, for example, tone, and final -*t* represents the glottal stop), nor again have I followed Burmese spelling too closely, which at times can be misleading.

INTRODUCTION

1   For consistency, I will use Rangoon throughout the book to refer to the city that is also known as Yangon. This is not an expression of colonial nostalgia but a recognition of the fact that "Rangoon" is a valid way to romanize the Burmese name especially if historical changes in phonetics are considered. (Thanks to Patrick McCormick for pointing out the importance of linguistic and phonetic changes through time.) As for the name of the country, I will generally refer to the country as Burma except when I am discussing the actions of the post-1988 government.
2   Thanks to ethnomusicologist Tasaw Lu for her advice in rendering the drumming into this onomatopoeic representation. In my nonexpert representation, the longer dash (—) is meant to represent a longer duration of the rhythm while the shorter dash (-) is a shorter duration. Any error in this representation is mine alone.
3   Although many scholars have discussed the porosity of boundaries and the non-territorial nature of traditional polities in Southeast Asia, the original analyses by Thongchai Winichakul and Stanley Jeyaraja Tambiah continue to influence the work Southeast Asianists. Beyond Southeast

Asia, the *territorial trap* as first articulated by John Agnew remains salient. As Agnew pointed out, the territorialized sovereign state as the appropriate container for society was not inevitable and in fact oversimplifies the various interactions within and between states that often cross nation-state boundaries. Winichakul, *Siam Mapped*; Tambiah, *World Conqueror and World Renouncer*; Agnew, "The Territorial Trap."

4   Mya Than, "Ethnic Chinese in Myanmar."

5   Conflict between ethnicity and nationalism is not unique to Burma/ Myanmar and has been studied in many other countries. In the context of Burma, primordialism remains central in constructing ethnic identities, and this ideological basis has periodically fueled violent conflict. While many scholars such as Thomas Hylland Eriksen, Lola Romanucci-Ross, and George De Vos have discussed this problem, particularly in postcolonial nation-states, I find the analysis provided by Arjun Appadurai most illuminating. In particular, my analysis of the Sino-Burmese framed around place fits nicely with his *production of localities*. Eriksen, *Ethnicity and Nationalism*; Romanucci-Ross and De Vos, *Ethnic Identity*; Appadurai, *Modernity at Large*.

6   Although *lifeworld* could be replaced by terms such as *habitus*, I prefer this concept from phenomenology to others for three main reasons: (1) It not only speaks to internalized structural forces such as style and taste that predetermine norms in society but also foregrounds dynamic intersubjectivity and the givenness of our world; that is, the lifeworld is already present and meaningful before rational analysis. (2) The intersubjective givenness of the lifeworld is an appropriate lens for examining life in Burma because most of the population has internalized Buddhist concepts such as impermanence and dependent origination. These two fundamental principles in Buddhist thought state that reality as experienced is at once constantly changing and apparently continuous, formed out of myriad forces that gather in each moment to give rise to life. As a Western-trained researcher studying Burma, I do not want to superimpose Western theories onto non-Western cultures without critically examining the appropriateness of my philosophical framework. It seems to me that the concept of lifeworld is able to accommodate the Buddhist ideas of impermanence and mutually constituted reality and is therefore an appropriate frame of reference. (3) Although *lifeworld* is not a common English term, it is sufficiently comprehensible as a combination of *life* and *world*, which evokes a sense of understanding that remains open for further investigation. I find this openness essential in trying to understand a so-called "other" or another culture because hard-lined definitions often preclude reflective understanding.

7   Conversation in Burmese with Kyaw Yin Hlaing, December 22, 2006. Unless otherwise noted, all translations are mine. *Ethos* is translated into

Burmese as (a) "a circle of family, friends, and relatives"; (b) "a group," "a block"; or (c) "morale," "spirit." These glosses approximate the common English understanding of a society's values and the spirit of the time or place. *Identity* as the Western concept of a "true self" or as practiced in identity politics has yet to be used by the Burmese. In English-to-Burmese dictionaries, there are numerous translations for the verb *to identify*. For *identity*, there are a few glosses that render the word as something like "being the same as." I cannot recall anyone in Rangoon talking about himself or herself in terms of identity.

8   Arendt, *Essays in Understanding*, 307–62.

9   These two ethnic nationalities are from the borderlands between Burma, China, and Thailand. As I discuss below, the identities of these people are flexible and often cross nation-state boundaries.

10   Arendt, *The Human Condition*, 52.

11   Scholars such as Wang Gungwu, Shu-mei Shih, and others have analyzed the hegemonic tendencies of *China* and *Chinese* and cautioned against the reification of Chineseness as a political identity centered on the nation-state of China. Although I came upon the concept of "place" from Martin Heidegger and phenomenology, I am using the concept in a similar manner to Wang and Shih. Place is an opening that allows for different practices, and these practices not only give rise to different ways of living (of being somehow Chinese), but they also create different places.

12   McGowan, *Hannah Arendt*, 139.

13   Malpas, *Place and Experience*, 40.

14   In 2014, the Myanmar government undertook and completed a national census. However, due to various sensitivities regarding ethnic nationalities and in particular the Rohingya, categories and regions were omitted from the census. For considered critiques of the 2014 census, see Callahan and Nyunt, "Political Risk Assessment"; Transnational Institute, "Ethnicity without Meaning, Data without Context."

15   An exonym is the name assigned to an ethnic group or to a geographical entity by another group of people. The exonym can be contested by members of the named group as inaccurate and can often be derogatory.

16   Luce, "Note on the People of Burma."

17   Goh, "The Question of 'China' in Burmese Chronicles"; Aung-Thwin, *Myth and History*.

18   Although China is often conceived of as a monolithic whole with a homogenous population, it is actually a diverse nation with a history of conflict between different ethnic groups. Since the founding of the People's Republic of China, these groups have been classified into fifty-six officially recognized nationalities, with Han being the dominant group. Han culture can be generally described as the culture originating in the Yellow River Valley built upon Confucianism, Taoism, and the mandarin

bureaucratic system. For insightful discussions, see, among others, Mullaney et al., *Critical Han Studies*; Harrell, *Cultural Encounters on China's Ethnic Frontiers*; Mueggler, *The Age of Wild Ghosts*.

19   For an introduction to the historical and contemporary issues of ethnic identity and self-determination in the southwest of China, see Harrell, *Cultural Encounters on China's Ethnic Frontiers*; McCarthy, *Communist Multiculturalism*.

20   Goh, "The Question of 'China' in Burmese Chronicles," 129.

21   Jones, "The Image of the Barbarian in Medieval Europe." The names *China* and *Chinese* have been debated since at least the turn of the twentieth century. For a thorough discussion of the various theories regarding the origin of the word *China/Cina*, which has been traced back to ancient Greece as well as to the *Mahabharata*, see Wade, "The Polity of Yelang," 6–13; Liu, *The Clash of Empires*, 75–80.

22   Many anthropologists and human geographers have focused on ethnic and sub-ethnic identities in China. See, among others, Cartier, *Globalizing South China*; Lipman, *Familiar Strangers*; Gladney, *Dislocating China*.

23   This sense of equation between "Chinese" and "China" is not new and has been discussed by many scholars such as Cartier, *Globalizing South China*; Kuhn, *Chinese among Others*; Tu, "Cultural China"; Wang, "Chineseness." Among these scholars there has been an effort to interrogate the words *Chinese* and *Chineseness* and to distinguish between "overseas Chinese" and "Chinese overseas." "Overseas Chinese" is generally understood to be the translation for *huaqiao*, a Chinese word for a Chinese person who is temporarily away from his or her home but fundamentally belongs in China. From around 1900, the government of China began to use *huaqiao* explicitly as a political tool to promote Chinese nationalism and loyalty toward China. In contrast, "Chinese overseas" is the translation for *huaren* or *huayi*, meaning a person of Chinese descent regardless of nationality or citizenship. That is, *huaren* defines belonging by culture, not politics. Although I respect and see the usefulness of this distinction, I do not follow this strict system for two reasons: (1) Except for two informants, the people of Chinese descent in Rangoon did not distinguish between *huaqiao* and *huaren*. In fact, people generally mixed terms such as *huaqiao*, *zhongguoren* (strictly, a Chinese national), and *tangren* (an old word used in southern China meaning "culturally Chinese people"). It seemed to me that only people who had read academic analyses about the Chinese diaspora made the distinction. (2) Maintaining the distinction between "overseas Chinese" and "Chinese overseas" is often cumbersome. To avoid burdening the reader with awkward prose, I employ both terms interchangeably.

24   The history of and contestations regarding the classification, naming, and rights of these different ethnic nationalities lie beyond the purview of this

book. Conflicts between the Burmese state and different ethnic groups have persisted since the founding of Burma in 1948. The status of ethnic nationalities as indigenous peoples coupled with specific territories has rendered their position problematic because different ethnic groups can threaten the territorial integrity of Myanmar through assertions of self-sovereignty. This book focuses on the position of the Chinese in Myanmar placed within the national system of ethnic nationalities and foreign residents. For an introduction to ethnic studies in Myanmar, see Gravers, *Exploring Ethnic Diversity in Burma*; Smith, *Burma: Insurgency and the Politics of Ethnicity.*

25 "The Union Citizenship Act, 1948," http://www.burmalibrary.org/docs/ UNION_CITIZENSHIP_ACT-1948.htm.

26 According to Mya Than and Fan Hongwei, the 1948 act was liberal compared to laws implemented in other Southeast Asian countries, and over 50 percent of the Chinese population qualified for citizenship in the 1950s. However, Fan's research indicates that few Chinese took up the opportunity to acquire citizenship in the 1950s because they could not see the benefits. See Fan, "Study on the Changes of Political Status of Chinese Community" and Mya Than "Ethnic Chinese in Myanmar."

27 Fan, "Study on the Changes of Political Status of Chinese Community"; Mya Than "Ethnic Chinese in Myanmar"; Taylor, "Do States Make Nations?"

28 As noted in the Preface, the Sino-Burmese in Rangoon speak different Chinese languages. Some of them said "kosuan" in the Hokkien pronunciation, while others said "kaoshan" in standard Chinese. These words are also found in written Chinese sources listed in the Bibliography.

29 Wang Gungwu covers the history of the Chinese in Southeast Asia in all of his writings but offers specific details in works such as "Southeast Asian Huaqiao in Chinese History-Writing" and "Merchants without Empires," both in *China and the Chinese Overseas.*

30 Ibid.

31 Reid, "Creating the Centre for the Study of the Chinese Southern Diaspora," 173.

32 Quoted in Mya Than, "Ethnic Chinese in Myanmar," 136. The irony of course is that Ne Win is supposed to be a mixed-blood Sino-Burmese. This suspicion regarding foreigners has been in the news for over a decade: both Daw Aung San Suu Kyi's marriage to an Englishman and her "half-bred" children have been given as reasons to question her loyalty and remain the reasons she cannot run for president.

33 Ministry of Religious Affairs, *Dictionary of Buddhist Terms.*

34 I am of course alluding to Ong, *Flexible Citizenship*; Ong and Nonini, *Ungrounded Empires.*

35 Lefebvre, *The Production of Space*, 38.

36 Casey, *The Fate of Place*, 242.

37 Eminent thinkers such as Michel Foucault, David Harvey, Gilles Deleuze, Félix Guattari, and Henri Lefebvre have all dedicated significant attention to space and place as sites of power and multiplicity. They have discussed the rational regulation of space as a technique of government and the everyday interactions in space as a countermeasure to political dominance. My analysis of place is particularly informed by Harvey's absolute and relational space, Lefebvre's conceived and lived space, and the more poetic examination of place as put forth by philosophers Edward S. Casey, Jeff Malpas, and Robert Mugerauer. It also draws from the "legibility" of space as provided by James C. Scott. Foucault, *Discipline and Punish*, *Language, Counter-Memory, Practice*, and "Space, Knowledge, and Power"; Harvey, "Space as a Key Word"; Deleuze and Guattari, *A Thousand Plateaus*; Lefebvre, *The Production of Space*; Casey, *The Fate of Place*; Malpas, *Heidegger and the Thinking of Place, Heidegger's Topology*, and *Place and Experience*; Mugerauer, *Interpretations on Behalf of Place* and *Interpreting Environments*; Scott, *Seeing like a State*.

38 Oakes, "Place and the Paradox of Modernity," 511.

39 Sarah Heminway Maxim in her unpublished dissertation, "Resemblance in External Appearance: The Colonial Project in Kuala Lumpur and Rangoon," discusses the civilizing project undertaken by the British colonial officials. This practice, however, was common in Europe around the eighteenth century. As Foucault shows, the rational ordering of space was employed as a means to discipline society. Foucault, *Discipline and Punish*, *Language, Counter-Memory, Practice*, and "Space, Knowledge, and Power."

40 As the limited research to date indicates, *Tayout-kabya* remains a slippery term, one that is less clear than *Tayout*. During my fieldwork, parentage was not a reliable determinant of who claimed to be Tayout versus Tayout-kabya. Those who had "pure" Chinese blood and those who had mixed Mon or Burmese plus Chinese blood both said they were Tayout-kabya. Therefore, the term pointed to both racial and cultural identity, and the two aspects did not necessarily coincide.

41 From 2007 to 2009, I attended a weekly group meditation with the grandchildren and great-grandchildren of Chan Mah Phee. These sessions held in the home of Daw Cho Cho, called *san-gaw* by members of her family, included afternoon tea and allowed me to observe their familial interactions. They spoke to one another in Burmese, although almost all of them were fluent in English. However, in addressing one another, they used Hokkien familial terms.

42 Conversation in standard Chinese with owner of pharmaceutical company, August 1, 2007.

43 The Chinese and hybrid Chinese populations in these countries have

greatly outnumbered the population in Burma since the eighteenth century. For example, Thailand is about 14 percent Chinese, while Malaysia is 25 percent Chinese, according to the Central Intelligence Agency's 2012 *World Factbook* figures, and these populations have historically exercised significant economic power. The populations in Indonesia and the Philippines have fluctuated throughout history due to pogroms (instigated by the Dutch and Spanish governments, respectively). Although the populations in Indonesia and the Philippines are only 1–3 percent of the national population, some of the largest multinational conglomerates are owned by people of Chinese descent.

44 Comparative studies on the Indian and Chinese populations in Burma remain scant; however, J. S. Furnivall, Robert H. Taylor, and Mya Than have all concluded that Indians dominated Rangoon. See Furnivall, *An Introduction to the Political Economy of Burma*; Taylor, *The State in Burma*; Taylor, "Do States Make Nations?"; Mya Than, "Ethnic Chinese in Myanmar." In addition, there is one macro-level comparison by Reneau Egreteau in Bhattacharya and Kripalani, *Indian and Chinese Immigrant Communities*.

45 Taylor, *The State in Burma*, 135.

46 Chakravarti, *The Indian Minority in Burma*, 78–79. The dominance of the Indian population is also discussed in Purcell, *The Chinese in Southeast Asia*.

47 Yegar, *The Muslims of Burma*.

48 Chakravarti, *The Indian Minority in Burma*, 19, table 2.4; Thant Myint-U, *The River of Lost Footsteps*.

49 Taylor, *The State in Burma*, 128. In these and other statistics, I have checked against some census figures via digitized archival collections available on the Internet but did not undertake independent demographic analysis. See India, Census Commissioner, "Census of India, 1911." For a demographic analysis, see Purcell, *The Chinese in Southeast Asia*, 41–48.

50 Feng, *Mianhua bainian shihua*, 12. I have provided the standard Chinese transliteration because this term was used in Chinese texts written by the Sino-Burmese. Many Sino-Burmese talked about how their forefathers had to travel a long way and had to try their luck in other locales first. One informant noted that his grandfather had actually gone to Hawaii and after failing to succeed in Hawaii headed back west, eventually landing in Rangoon.

51 Taylor, *The State in Burma*; Mya Than, "Ethnic Chinese in Myanmar."

52 Chen, "The Chinese in Rangoon." He also authored *A Model Burmese-Chinese Dictionary*.

53 Conversations in English with U Thaw Kaung, historian and former head librarian of Myanmar, 2008–9.

54 Chen, "The Chinese in Rangoon." Purcell refers to these as the maritime Chinese, a term that has generally stuck in the study of the Chinese in Burma. Purcell, *The Chinese in Southeast Asia.*

55 Hill, *Merchants and Migrants.*

56 Toyota, "Contested Chinese Identities."

57 Conversation with a Kachin/Shanba Tayout woman on February 13, 2008, at a restaurant that I frequented in my neighborhood.

58 Purcell, *The Chinese in Southeast Asia*, 41–79. The Mountain Chinese migrated to Burma overland from the north. In contrast, the Maritime Chinese came by sea through the Straits Settlements.

59 Chang has focused on the Chinese and Nationalist troops in the border regions between China, Thailand, and Burma. Duan, a Chinese anthropologist, focused on the Chinese in Mandalay. Fan, a scholar based at Xiamen University, has tended to examine macro-level political factors. Li completed a historical thesis on the Chinese during the colonial era. Daw Win, a Sino-Burmese, is currently an associate researcher at the Chinese Heritage Centre, Nanyang Technical University, Singapore. She contributed many entries to the biographical dictionary by Leo Suryadinata, *Southeast Asian Personalities of Chinese Descent.*

60 As noted above, the absence of reliable census data makes discussions of populations problematic. Fan uses a 1956 report on the overseas Chinese population in southern Burma, which states the following percentages: Hokkien, 55 percent; Cantonese, 35 percent; Yunnanese, 6 percent; and other, 4 percent. See Fan, "A Study on the Changes of Political Status of Chinese Community." Contemporary Sino-Burmese agree that although Hokkien people constitute the majority population in Yangon, they might soon be outnumbered by the Yunnanese.

61 In particular, a Hakka woman in her sixties said that when she was growing up, if one wanted to succeed, one had to speak Hokkien because it was the language of commerce. Conversation, November 12, 2008.

62 Qingfu Gong Executive Committee, *Qingfu Gong baizhounian qingdian tekan*; the emphasis is mine.

63 Fan, "A Study on the Changes of Political Status of Chinese Community," 48–51.

64 *Myanmar-English Dictionary.*

65 Mya Maung, "On the Road to Mandalay."

66 U Thaw Kaung first pointed out these short stories to me in 2008. For a cogent discussion about these short stories, see Maung Aung Myoe, *In the Name of Pauk-Phaw*, 124, 171–73. Anti-Chinese sentiments as expressed through literature and other media are also discussed in Min Zin, "Burmese Attitude toward Chinese."

67 Maung Aung Myoe, *In the Name of Pauk-Phaw.*

68 The cease-fire agreements brokered by Khin Nyunt gave armed ethnic

groups such as the Kokang and Wa much greater mobility within Myanmar. The privileges provided through the cease-fires contributed toward the migration of Chinese-looking people to central Burma and later Lower Burma as well. Several commentators and scholars have analyzed these events; among them Maung Aung Myoe provides a measured analysis in *In the Name of Pauk-Phaw*. Chinese anthropologist Duan Ying undertook his fieldwork in Mandalay among Chinese residents in 2010. He emphasizes that it was a massive fire that destroyed many of the buildings in downtown Mandalay and that government decisions in the sale of those properties after the fire brought in many Chinese residents. Personal conversation, December 2, 2012.

69   Maung Aung Myoe, *In the Name of Pauk-Phaw*. The Kokang are culturally Han and speak a variant of standard Chinese as their native tongue, although anecdotal evidence suggests that Kokang see themselves as belonging to their own country, Kokang, not a part of China or Myanmar. Wa people belong in the Austroasiatic language family, but due to the diversity of dialects within their various subgroups, standard Chinese is used as their work language along with some Burmese and Shan. The Wa areas were a stronghold of the Burmese Communist Party, which was supported by the Chinese Communist Party. Due to this politico-military connection, many Wa were educated in standard Chinese and much of their military culture is based on Communist Chinese culture. See Renard, "The Wa Authority and Good Governance."

70   For a cogent analysis of the Burman-Chinese tension in Mandalay, see Maung Aung Myoe, *In the Name of Pauk-Phaw*, 123–25.

71   Conversation in standard Chinese with a Teng clan elder, November 20, 2007.

72   Conversation in Burmese with a Burman architect, January 28, 2008.

73   *Le* in Burmese means "little" or "small" and is often used as a diminutive, rendering the modified noun more endearing. In this case, *pauk hpaw le* should be understood as "cute little *pauk hpaw*," carrying the warmheartedness one would associate with enjoying the presence of a small child.

74   Excerpted from Xiao Cao, "Record of Random Thoughts: My Thoughts on 'Baobo,'" posted on Mianhuawang (Myanmar Chinese), the only website created and maintained by the community of Sino-Burmese in Rangoon. I have translated the name of the website as "Myanmar Chinese," not "Burmese Chinese" or "Sino-Burmese," because several members of the committee that manages the website are members of the Mianhua Shanghui, which they translate as Myanmar Chinese Chamber of Commerce. Several elders in the Sino-Burmese community referred me to this website, and the organizers explicitly stated that this site is meant to represent the Sino-Burmese.

75   There are also lucrative deals struck with Thai and French companies.

These business ventures have been well covered in the news and are peripheral to this study of the Sino-Burmese.

76 Conversation with Dai Minqin in standard Chinese, August 4, 2007.

77 This is changing quickly in post-2011 Myanmar. Before 2011, Chinese businesses entered Burma, but, as already stated, they worked with the military junta, not with everyday people. After 2011, it appears that overseas Chinese networks are being reactivated. However, the largest projects, particularly real estate development, remain in the hands of those with connections with the generals.

78 Ong, *Flexible Citizenship*.

79 Anecdotal evidence suggests that Sino-Thai business families have already invested in five-star hotels and that Malaysian Chinese entrepreneurs are actively growing their businesses in Myanmar. For example, Chatrium Hotel, next to Kandawgyi Lake, is owned by a Sino-Thai family, and Capital Hypermart is owned by Malaysian Chinese. In addition, Dagon City, the high-end multiuse development project around the Shwedagon Pagoda, was jointly owned by the Marga Group based in Hong Kong and Thu Kha Yadanar, a shell corporation with ties to illicit trade in the China-Myanmar border region. As of July 2015, President Thein Sein instructed the Myanmar Investment Commission to cancel the Dagon City project. I analyze the process and significance of the popular and Buddhist protests surrounding this project in my conference paper "Power, Participation and Yangon" presented at the Burma/Myanmar Update Conference on June 6, 2015.

80 The residence of these Chinese near the Yayway Cemetery is significant because, according to Chinese tradition, living near graves brings bad luck and must be avoided.

1. HYBRID CHINESE PLACES IN A FORMER COLONIAL CAPITAL

1 During my residence in Rangoon, between 2006 and 2009, most downtown residents received electricity for only eight to twelve hours per day and had no choice as to when the power was delivered. Sometimes power was available in the middle of the night, when most people had no use for electricity. In the suburban areas most people had no power, unless they were in elite neighborhoods such as Shwedaungkya (Golden Valley) or Kamayut.

2 De Certeau, *The Practice of Everyday Life*, xi–xix.

3 Maxim, "Resemblance in External Appearance," 322.

4 Tagore, *Japane-Parashye (In Japan and Persia)*, 17–25.

5 Maxim, "Resemblance in External Appearance," 47.

6 This is the "absolute space" defined by Harvey and the "representation of space" defined by Lefebvre. British colonialists, like other European pow-

ers, dictated the forms of colonial cities to exert hegemonic control over their subjects. My analysis of Rangoon as a space of power and contestation follows in the footsteps of Foucault, Harvey, and Lefebvre. It also uses the concept of legibility as seen in Scott's work. Harvey, "Space as a Key Word"; Lefebvre, *The Production of Space*; Foucault, *Discipline and Punish*, *Language, Counter-Memory, Practice*, and "Space, Knowledge, and Power"; Scott, *Seeing like a State*.

7   Phayre to the Marquis of Dalhousie, 25 December 1852, Dalhousie-Phayre Correspondence, letter 3, as quoted in Maxim, "Resemblance in External Appearance," 46.

8   Maxim, "Resemblance in External Appearance," 46.

9   Scott, *Seeing like a State*.

10   Henry Keighly, "Appendix R: Report on the City of Rangoon," p. XXVII, in "Report of the Administration of the Province of Pegu for 1855–56," Administration Reports of the Government of India, 1855–56 (Calcutta: John Gray, "Calcutta Gazette" office, 1857), IOR V/10/2, as cited in Maxim, "Resemblance in External Appearance," 49.

11   Maxim, "Resemblance in External Appearance," 49.

12   Ibid., 51.

13   Pearn, *A History of Rangoon*.

14   *Pukka* (or *pucka*) was a term borrowed from British India that meant "solid," "substantial," or "properly constructed."

15   Phayre to Government, "Rules for the Grant of Town and Suburban Allotments within the Limits of the Jurisdiction of the Town Magistrate of Rangoon," IPP/200/40, 21 October 1853, no. 104, as quoted in Maxim, "Resemblance in External Appearance," 66.

16   AR Pegu 1858–59, p. 575, as quoted in ibid., 110.

17   Pearn, *A History of Rangoon*, 41–49.

18   McGee, *The Southeast Asian City*, 31–36.

19   Abbott, *The Traveller's History of Burma*; Oertel, *Note on a Tour in Burma*; Kelly, *Burma, Painted and Described*.

20   McGee, *The Southeast Asian City*, 34. For insightful analysis regarding Mandalay, the last dynastic capital of Burma, see Tainturier, "The Foundation of Mandalay by King Mindon."

21   The centrality of monasteries in Burmese culture is well known and discussed in Spiro, *Buddhism and Society*, sec 4. In terms of the physical layout of villages, I am not aware of any architectural or scholarly studies, but a general Burmese mental map situates the monastery at the head (eastern side) of a village, as seen in the first-grade reader lesson "Nyaung-bin-tha Village," in Okell, *Burmese: An Introduction to the Literary Style*, 36. In this simple text, Burmese children are taught that, in addition to the monastery, the village is surrounded by a pond to the south, woods to the north, and paddy fields to the west. Maxim makes a similar argument

in "Resemblance in External Appearance," stating that the entire plan of the city was directed toward serving the needs of the new and alien government.

22 Pearn, *A History of Rangoon*, 190–94.

23 Ibid., 234, 255, 287; Taylor, *The State in Burma*.

24 Pearn, *A History of Rangoon*, 67.

25 Chen, "The Cantonese People in Burma."

26 Ibid., 102; Pearn, *A History of Rangoon*, 55.

27 Captain Michael Symes wrote, "All of the officers of the Government, the most opulent merchants, and persons of consideration, live within the fort; shipwrights and persons of inferior rank inhabit the suburbs." Quoted in Wright, *Twentieth Century Impressions of Burma*, 279.

28 Chen, "The Cantonese People in Burma," 98. *Tang people* (or *tangren*) is an older term that Hokkien and Cantonese people used to refer to themselves and is based on a cultural rather than a national sense of self-understanding.

29 Pearn, *A History of Rangoon*, 234, 255, 287.

30 All of the successful Chinese merchants featured in *Twentieth Century Impressions of Burma* either came from Penang or arrived in Rangoon after working in Penang or the Straits Settlements in general.

31 Wright, *Twentieth Century Impressions of Burma*, 280

32 Fei, Hamilton, and Wang, *From the Soil, the Foundations of Chinese Society*, vii.

33 Ibid., 62–63.

34 Kuhn, *Chinese among Others*, 42.

35 Interview with leader of Teng Clan Association, August 27, 2007. In the commemorative books published by Kheng Hock Geong, Kiuliong Tong, and other clan / native place associations, those with multiple surnames all provide a history of their particular lineages and how they were joined in the past. These records often read like hagiographies because they tend to trace their ancestry back to the Han dynasty (206 BCE–220 CE) or earlier and usually include some significant historical figures such as a royal minister or general.

36 Cartier, *Globalizing South China*, 27.

37 Goodman, *Native Place, City, and Nation*.

38 DeBernardi, *Rites of Belonging*.

39 Many scholars have commented on the centrality of native place in the Chinese imaginary; see Cartier, *Globalizing South China*; Naquin and Rawski, *Chinese Society in the Eighteenth Century*; Ebrey and Watson, *Kinship Organization in Late Imperial China*; Kuhn, *Chinese among Others*. Translated as "native place" or "hometown," the terms *laojia* (old family home), *jiaxiang* (home village), *guxiang* (literary term for "home village"), and *qiaoxiang* (home village for Chinese overseas) are signifi-

cant markers for a family's history and legacy. As the mobility of Chinese populations increases, both within and beyond China, the significance of native place might decrease. However, the *hukou* (household registration) system in China and the national identification card system in Taiwan explicitly define their citizens according to their ancestral native places even if a person was not born in the city or province of his or her fore-fathers. This technique of control will ensure the salience of native place in the foreseeable future. In regions such as Southeast Asia, native place is often intimately bound to religious organizations such as native place temples. This connection has and will likely continue to maintain the significance of native place for Chinese overseas (discussed in more detail in Chapter 2).

40 Interview in English and Burmese with U Aung Myint, February 16, 2007. U Aung Myint does not speak Hokkien or standard Chinese.

41 Chen, "The Cantonese People in Burma."

42 Hsin-chun Tasaw Lu, an ethnomusicologist, has examined the influence of music on the Chinese population in Rangoon. See Lu, "Performativity of Difference." While we have studied similar events in the history of this population, we draw some different conclusions regarding their degree of political activism. There are two main reasons for this difference: (1) the population I focus on have remained in Rangoon and lived under the rule of the military junta, making them more circumspect in taking political action and expressing political views; and (2) Lu's informants in Taiwan and Rangoon were specifically involved in the political activities promoted by the Chinese Communist Party and the Nationalist Party, and therefore politics is in the forefront of their narratives. While I also con-ducted interviews in Taiwan and Macao among those who left Rangoon in the 1960s and 1970s, their interpretation of Chinese life plays a much less significant role in my analysis. I focus on the Sino-Burmese who not only identify with Burma but either have decided to stay or could not leave the country. Their perspective in the late 2000s is understandably different from that of those who left in the 1960s and 1970s.

43 Lin and Zhang, *Mianhua shehui yanjiu*, 121–26.

44 I was invited to the two services held for the leader, Din Tin Lok, on November 20 and 21, 2008. Both ceremonies were very elaborate and involved martial-arts-like rituals performed first by Ho Sing and then by Kien Tek brothers.

45 Since Burma and China officially reestablished diplomatic relations in 1978 and the SLORC opened up the Myanmar economy, Sino-Burmese Rangoonites have been actively rebuilding connections with distant fam-ily members in Fujian, Hong Kong, and Taiwan.

46 Chinese populations in Penang, Melaka, and Singapore can be traced back to the early 1500s, and their numbers increased dramatically after

the British seized Malaya. In the nineteenth and early twentieth centuries, these three territories in the Straits Settlements were the most popular destinations for Chinese migrants. The Peranakan also include the descendants of migrants who settled in the Indonesian archipelago. During my fieldwork, some informants used the word *Baba* to describe different types of Chinese in Rangoon, but no one used the word *Nyonya*.

47 *Pashu* is a word used to designate the place (Malaya) and as an attribute of the people and cuisine from the place. In addition to the Peranakan, people explained that *jaukjaw*, a gelatin-like dessert made of coconut milk and agar-agar, is Pashu.

48 Straits Eclectic style was popular between the 1890s and 1940s. See Knapp, *Chinese Houses of Southeast Asia*.

49 Chen, "The Cantonese People in Burma."

50 Wright, *Twentieth Century Impressions of Burma*, 314–22.

51 Interviews with the grandchildren of Chan Mah Phee, 2007–9.

52 Ibid. In addition, the family showed me the antique candleholders, incense urns, and other ritual paraphernalia they still use to worship the gods during Chinese New Year.

53 In actual practice, the British government controlled the various populations in British Malaya through intermediaries such as Malay village headmen, Muslim judges, and Chinese *kapitans* (*kapitan cina*), who were expected to keep their own people in line. See, among others, Khoo, *The Straits Chinese*; Lees, "Being British in Malaya."

54 Mansions are the large homes built within the grid of central Rangoon; villas are the large estates built in suburban areas.

55 Although I was not able to learn any details about Lim or his family during my fieldwork, I later discovered that his progeny left Burma and are now living in Penang, Singapore, and Canada. One of his great-grandsons, Davey Lim, maintains a website about the Lim family (http://www.geocities.ws/davey_lim/Davey_LimHomepage.html). In addition, the Anglo-Burmese Library provides an overview of Lim Chin Tsong's troubled relationship with the Burmah Oil Company (http://www.angloburmeselibrary.com/burmah-oil-company.html). Finally, there is an entry about Lim Chin Tsong in Suryadinata, *Southeast Asian Personalities of Chinese Descent*, 1:601–2.

56 This decorative use of Chinese architectural elements is also seen in Quanzhou, the native place of these various Chinese overseas. I saw this firsthand when in 2008 I assisted in a research project titled "Huaqiao Influence on Housing Policy and the Development of a Globalized Domestic Architecture in Quanzhou, Fujian," led by Daniel Abramson of the University of Washington; Chiang Bo-wei of the National Kinmen Institute of Technology, Taiwan; and Wang Lianmao, curator of the Quanzhou Maritime Museum, China. The project was funded by the

Chiang Ching-kuo Foundation for International Scholarly Exchange.

57 "The Union Citizenship Act, 1948," http://www.burmalibrary.org/docs/ UNION_CITIZENSHIP_ACT-1948.htm.

58 As already stated, much more research is necessary to uncover the history of the Chinese in Burma. As my interviews between 2007 and 2009 revealed, most Chinese of mixed descent had a grandmother or great-grandmother who was Mon.

59 Fan, "A Study on the Changes of Political Status of Chinese Community," 50.

60 Wealthy Indians were affected more dramatically because they were not allowed to reenter Burma after they sought refuge in India during World War II and were specifically targeted as colonial collaborators.

61 Lim is mentioned in a short editorial in Huang, *Huang Chouqing shiwen xuan.*

62 Conversation in standard Chinese with Huang Xiangquan on November 16, 2008, while touring Chin Tsong Palace, Rangoon.

63 It is likely that members of those families emigrated from Burma as the economic situation worsened in the 1960s. Because there are no reliable statistics for Burma after 1931, this discussion is based on the qualitative research conducted between 2006 and 2009.

64 Conversation in Burmese with a cab driver of Indian descent, March 10, 2007.

65 Yu, *Yangguang Guangdong Gongsi.* Within this commemorative book, Chen Yi-Sein provides a detailed list of businesses (140–44), but it is unclear whether he generated a complete list.

66 I am referring to Arendt's definition of the public realm as in, among other sources, *The Human Condition.*

67 If the reader familiar with Burma and Southeast Asia is wondering why there is not a discussion of John Sydendam Furnivall and plural society at this point, the influence of the market on Rangoon's urban society will be discussed in Chapter 4.

68 These garden-like neighborhoods north of downtown Rangoon still house stand-alone units and large villas. They are in Ahlone and Kamayut Townships and Golden Valley. Newer wealthy neighborhoods and gated multi-unit estates have arisen since the early 1990s, but they do not compare to old money neighborhoods.

2. THE HOKKIEN KUANYIN TEMPLE AS A CENTER OF BELONGING

1 Kuhn, *Chinese among Others.*

2 Although it has become standard to refer to the bodhisattva Kuanyin as Guanyin, based on standard Chinese pronunciation, I maintain the older romanization because my informants were mainly of Hokkien heritage,

so they pronounced the name of the goddess with more of an initial *k* sound. Furthermore, Kuanyin has remained a region-based deity that has escaped the nationalist Chinese discourse. Therefore, a more localized representation is appropriate. Kuanyin is also known as Avalokitesvara and Kannon.

3   Interview with Yang Min in standard Chinese and Hokkien, January 10, 2008.

4   Many scholars of the Chinese diaspora have noted theses historical trends. For a clear and updated overview, see Kuhn, *Chinese among Others*; Ma and Cartier, *The Chinese Diaspora*.

5   Kuhn, *Chinese among Others*, 247.

6   This is common knowledge among contemporary Sino-Burmese Rangoonites. It is also recorded in Feng, *Mianhua bainian shihua*. This spatial division between different groups of Chinese also occurred in Singapore.

7   Huang, *Huang Chouqing shiwen xuan*, 68–69; *Rangoon Times*, "The Chinese in Burma," July 20, 1912.

8   Interview in standard Chinese with Cao Weiguo, January 10, 2009. Cao is a first-generation Sino-Burmese whose father migrated from Guangdong Province. He speaks standard Chinese and Cantonese fluently and was one the most eloquent interlocutors for the Sino-Burmese community. Many other informants provided the same assessment in similar words. Again, without reliable statistics, it is difficult to determine if the Hokkien were always numerically and financially dominant. Many informants said the Hokkien determined what it meant to be Sino-Burmese, but there is also the above view.

9   Dean, *Taoist Ritual and Popular Cults*.

10   There is one more deity of sorts called Ho Yah (Tiger Lord), who sits under the altar below Kuanyin and Matso. Not everyone pays respect to Ho Yah, who is seen as a lower-level deity. The temple attendants say that praying to him can prevent bad things from happening. He is also known as Matso's royal mount or vehicle (*vahana*).

11   Faure, *The Structure of Chinese Rural Society*, 10.

12   Burmese residents know the Kokine Chinese Temple for the vegetarian restaurant that is attached to the temple. I was surprised to learn that even people who lived in predominantly Burman neighborhoods such as Pazundaung knew about the restaurant. A friend said that her family went to the Kokine Chinese Temple periodically to have vegetarian Chinese food.

13   On special holidays such as Kuanyin's birthday or Chinese New Year, worshippers do their best to pay respect to the goddesses and gods in the proper sequence but have no qualms about changing the order if particular gods have too many people crowded in front of them.

14   Interviews with the grandchildren of Chan Mah Phee and other Sino-Burmese families, 2008–9; Feng, *Mianhua bainian shihua*, 18.

15 Mugerauer, *Interpretations on Behalf of Place*, 72.

16 My interpretation of Kuanyin Ting as a "nested place" has been influenced by Jeff Malpas's work on place and topology and particularly in his exposition on the connection between place and memory in *Place and Experience*, 34.

17 Weinsheimer, *Gadamer's Hermeneutics*, 171.

18 Dean, *Taoist Ritual and Popular Cults*; DeBernardi, *Rites of Belonging*; Goodman, *Native Place, City, and Nation*.

19 Interview in Hokkien and standard Chinese with members of the Kheng Hock Keong Executive Committee, December 10, 2006.

20 Many members of the executive committee lamented that their predecessors did not do a better job of recording the events of the temple and *gongsi*. There has been some internal rivalry between the various families that have been the leaders of the temple, and apparently some of the records those families kept in their own clan halls have been lost or destroyed.

21 The emphasis is mine. The golden temple is the Shwedagon Pagoda.

22 Although *gongsi* is understood as a private business in contemporary Chinese, it originally designated the manager or management committee of a public enterprise. As Philip A. Kuhn explains, it was "used as a metonym for the enterprise as a whole. The term could designate a lineage association, a brotherhood organization, or (in commercial use) a business firm." Kuhn, *Chinese among Others*, 105.

23 This kind of stone column can be seen in many temples throughout southern Fujian, Taiwan, and Southeast Asia where people worship Matso, Kuanyin, Po-sin-tai-tei, Tsing-tsui-tso-su, and other Hokkien deities.

24 Qingfu Gong Executive Committee, *Qingfu Gong baizhounian qingdian tekan*, 6.

25 Known mainly as Xiamen today, it was a treaty port between 1842 and 1912 and a center of transnational exchange, especially for overseas Chinese.

26 Qingfu Gong Executive Committee, *Qingfu Gong baizhounian qingdian tekan*, 6.

27 Conversation with Teng Ki Hua, March 11, 2007.

28 Cartier, *Globalizing South China*; Goodman, *Native Place, City, and Nation*; DeBernardi, *Rites of Belonging*.

29 Most migrants were male, so the use of *him* is appropriate.

30 Qingfu Gong Executive Committee, *Qingfu Gong baizhounian qingdian tekan*, 4.

31 This list of surname associations is presented in the order provided by the executive committee as posted on the wall of the Hokkien Gongsi. As noted before, some of these surname associations include two surnames;

therefore, the number of surnames is twenty-five rather than twenty-four. In addition, some surnames such as Yeoh belong to two different surname associations.

3. CHINESE SCHOOLS AND CHINESENESS

1   Of course, I am not arguing that these attributes are coterminous. As seen in the "scientific classification" of different ethnicities in Asia, language has often been interpreted as coinciding with a specific territory and religion. This simplification has resulted in many problems for different ethnic groups in China and Burma. Contestation over language, territory, and culture has taken on ideological overtones in the identity politics that plague Burma/Myanmar.

2   Young children began their education with texts such as *Sanzijing* (Three Character Classic) that taught moral rectitude and proper behavior and eventually progressed to the Four Books and Five Classics.

3   It is worth noting that in Theravada Buddhist countries such as Burma and Siam/Thailand, young boys gained basic literacy through schooling by monks in Buddhist monasteries. The prevalence of basic education via religious institutions probably facilitated Chinese education in Burma. As my fieldwork revealed, some Chinese boys underwent Burmese *shinbyu* (the ordination ceremony for young boys), but it was uncommon for them to attend monastic schools.

4   As already discussed by S. Robert Ramsey in *The Languages of China* (243), the dialects of southern China such as Cantonese, Hokkien, and Hakka are actually different languages. They have been Sinified, to greater and lesser degrees, through northern encroachment since about the first millennium BCE, but speakers of Cantonese and Hokkien have asserted their linguistic independence against the dominance of standard Chinese. This contestation between different Chinese languages continued into the modern era of Chinese history and was only officially resolved in the People's Republic of China in 1956. Since this book does not focus on linguistics, I will use the word *dialect* (1) to minimize confusion and (2) to prioritize the shared Han culture between the Chinese in Rangoon. As will be evident in this chapter, the Chinese language has been a major force of Sinification at different scales: regional, national, and transnational.

5   Huang was a reporter for Chinese newspapers in Rangoon and is considered a reliable source for the history of the Chinese in Burma. This reference to the study halls in temples is from Lin and Hong, *Mianhua shehui yanjiu*, 1:68.

6   Ibid. Organization for the Righteousness School began in 1903, but the school did not open its doors to students until 1904. Taw Sein Ko was

a Sino-Burmese scholar literate in Chinese, Burmese, and English. He served as an official in the British colonial government and as an interlocutor between the three cultures in which he lived. See Edwards, "Relocating the Interlocuter: Taw Sein Ko." As noted in the Preface, transliteration for the names of institutions abides by the following list of priorities: (a) standardized transliteration or transliteration by the institution itself if an English-language source was found; (b) transliteration from Hokkien pronunciation if the institution was established before the founding of the first standard Chinese–medium school in 1921; and (c) transliteration from standard Chinese after 1921.

7   Feng, *Mianhua bainian shihua*, 26–27.
8   Fan, "A Study on the Changes of Political Status of Chinese Community." Maung Aung Myoe stated that as of 1962, there were 259 Chinese schools; see Maung Aung Myoe, *In the Name of Pauk-Phaw*, 66. I am foregrounding the Chinese source because Chinese surveyors probably had better access.
9   Fan, "A Study on the Changes of Political Status of Chinese Community," 28–29.
10 Ramsey, *The Languages of China*, 8–27.
11 Taylor, *The State in Burma*; Callahan, *Making Enemies*.
12 Anderson, *Imagined Communities*; Baker and Pasuk, *A History of Thailand*. Although Siam was never officially colonized, it was under tremendous pressure from the West and modernized to counter colonial encroachment.
13 According to Daw Win, Aung San was sailing to Japan; see Suryadinata, *Southeast Asian Personalities of Chinese Descent*, 557. However, Huang Chouqing stated that the *M. V. Haili Rangoon* was bound for Amoy.
14 Huang, *Huang Chouqing shiwen xuan*, 387–80. This book is a collection of some of his articles in the *New Rangoon Times*.
15 Fan, "The 1967 Anti-Chinese Riots," 237.
16 Keyes, "The Politics of Language in Thailand and Laos."
17 Ibid.
18 As Mary P. Callahan argues in "Making Myanmars," the post-1988 regime of Burma has been more coercive than prior governments in manufacturing a homogenous Myanmar citizenry. Whereas the Parliamentary and Socialist governments of Burma exerted some effort to Burmanize all the people within the territorial boundaries of Burma, insurgencies within the country, practical limitations, and the promotion of the Burmese form of Socialism blunted the effect of Burmanization. Standardized education as an apparatus of control has been deployed much more aggressively since 1988. Therefore, I am following Callahan's lead in using *Myanmar* rather than *Burmese* as the designation of the desired citizenry.
19 Cheesman, "Legitimising the Union of Myanmar," 65.

20 Callahan, "Language Policy in Modern Burma."

21 Among the Hokkien Sino-Burmese in Rangoon, many speak standard Chinese with a noticeable Hokkien or Hokkien-Burmese accent, meaning they fail to distinguish between the *z* and *zh*, *s* and *sh*, *f* and *p* sounds or add unnecessary nasalization. For those of the older generation who don't speak standard Chinese, such as the descendants of Chan Mah Phee who donated the land for the Overseas Chinese Middle School, they say "Hwa-chong," which maps onto Burmese sounds more easily.

22 On October 2, 2007, I was given a ride by two graduates of the Overseas Chinese Middle School. While telling me about their youth, the couple, in their late sixties, simultaneously broke out in song and belted out their school anthem with great abandon. After they finished the song, I asked them why they were so animated in their singing. They explained that going to school was one of the best periods of their lives, that there was a strong sense of camaraderie among the students and teachers, and that they lived as one big family.

23 Lin and Hong, *Mianhua shehui yanjiu*, vols. 1–2; Lin, *Mianhua shehui yanjiu*; Lin and Zhang, *Mianhua shehui yanjiu*.

24 Chan went by two names, Chan Mah Phee and Chan Gong Phee (both in Hokkien pronunciation). Although he achieved great financial success, he might have been illiterate in Chinese. In his family's estate in Shwedaung-kya (Golden Valley), there is a copy of a document that Chan signed with an *X*.

25 The Chinese secondary sources note that the estate was worth about Rs 500,000 in 1919.

26 Lin, *Mianhua shehui yanjiu*, 135–41; Feng, *Mianhua bainian shihua*, 218–19.

27 Lin, *Mianhua shehui yanjiu*. Burmese language classes were introduced in 1957; see Fan, "A Study on the Changes of Political Status of Chinese Community," 91.

28 Lu, *Huaqiao zhi—Miandian*; Lu, *Miandian Huaqiao gaikuang*.

29 Lu, *Huaqiao zhi—Miandian*, 180. The name of the organization, Mianhua Wenjiao Cujinhui, is translated as Burma Overseas Cultural and Educational Advancement Association by Maung Aung Myoe in *In the Name of Pauk-Phaw*, 66.

30 Lu, *Huaqiao zhi—Miandian*, 180–81.

31 Feng, *Mianhua bainian shihua*; Lin and Hong, *Mianhua shehui yanjiu*, 1:74–77.

32 Lin, *Mianhua shehui yanjiu*, 142–45; interviews with alumni from Huazhong and Nanzhong, 2007–9.

33 Huang Yanfeng, "Recalling My Life Learning at Nanzhong," in Lin, *Mianhua shehui yanjiu*, 143.

34 One of the alumni posted a video of their visit on YouTube: http://

youtu.be/v64ARP89W3E (accessed February 10, 2014). By good fortune, I was invited to the annual Nanyang Zhongxue Alumni Association dinners in January 2009 and 2013, but did not participate in the tour of the old campus.

35   Callahan, *Making Enemies*, 155, 156, 221; Taylor, *The State in Burma*, 239, 251, 265; Maung Aung Myoe, *In the Name of Pauk-Phaw*, 32–39.

36   Conversation with Jimmy, February 26, 2007. Jimmy, a Cantonese Sino-Burmese said that because he could speak English and Burmese; he was interpreting for the Flying Tigers.

37   Lin and Hong, *Mianhua shehui yanjiu*, vols. 1–2; Lin, *Mianhua shehui yanjiu*; Fan, "The 1967 Anti-Chinese Riots"; Maung Aung Myoe, *In the Name of Pauk-Phaw*. More research is necessary, but my fieldwork indicates that most teachers who were pro-Communist returned to China in the 1960s. Lin Qingfeng and Zhang Ping, two teachers who now live in Macao, said that after they returned to China, they found themselves "sent down" to very impoverished rural areas. After struggling for a few years in southern China, they managed to migrate to Macao, where they had to learn Cantonese to survive. Interview, September 20, 2008.

38   Both pieces are politicized dramas designed to promote the Chinese brand of Communism. They were a part of the "eight model plays," the only operas and ballets permitted during the Cultural Revolution. Ethnomusicologist Hsin-chun Tasaw Lu analyzes the culture around these performances in "Performativity of Difference."

39   Huang, *Huang Chouqing shiwen xuan*; Lin and Hong, *Mianhua shehui yanjiu*, vols. 1–2; Lin, *Mianhua shehui yanjiu*; Lu, *Huaqiao zhi—Miandian*.

40   Interview with Chen Minhui in standard Chinese, Taipei, March 18, 2009.

41   Chinese sources published in Hong Kong, Macao, and China use the typical revolutionary and patriotic language to describe events in the 1950s and 1960s. Sino-Burmese who have never left Rangoon are much more restrained in their descriptions of the 1960s. However, those who spoke about the rise of New China did so with noticeable pride. Among the men interviewed, several mentioned that male Chinese youth returned to China to join the revolution. Two men in particular said that their elder brothers returned to China but thought that it was not right for the eldest males to leave their mothers and families behind.

42   Maung Aung Myoe, *In the Name of Pauk-Phaw*, 67; Fan, "The 1967 Anti-Chinese Riots," 247.

43   Interview with Yang Min, March 10, 2007. Hsin-chun Tasaw Lu's research yielded similar findings; see Lu, "Performativity of Difference."

44   Cited in Fan, "Analysis of the June 26, 1967, Anti-Chinese Riots," 52. Anti-Chinese riots also spread to other cities in Burma, reaching Magwei on

June 29 and Mandalay on June 30. In Pyinmana, Toungyi, Mawlamyiang, and about 280 other towns, anti-Chinese demonstrations also occurred but at smaller scales.

45 Maung Aung Myoe, *In the Name of Pauk-Phaw*, 72. Maung Aung Myoe states that PRC support for the Burma Communist Party did not completely stop until 1989.

46 A comparative analysis regarding the threat of a Communist takeover in Southeast Asia is beyond the scope of this book. However, similar anti-Chinese riots in Indonesia (1965) and discussions of the Fifth Column would be important to consider in future research about the Chinese in Burma/Myanmar.

47 Quoted in Fan, "The 1967 Anti-Chinese Riots," 243

48 Ibid.

49 Interviews in standard Chinese and Hokkien, Rangoon, 2006–9, and Taipei, March 2009.

50 Ibid. Fan also found that the Sino-Burmese separated government action from the action of everyday Burmese. See Fan, "The 1967 Anti-Chinese Riots"; Fan, "Analysis of the June 26, 1967, Anti-Chinese Riots."

51 Interviews with leaders in the Hokkien Kuanyin Temple, Eastern Language and Business Center, and Fuxing Technology Center, between 2006 and 2009; Fan, "The 1967 Anti-Chinese Riots"; Fan, "Analysis of the June 26, 1967, Anti-Chinese Riots."

52 Skinner, *Chinese Society in Thailand*, 38; emphasis in original.

53 Interviews with Dai Minqin, Taw Tsi Ming, Yang Min, and Eng Yian Tsing in Yangon, between 2007 and 2009; Fan, "The 1967 Anti-Chinese Riots," 242.

54 Keyes, "The Proposed World of the School."

55 Some informants described Japanese and French fluency along these lines, with a particular focus on working as tour guides for foreigners.

56 Conversation in Burmese and standard Chinese with Daw Tin Tin, a Sino-Burmese woman whose family owns the City Mart franchise, on December 10, 2008. I was struck by her use of the word *waiguoren* (foreigner) rather than *Zhongguoren, Xianggangren, Taiwanren*, or *Xinjiaporen* ("Chinese," "Hong Kong person," "Taiwanese," or "Singaporean," respectively). I interpreted her choice of words as an indication that she saw everyone from outside of Burma as a foreigner, regardless of descent. She is most comfortable conversing in Burmese, and the language of her home is Burmese. When talking about herself, she says that she is Tayout but from Burma. The City Mart family will be discussed in chapter 4.

57 Interviews with successful Sino-Burmese merchants who now own supermarkets, small hotels, and other businesses, 2007–9. In one particular conversation, the owner of City Mart said that the company opened a karaoke restaurant on Shwedagon Pagoda Road because it was clearly

a profitable business. However, once the company saw how the young women were being mistreated, it decided that it could not continue running that type of operation.

58 However, Chinese does not enjoy the prestige of English. Whereas English still maintains an aura of advancement or modernity, Chinese is purely utilitarian.

59 The history and recent developments in Chinese-language education in Myanmar require much more research. Hanban and the Confucius Classrooms (the nonuniversity version of Confucius Institutes) are significantly influencing conceptions of China as delivered through standard Chinese–language education. In Myanmar, the PRC Ministry of Education is providing significant financial and curriculum support to Sino-Burmese who want to establish and operate Chinese schools. As of 2014, there are three Confucius Classrooms in Myanmar: two in Rangoon and one in Mandalay. However, the school in Mandalay exercises significant independence in its curriculum (it writes its own) and explicitly states that its students are learning Chinese as a second language, not as a practice of returning to their fatherland. In contrast, the schools in Rangoon take the Hanban curriculum wholesale because Sino-Burmese Rangoonites do not know enough Chinese to write their own curriculum. I presented my preliminary findings about contemporary Chinese-language education at the "Myanmar in Reform 2013 Symposium" in Hong Kong.

60 The majority of students are still Sino-Burmese, but those interviewed all commented on the fact that many people, regardless of heritage, are studying Chinese to gain a market advantage.

61 Shih, "Against Diaspora," 25.

62 Interview with Yin Min Aye, April 4, 2009. Yin Min is Mon and Burman by descent.

63 The vicarious satisfaction of seeing wrongdoers rightly punished must have provided some sense of solace and contributed to the popularity of the TV series.

64 The resurgence of Chinese-language education after 1990 is particularly notable because ethnic minority languages such as Mon have been suppressed. The post-1988 regime has been more coercive than prior governments in manufacturing a homogenous Myanmar citizenry and more extensive in its reach, deploying standardized education in the Myanmar language beyond central Burma into the former Frontier Areas. I am currently conducting further research on Chinese-language education in Myanmar. My hypothesis is that Chinese as a *foreign* language with no connection or rights to a territory, unlike ethnic minority languages, is less threatening to the nation-state.

4. SINO-BURMESE COMMERCE AND CITY MART

1   Interview with Eng Tsing Yian in a mixture of Hokkien and standard Chinese, January 14, 2009.

2   *Kala* is a very common exonym for Indians and descendants of Indians in Burma. Largely a derogatory term, it means "dark-skinned foreigner." Another explanation is that *kala* comes from *ku*, "to cross," and *la*, "to come," and means those who have crossed an ocean to come to Burma.

3   Furnivall, *Colonial Policy and Practice*, 312.

4   In February 2007, some organizers of Chinese New Year events mentioned that it was harder for them to celebrate their own holidays because Chinese holidays are not recognized as national holidays by the Myanmar government. They also said that Islamic organizations have managed to gain more rights for themselves and pointed to the fact that the entrance of the Surti Sunni Jamah Mosque sticks out onto Shwebontha Street as evidence of Muslims gaining concessions from the Parliamentary government. Given the post-2011 violence against Muslims in Myanmar, this kind of statement must be analyzed thoroughly. In this study of the Sino-Burmese, it is worth mentioning because it indicates their own understanding of their status in Burmese society relative to the other major group of foreigners.

5   If the topic of marriage came up in conversation, everyone, whether Burmese, Sino-Burmese, Indo-Burmese, Karen, or Mon, noted that many local women married Chinese men because they know that Chinese men work harder than Burmese men and are generally wealthier. Also, many Burmese people said that if a family is still wealthy after one generation, that family must be Chinese, because a Burmese family would have frittered away their money.

6   Wang, *China and the Chinese Overseas*.

7   Ibid. Merchant families educated their sons in the hope that they could pass examinations and become members of the literati. They also sought official titles and bought them whenever they could.

8   *Kapitan*, or *kapitan cina*, was explained in Chapter 1. *Compradors* is a term used mainly in Hong Kong and Macao to designate Chinese men who served as middlemen for European businesses. They became a local elite class and adopted English mannerism.

9   The comparison between the Indian and Chinese communities was introduced in Chapter 1. In addition to the forceful expulsion of Indians and particularly Indian businesses in the 1960s, many Indians who had sought refuge in India during the Japanese invasion were not allowed to return.

10   Wang, *China and the Chinese Overseas*, 188. Scholars such as Carolyn L. Cartier and Ying-shih Yu have pointed out that the idealized Confucian social order has not prevailed uniformly across China in time or place and

that ideas about *shidao* (market way) have also been influential in Chinese society. Cartier, *Globalizing South China*; Yu, "Business Culture and Chinese Traditions"

11   Wang, *China and the Chinese Overseas*, 187.

12   Many scholars of the Chinese diaspora have discussed this subject including Kuhn, *Chinese among Others*; Wang, *China and the Chinese Overseas*.

13   Bolton and Hutton, *Triad Societies*.

14   As seen in Ara Wilson's ethnography of multiple market venues in Bangkok, global capitalism is neither external nor impersonal. It is a social and cultural process that affects and is mediated by intimate relations in specific places. One such relation is the family, the primary unit of commerce in overseas Chinese communities. Wilson in her case study of the Sino-Thai Chirathivat family and the tremendous growth of their business deconstructs the separation of "the economy" from family, home, and private life. By tracing how family has always been intertwined with work, she proposes intimate economies as a critical framework that foregrounds relational life. See Wilson, *The Intimate Economies of Bangkok* and "Intimacy: A Useful Category of Transnational Analysis."

15   Among Chinese overseas in Southeast Asia, Tan Kah Kee, the founder of Xiamen University, is known as the highest exemplar. Although he returned to Xiamen from Singapore, he is claimed by the Sino-Burmese in Rangoon as a compatriot. Except for the founder of Tiger Balm, Aw Boon Haw, the Chinese from Burma are not known.

16   These numbers for those who fled and the total population are rough estimates drawn from Fan, "A Study on the Changes of Political Status of Chinese Community"; Taylor, *The State in Burma*; Chakravarti, *The Indian Minority in Burma*.

17   Fan, "A Study on the Changes of Political Status of Chinese Community," 33–39.

18   Many Sino-Burmese expressed this sentiment, particularly older men who had lived through World War II and the Socialist period. This sentiment is also found in Lin, "Miandian huaren jingji de fazhan yu bianhua"

19   Taylor, *The State in Burma*, 274.

20   Ibid.; Tinker, *The Union of Burma*. Although no reliable census is available for postcolonial Burma, scholars agree that whereas Rangoon was a predominantly Indian city prior to World War II, it became a Burmese city after the war, with a much-reduced foreign/immigrant population.

21   Fan, "A Study on the Changes of Political Status of Chinese Community."

22   Callahan, *Making Enemies*, 21–44. In principle, this new nation included all the various ethnic groups within the national boundaries—Burman, Chin, Kachin, Karen, Mon, Rakhaing, Shan, and so on—but its leaders were mainly of Burman descent and held a strong distrust of Kachin and Karen peoples who served as soldiers under the British.

23 "The Union Citizenship Act, 1948," http://www.burmalibrary.org/docs/ UNION_CITIZENSHIP_ACT-1948.htm.

24 The 1948 Citizenship Act was also discussed in the Introduction.

25 Kyaw Yin Hlaing, "The Politics of State-Business Relations."

26 Ibid.; Fan, "A Study on the Changes of Political Status of Chinese Community," 48–113.

27 Kyaw Yin Hlaing, "The Politics of State-Business Relations."

28 Quoted in Fan, "Overseas Chinese during the Period of Industrial Development," 118; Lin, "Miandian huaren jingji de fazhan yu bianhua."

29 Interviews with Sino-Burmese leaders and merchants, 2006–9; Lin, "Miandian huaren jingji bianqian de huangjinsuiyue."

30 Chakravarti, *The Indian Minority in Burma*, 186. However, it should be noted that many scholars, including Nalini Ranjan Chakravarti, note that there are no reliable statistics for the Indian population in Burma after World War II.

31 Ibid; interview with U Khin U, March 19, 2007. U Khin U is the son of a Muslim Indian merchant whose property (both his home near Inya Lake and business) was taken. Conversations with Indian taxi drivers, 2006–7.

32 Fan, "The 1967 Anti-Chinese Riots," 237.

33 Interview with the grandchildren of Chan Mah Phee, February 3, 2009.

34 Interview with Stephan Chua, Seattle, September 18, 2006; interview with Yang Rongguo, Rangoon, November 20, 2008. Chua was born in Burma but left in the late 1970s. Other men also mentioned this system and generally spoke about "the bank" with noticeable nostalgia. They remember it as a time when the riverfront was much livelier.

35 The plight of the Rohingya has been in the news since 2012. Their profound suffering is difficult for me to reconcile. As someone who has not directly investigated the history or current situation in Arakan, I am unable to comment.

36 All of the Sino-Burmese I spoke with commented on this fact. See also Fan, "A Study on the Changes of Political Status of Chinese Community," 123–52.

37 The limited scholarship on the Sino-Burmese agrees with this assessment. See Taylor, "The Legal Status of Indians in Contemporary Burma"; Mya Than, "Ethnic Chinese in Myanmar"; Fan, "A Study on the Changes of Political Status of Chinese Community."

38 Conversations with Sino-Burmese residents, Rangoon, 2006–9.

39 Lin, Miandian huaren jingji de fazhan yu bianhua"; Steinberg, *Burma/ Myanmar*, 76.

40 Conversation with the chairman of the Myanmar Chinese Chamber of Commerce, October 29, 2008.

41 Conversation with Eng Tsing Yian, January 14, 2009.

42 Among the Sino-Burmese, Aik Tun, who owned Asia Wealth Bank and

now owns the Shwe Taung Group, is identified as Yunnanese. He is listed as a man of Chinese descent in Suryadinata, *Southeast Asian Personalities of Chinese Descent*, 3–4.

43   For an in-depth discussion from a historical perspective, see Turnell, *Fiery Dragons*, 256–315, and "Myanmar's Banking Crisis."

44   Several informants said that the owner of Yadanar Garden has Chinese blood, but he is really not Chinese anymore. However, some Sino-Burmese have done business with him because he has connections with the generals.

45   Conversation with Taw Tsi Ming, January 12, 2007.

46   Conversation with Eng Tsing Yian, January 14, 2009.

47   Conversation with Burmese owners of shipping company in Sanchaung Township, December 11, 2007.

48   Conversation with U Kyaw, December 1, 2008.

49   It is a family business that owns and operates City Mart Holdings and Pahtama Group Company Limited.

50   Sung, "Myanmar's Supermarket Queen"; McLaughlin, "Supermarket Entrepreneur Eyes Expansion."

51   During my fieldwork in 2007–9, I did some of my morning grocery shopping with Daw Tin Tin and with other Sino-Burmese women whose families own hotels and large businesses.

52   Conversation in Burmese with Daw Tin Tin at a New Year's Eve party, December 31, 2008. Ensure is a nutritional drink often consumed by elderly people to make sure they are getting the proper nutrition.

53   If someone is living a good life, blessed with wealth and health, Burmese people say that particular person is *kan kaunde*. Educated Burmese and Burma scholars have sometimes criticized this luck-based conception of life as fatalistic, but it remains a central belief in Burmese society.

54   It must be noted that Chinese from southeastern China also believe that the events in one's life are determined in part by actions in the past. The Chinese term is *ming* (or *mingyun*), often translated as "fate." Therefore, the adoption of *kan/kamma* by Sino-Burmese would seem a natural extension of the southeastern Chinese belief system.

55   U Kyaw and Daw Tin Tin were very warm and welcoming but generally avoided serious conversations. While riding in the car with them after our morning workouts at Inya Lake, they often talked about their family or business casually. If, however, I tried to probe, they generally changed the topic. The SLORC/SPDC government had taught them to be cautious. Luckily, through our post-workout breakfasts, I met their four children and learned that they all worked in City Mart Holdings.

56   *Lunpian* is also romanized as *lumpiah* and *lunpiah*. *Lumpiah*, the version best known in the United States, is generally understood as a Filipino dish that is very similar to the fried spring roll served in Chinese restaurants.

In Taiwan, Quanzhou, and Rangoon, *lunpian* is a soft roll that must be eaten quickly before the moisture in the stuffing soaks through the spongy wrapper. Among the Hokkien people, *lunpian* is considered a difficult dish to make well and is reserved for special occasions.

57 I was in the buffet line next to this employee, who was introduced to me as a senior manager in the company. I overheard this exchange in Burmese.

58 Conversation at post-workout breakfast with Lau Hongli, February 14, 2009.

59 Conversation with Yang Rongguo, January 2, 2009.

60 I spoke with delegates who went to the Osaka convention in 2007 and the Manila convention in 2009 and was told that members of the chamber of commerce have been attending these conventions for several years.

61 I served as a volunteer for the anniversary celebration. Therefore, I was involved in some of the preparation and attended all the various meetings, banquets, and tours from December 31, 2008, to January 2, 2009. Although the large organizing committee spared no expense in putting on the celebration, the outcome was disappointing. Top officials from the Rangoon government cancelled at the last minute, and very few representatives came from Singapore or Hong Kong, the most desirable business partners. Indeed, owners of the most successful Sino-Burmese businesses said that the celebration was fairly useless because it did not enable them to build new connections.

5. CHINESE NEW YEAR AND PUBLIC SPACE

1 Gadamer, *Truth and Method*, 261.

2 Tradition as practiced by the marginalized is embodied and sometimes unconsciously perpetuated but is rarely a pure rhetorical exercise or performance. Ceremony is certainly a part of the practice, but in my fieldwork no informant discussed his or her practices as a pure performance to achieve a predetermined agenda. The practices surrounding Chinese New Year in Rangoon do not fit within the concept of the invention of tradition as defined in Hobsbawm and Ranger, *The Invention of Tradition*.

3 Conversation with Yang Rongguo, January 26, 2009. I asked him if the Chinese New Year market usually ran for three or four days. Yang said that the township officials had declared it a three-day market, but people don't always follow the rules.

4 There are many people in Rangoon of mixed Chinese and Burmese descent, but most are leading very localized or "Burmese" lives. None except those who were selling *duilian* could speak standard Chinese or Hokkien, and they do not distinguish themselves as different in public space.

5   Conversation with six Burmese artists, April 3, 2007; multiple conversations with my landlords and neighbors, 2007.
6   I tried to ascertain how much the vendors must pay but was unable to get an answer. For fear of drawing too much attention to myself or unintentionally making enemies, I did not pursue the question of fees aggressively. The Sino-Burmese who do not operate stalls did not know how much the vendors pay.
7   It is possible that some Rangoonites would find the loud drumming annoying, but noise of all sorts—mechanical, human, Buddhist, and animal (e.g., stray dogs)—is an accepted part of everyday life. I would argue that the Western sensitivity to noise pollution has yet to arise in Rangoon.
8   Conversations with Yang Quanmin, November 11 and 22, 2008. His recollection of the past matches those presented in Huang, *Huang Chouqing shiwen xuan*; Feng, *Mianhua bainian shihua*.
9   This attitude toward tradition and modernity has been discussed by many scholars including Spence, *The Search for Modern China*, and Mueggler, *The Age of Wild Ghosts*.
10 Sheng, "Remembering the Chinese New Year Culture and Entertainment Carnival."
11 Conversations with Yang Quanmin, November 11 and 22, 2008.
12 For a detailed discussion focused on the performances, see Lu, "Performativity of Difference."
13 Ibid.
14 Ibid.; Sheng, "Remembering the Chinese New Year Culture and Entertainment Carnival."
15 Lin and Zhang, *Mianhua shehui yanjiu*; Lin, "Miandian huaren jingji de fazhan yu bianhua"; Maung Aung Myoe, *In the Name of Pauk-Phaw*.
16 Conversations with Yang Quanmin, November 11 and 22, 2008. Yang was one of the organizers of the New Year greetings float.
17 Ibid.
18 Ibid.
19 Ibid.
20 In Burma, as in much of Southeast Asia, when outdoor lighting is needed, fluorescent tube lights are used because they are cheap and easy to obtain.
21 Again, I argue that the Sino-Burmese are not inventing tradition but are trying to maintain past practices while also becoming modern. This practice is mainly undertaken at the personal and communal scale. They are making sense of how they are Chinese to themselves and to the other hybrid Chinese in Rangoon. Sino-Burmese people, like all Burmese, have a keen sense of being behind the times, and this sense of insecurity undergirds much of their action. Their pursuit of legitimacy is largely internalized and has not reached the scale of the nation. Furthermore, this tension between tradition and modernity has been examined by many

scholars; see, among others, Kusno, *Behind the Postcolonial*; Hosagrahar, *Indigenous Modernities*.

22   Interviews with the organizers of the Sint Oh Dan Lion Dance Competition and with lion dancers, 2007–9.

23   Ibid. Lion dancing is proving to be a powerful transnational and transcultural phenomenon. During the period of my fieldwork, lion dancing in shopping malls and other public space had become unproblematic in Indonesia and was increasingly popular in Malaysia. A comparative study of lion dancing in Southeast Asia would be fruitful but is beyond the scope of this book. For some insights, see Tan, "The Lion Dances to the Fore"; Carstens, "Dancing Lions and Disappearing History."

24   According to ethnomusicologist Tan Sooi Beng, this form of lion dancing on posts is called *meihua zhuang* and was created in Malaysia specifically for lion dance competitions. This new form has proved to be very popular and has also traveled to Medan, Indonesia, via VCDs. See Tan, "The Lion Dances to the Fore."

25   Interviews with the organizers of the Sint Oh Dan Lion Dance Competition and with lion dancers, 2007–9. Also, see Carstens, "Dancing Lions and Disappearing History"; Tan, "The Lion Dances to the Fore."

26   A web survey reveals that lion dance associations generally claim to be martial arts organizations even though they provide no explanation of their training in kung fu. They do, however, provide details and even lessons about drumming techniques and lion dance movements. Most of these web-based representations are created by teams in Malaysia, Singapore, and the United States. Material culture specialist Heleanor B. Feltham provides a good introduction to the history and significance of lion dancing in "Everybody Was Kung-Fu Fighting."

27   Conversation in Burmese with Huang Meimei, October 29, 2008. A thirteen-year-old Sino-Burmese student, she was clearly proud of her Chinese descent. She could speak some standard Chinese and no Hokkien.

28   Several Burmese men and women made this comment to me. The first time was when I first arrived in Rangoon in 2006 to study Burmese. While watching TV with the service staff at the motel, two of the receptionists said to me that Chinese people are good at martial arts. The most memorable incident was when I caught a falling object and the male housekeeper of the guest house I was living in said something like, "Look at her kung fu. She is Chinese, and all Chinese know kung fu" (December 8, 2008).

29   Interviews with lion dance competition organizers, lion dancers, and Yang Rongguo, 2007–9.

30   Interview with Ko Myo, January 18, 2009.

31   Interview with Ko Japan, January 24, 2009.

32   When I asked the lion dancers in Burmese what *dailou* means, they said in English "captain." Their use of these terms demonstrates the transfor-

mation of understanding and equating of words from different languages. Historian Patrick McCormick and linguist Justin Watkins have begun to study the use and significance of English in contemporary Myanmar. *Hoya* is literally "good-ah."

33 That language is not a barrier in lion dancing has been identified by Tan, "The Lion Dances to the Fore."

34 This long and rather cumbersome name is a direct translation of the Burmese title given by the organizers. It should be noted that the name was only in Burmese, with no Chinese or English translation. I have included the name in full because the explicit inclusion of the word *family* is significant and will be discussed later in this chapter. It should also be noted that the competition included only the lion dances. The dragon dances were a part of the exhibition.

35 Conversations with organizers during line dance competition, January 27, 2009.

36 Other researchers have also found an openness in lion dancing, with people of different descent participating in and even leading lion dance troupes. See Tan, "The Lion Dances to the Fore."

37 I discuss the marginality of the lion dancers in more depth in Roberts, "The Sin Oh Dan Street Lion Dance Competition."

38 Interviews with lion dancers, 2007–9. When I asked them how they find their team members, they said that they asked their friends and other people they knew.

39 When I asked the lion dancers about the meaning and history of the lion dance, many pointed me to this set of VCDs.

40 Interview with Si Kim Hua in Burmese and Hokkien, November 25, 2008.

41 It should be noted that unlike the politics that have surrounded lion dancing in Malaysia, the revitalization of lion dancing in Rangoon is explicitly apolitical. The lion dancers and organizers of the lion dance competition have described their practice as purely cultural, celebratory, and focused on generating good luck. For the history of the Malaysian Chinese attempt to have lion dancing included as a part of Malaysian national culture, see Carstens, "Dancing Lions and Disappearing History."

42 The general manager of Capital Hypermart at that time was Malaysian Chinese. In response to my question, "Why did you decide to sponsor a lion dance competition?" he said he wanted to introduce Chinese tradition to the Chinese people in Rangoon so they could better know their own culture (interviewed on January 24, 2009). It is worth noting that a Malaysian Chinese person found the Sino-Burmese lacking in Chineseness. However, comparatively speaking, Malaysian Chinese people have a complete standard Chinese–medium education system that parallels the Malaysian national education system and have maintained very vibrant Chinese folk and popular cultures.

43 Research based on random and/or representative surveys was not possible in Myanmar during my fieldwork and remains an extremely difficult research method to implement in the country.

44 Philosopher Tu Weiming has already criticized the political state of China and asserted that overseas Chinese can lead the way in constructing a new vision of Chineseness that is better attuned with modernity. See Tu, "Cultural China."

45 The Sint Oh Dan Street lion dance organizers have taken a Myanmar team to the Genting Highlands since 2012. In fact, the Chinese New Year lion dance competition has grown significantly in scale and is now widely broadcast on Myanmar television. For how the Sint Oh Dan Street family troupe represents itself, see its Facebook page: http://www.facebook.com/sintohdanstreet.

CONCLUSION

1 I am again referring to the Burmese trope "There are five enemies: water, fire, kings, thieves and ungrateful heirs," mentioned in the introductory chapter (see page 9).

2 The burning of Tai Su Yah is a common practice in the former Straits Settlements such as Penang and Singapore. In Yangon, Teng clan members who were responsible for the 2007 Hungry Ghost Festival could not explain why they did what they did. In fact, without the direction of a ritual specialist, who was also the person who produced the various effigies, Teng clan elders would have been at a loss as to what to do. Although some scholars such as Jean DeBernardi (*Rites of Belonging*) and Cheu Hock Tong (*Chinese Beliefs and Practices*) have discussed Chinese religious practices in Southeast Asia, I have yet to come across a scholarly analysis about Tai Su Yah.

3 Foucault, *Language, Counter-Memory, Practice*, 154.

4 As evident in Ingrid Jordt's *Burma's Mass Lay Meditation Movement: Buddhism and the Cultural Construction of Power*, Vipassana meditation has become a defining characteristic of modern Burmese culture and provides an alternative moral order to counter the abuses of the military government. Everyone I spoke with in Burma had some knowledge of Vipassana meditation, and many had undertaken meditation courses. Those who practice Vipassana meditation are respected for their self-discipline.

5 Conversation with Huang Aihui, October 3, 2008.

6 Interviews with Ko Japan, 2007–9.

7 It is very common for Burmese people to donate money, food, or necessities to monks and nuns. Many people provide a large meal for all nuns and monks in an institution to celebrate their birthdays or commemorate the passing of family members.

8   Interview with Lin Qingfeng and Hong Xinye, editors of the series *An Analysis of Sino-Burmese Society*, September 20, 2008.

9   Interviews with self-identified Sino-Burmese in Zhonghe, Taipei, March 2009.

10   Conversation with Jiaoyan, September 8, 2009. Jiaoyan's family left Burma when she was nine years old. She described the sense of alienation and shame she felt as someone whose standard Chinese was judged strange and inadequate.

11   This situation is not unique to the Sino-Burmese. For other Chinese such as Malaysian Chinese and Vietnamese Chinese who have undertaken a second leg of migration from their Southeast Asian homes, their primary source of identification is not China but Malaysia and Vietnam.

12   Conversation with Daw Tin Tin, December 31, 2008.

13   Conversation with Teng Ki Hua, July 5, 2007.

14   McGowan, *Hannah Arend*, 17.

15   Conversation with Eng Tsing Yian in Hokkien and standard Chinese, January 14, 2009. I followed up with this question: "Wouldn't it be a shame if a Hokkien person couldn't speak Hokkien?" He answered: "If you take time to study Hokkien, you could also use that time to study English or French. Wouldn't those languages be better to study? They can be used in other countries." This pragmatism is understandable given their marginal status. As scholars of ethnic minorities have discussed, the language of the state is often hegemonic and the maintenance of minority languages often demands crude calculations based on livelihood. See, among others, Bulag, "Mongolian Ethnicity and Linguistic Anxiety in China."

16   Lin, *Mianhua shehui yanjiu*, 130–31.

17   The overseas Chinese person's willingness to take risks is a standard trope that is used to explain why overseas Chinese businesses have been able to succeed despite significant challenges. It is usually paired with Chinese industriousness. For an anthropologically grounded analysis on this characteristic, see Oxfeld, *Blood, Sweat and Mahjong*.

18   Conversation with Lai Yansong, September 23, 2007.

19   Hall, "New Ethnicities," 448.

20   Kyaw, "Government to Charge Wine Distributor."

21   Quoted in ibid.

22   Kyaw, "After Arrest in Govt Crackdown, Retailer Points to Alcohol Imports by Tycoons."

23   Interview with Taw Tsi Ming, January 12, 2007.

GLOSSARY

ABBREVIATIONS

B   Burmese
H   Hokkien
SC   Standard Chinese (Mandarin)

Ankue (H) Anxi (SC) 安溪 county in the Quanzhou Prefecture, China

bahuthuta (B) common knowledge
Baohuangpai (SC) 保皇派 Save the Emperor Society
Bun-tsong-kun (H) Wenchangjun (SC) 文昌君 god of examinations

Chamadao (SC) 茶馬道 Tea Horse Road
Chan Mah Phee (H, B) Zeng Guangbi (SC) 曾廣庇 successful Hokkien merchant who supposedly owned most of the property in Chinatown
Chunjie (SC) 春節 Chinese New Year

Dongfang yuyan yu shangye zhongxin (SC) 東方語言與商業中心 Eastern Language and Business Center

eingyi-do (B) Cantonese Chinese (lit. "short sleeve")
eingyi-shei (B) Hokkien Chinese (lit. "long sleeve")

Fuxing Jishu Zhongxin (SC) 福星技術中心 Fuxing Technology Center

Guangdong Guanyin Gumiao (SC) 廣東觀音古廟 Cantonese Guanyin Temple
Guan-tei-gun (H) Guandi (SC) 關帝 deification of Guanyu, who was known for his loyalty

Guoyu (SC) 國語 standard Chinese as the designated "National Language" under the Nationalist governments in China and Taiwan

hiunong (H) xiangwang (SC) 香旺 profuse incense

Ho Sing Gongsi (H) Hesheng Gongsi (SC) 和勝公司 Hesheng Association (secret society)

Hock Suan Si (H) Fushan Si (SC) 福山寺 Fushan Temple, subsidiary temple of Qingfu Gong, where the Patriarch of the Clear Stream is the central deity

Hokkien Gongsi (H) Fujian Gongsi (SC) 福建公司 Fujian Native Place Association

hpoungyi kyaung (B) monastery

Huaqiao Lianhehui (SC) 華僑聯合會 Overseas Chinese Allied Association

Huaqiao Zhongxue (SC) 華僑中學 Overseas Chinese Middle School

huashang wenhua (SC) 華商文化 Chinese merchant culture

hunhiun (H) fenxiang (SC) 分香 divide incense ash to establish a new sacred space

juetougang (SC) 絕頭港 port of last hope

kan (B) kamma in Pali and karma in Sanskrit, which is often translated as "law"

kan kaunde (B) good luck

Kheng Hock Keong (H) Qingfugong (SC) 慶福宮 Hokkien Guanyin Temple on Strand Road

Kien Tek Tsonghue (H) Jiande Zonghui (SC) 建德總會 Jiande Association (secret society)

Kisiong Yiahak (H) Yishang Yexue (SC) 益商夜學 Yishang Night School

Kiu Liong Tong (H) Jiulongtang (SC) 九龍堂 Jiulong Clan Hall

Kokogo belo nale dele? (B) How do I understand myself?

kosuan (H) kaoshan (SC) 靠山 powerful person or institution to rely on (lit. "mountain to lean on")

Kuanyin (H) Guanyin (SC) 觀音 Guanyin

kudho (B) good work or meritorious deed

Kwamyin Medaw Hpayakyaung (B) Kuanyin Ting (H) Guanyinting (SC) 觀音亭 colloquial name for the Hokkien Guanyin Temple

kyezushin (B) benefactor

lao-le (H) renao (SC) 熱鬧 lively, bustling, festive

let-shei (B) Hokkien Chinese (lit. "long sleeve")

let-to (B) Cantonese Chinese (lit. "short sleeve")

Lim Chin Tsong (H, B) Lin Zhenzong (SC) 林振宗 tycoon who built the Chin Tsong Palace

Lim Chin Tsong Tiongse Ingbun Hakhao (H) Lin Zhenzong Zhongxi Ying-wen Xuexiao (SC) 林振宗中西英文學校 Lim Chin Tsong Chinese and Western English School

ling (H, SC) 靈 efficacious in granting wishes

Liong San Tong (H) Longshantang (SC) 龍山堂 Longshan Clan Hall

lumyo (B) biologically determined "kinds of people" or races

Matso (H) Mazu (SC) 媽祖 protectress of seafarers

Myanmapyi/Bamapyi-ga khit ma hmi bu. (B) Myanmar/Burma is behind the times / not modern.

Nanyang Zhongxue (SC) 南洋中學 Nanyang Middle School

Pauk Chin (B) Bao Qingtian (SC) 包青天 the legendary Judge Bao from the Song dynasty

pauk-hpaw (B) pao-pou (H) baobo (SC) 胞波 people born of the same womb or kinsfolk (the various Chinese versions are transliterated from Burmese)

Po-sin-tai-tei (H) Baoshengdadi (SC) 保生大帝 the Great Emperor Who Protects Life

Putonghua (SC) 普通話 standard Chinese as the "common" and national language in Communist China

Rohingya (B) Rohingya, an ethnic minority group that is not recognized by the state of Myanmar

Shan Tayout (B) Shan Chinese

Tai Su Yah (H) Dashiye (SC) 大士爺 Lord of Hades, who is appeased on Hungry Ghost Day

tainyintha lumyo (B) sons or offspring of the geographical division or ethnic nationality

Taw Sein Ko (H) Du Chenggao (SC) 杜誠誥 first archaeologist in Burma who was fluent in Burmese, Chinese, and English

Tayout (B) Chinese

Tayout Hpongyi Kyaung (B) literally Chinese Monastery, but usually refers to Kuanyin Ting

Tayout ka hpaya ma shi, taya ma shi. (B) The Chinese have no Buddha and no law.

Tayout lo lout. Kala lo su. Bama lo ma hpyoun ne. (B) Work like the Chinese. Save money like the Indians. Don't throw away money like the Burmese.

Tayout Tan (B) Chinatown

Tayout-kabya (B) mixed Chinese

Tazaundaing (B) holiday for end of Buddhist Lent

Tazaundaing Labyeinei (B) full moon day around November

Thadingyut (B) Festival of Lights

Tin-gong-tso (H) Tiangongzu (SC) 天公祖 Lord of Heaven

Tionghua Kihak (H) Zhonghua Yixue (SC) 中華義學 Zhonghua Righteousness School

Tionghua Outeng (H) Zhonghua Xuetang (SC) 中華學堂 Zhonghua Study
Hall

Tongmenghui (SC) 同盟會 Chinese Revolutionary Alliance

Tsingtsiu (H) Zhangzhou (SC) 漳州 prefecture in southern Fujian

Tsing-tsui-tso-su (H) Qingshuizushi (SC) 清水祖師 Patriarch of the Clear
Stream

tsi-siok (H) shushu (SC) 書塾 study hall

Tsuantsiu (H) Quanzhou (SC) 泉州 prefecture in southern Fujian

Tsu-tsin-niu-niu (H) Zhushengniangniang (SC) 註生娘娘 goddess of
fertility

Tua-pei-gong (H) Dabogong (SC) 大伯公 deity of place who is worshipped
in Southeast Asia

Wenyu Guangchang (SC) 文娛廣場 Culture and Entertainment Festival

Zhongguo Nüzhong (SC) 中國女中 Chinese Girls Middle School

BIBLIOGRAPHY

Abbott, Gerry. *The Traveller's History of Burma*. Orchid Guides. Bangkok: Orchid Press, 1998.

Agnew, John. "The Territorial Trap: The Geographical Assumptions of International Relations Theory." *Review of International Political Economy* 1, no. 1 (1994): 53–80.

Anderson, Benedict R. *Imagined Communities: Reflections on the Origin and Spread of Nationalism*. Rev. and extended ed. New York: Verso Books, 1991.

Appadurai, Arjun. *Modernity at Large: Cultural Dimensions of Globalization*. Minneapolis: University of Minneapolis Press, 1997.

Arendt, Hannah. *Essays in Understanding, 1930–1954*. Edited by Jerome Kohn. New York: Schocken Books, 1994.

———. *The Human Condition*. Chicago: University of Chicago Press, 1998.

Aung San Suu Kyi. *Freedom from Fear, and Other Writings*. Edited by Michael Aris. London: Penguin Books, 1995.

Aung-Thwin, Michael. *Myth and History in the Historiography of Early Burma: Paradigms, Primary Sources, and Prejudices*. Athens: Ohio University Press, 1998.

Baker, Christopher John, and Pasuk Phongpaichit. *A History of Thailand*. 2nd ed. Cambridge: Cambridge University Press, 2009.

Bhattacharya, Jayati, and Coonoor Kripalani, eds. *Indian and Chinese Immigrant Communities: Comparative Perspectives*. Anthem-ISEAS India-China Studies. London: Anthem Press; Singapore: Institute of Southeast Asian Studies, 2015.

Bolton, Kingsley, and Christopher Hutton, eds. *Triad Societies: Western Accounts of the History, Sociology and Linguistics of Chinese Secret Societies*. Colonial Encounters, vol. 5. London: Taylor and Francis, 2000.

Bulag, Uradyn E. "Mongolian Ethnicity and Linguistic Anxiety in China." *American Anthropologist* 105, no. 4 (2003): 753–63.

Callahan, Mary P. "Language Policy in Modern Burma." In *Fighting Words:*

Language Policy and Ethnic Relations in Asia, edited by Michael E. Brown and Šumit Ganguly, 143–75. Cambridge, MA: MIT Press, 2003.

———. *Making Enemies: War and State Building in Burma*. Ithaca, NY: Cornell University Press, 2003.

———. "Making Myanmars: Language, Territory, and Belonging in Post-Socialist Burma." In *Boundaries and Belonging: States and Societies in the Struggle to Shape Identities and Local Practices*, edited by Joel S. Migdal, 99–120. New York: Cambridge University Press, 2004.

Callahan, Mary P., and Daw Tin Tin Nyunt. "Political Risk Assessment: Myanmar 2014 Population and Housing Census." Yangon: United Nations Population Fund (UNFPA), 2013.

Carstens, Sharon. "Dancing Lions and Disappearing History: The National Culture Debate and Chinese Malaysian Culture." *Crossroads: An Interdisciplinary Journal of Southeast Asian Studies* 13, no. 1 (1999): 11–63.

Cartier, Carolyn L. *Globalizing South China*. Oxford, UK: Blackwell, 2001.

Casey, Edward S. *The Fate of Place: A Philosophical History*. Berkeley: University of California Press, 1997.

Central Intelligence Agency. *The World Factbook 2012: CIA's 2011 Edition*. Washington, DC: Potomac Books, 2012.

Chakravarti, Nalini Ranjan. *The Indian Minority in Burma: The Rise and Decline of an Immigrant Community*. London: Oxford University Press, 1971.

Cheesman, Nick. "Legitimising the Union of Myanmar through Primary School Textbooks." MEd diss., University of Western Australia, 2002.

Chen Yi-Sein. "The Chinese in Rangoon during the Eighteenth and Nineteenth Centuries." In *Essays Offered to G. H. Luce by His Colleagues and Friends in Honour of His Seventy-Fifth Birthday*, edited by Ba Shin, Jean Boisselier, and A. B. Griswold, vol. 1, *Papers on Asian History, Religion, Languages, Literature, Music Folklore, and Anthropology*, 171–76. Ascona, Switzerland: Artibus Asiae, 1966.

———. "Guoqu sangeshiji (sanbainian) qijiede Miandian Guangdongren" 過去三個世紀（三百年）期間的緬甸廣東人 (The Cantonese people in Burma in the past three centuries). In *Yangguang Guangdong Gongsi (Guanyin Gumiao) yibaiqishijiu zhounian chongxiu luocheng jinian tekan* 仰光廣東公司（觀音古廟）一百七十九週年重修落成紀念特刊 (The 179th anniversary and rebuilding of the Yangon Guangdong Gongsi [Guanyin Temple], special edition), edited by Yu Reirong. Yangon: Yangon Guangdong Gongsi, 2004.

———. *Mofan Miandian dacidian* 模範緬華大辭典 (A model Burmese-Chinese dictionary). Tokyo: Dongyang Wenku 東洋文庫, 1962.

Cheu Hock Tong. *Chinese Beliefs and Practices in Southeast Asia*. Selangor Darul Ehsan, Malaysia: Pelanduk Publications, 1993.

Dean, Kenneth. *Taoist Ritual and Popular Cults of Southeast China*. Princeton, NJ: Princeton University Press, 1993.

DeBernardi, Jean. *Rites of Belonging: Memory, Modernity, and Identity in a Malaysian Chinese Community.* Stanford, CA: Stanford University Press, 2004.

de Certeau, Michel. *The Practice of Everyday Life.* Translated by Steven Rendall. Berkeley: University of California Press, 1988.

Deleuze, Gilles, and Félix Guattari. *A Thousand Plateaus: Capitalism and Schizophrenia.* Translated by Brian Massumi. Minneapolis: University of Minnesota Press, 2004.

Ebrey, Patricia Buckley, and James L. Watson, eds. *Kinship Organization in Late Imperial China, 1000–1940.* Berkeley: University of California Press, 1986.

Edwards, Penny. "Relocating the Interlocutor: Taw Sein Ko (1864–1930) and the Itinerancy of Knowledge in British Burma." *South East Asia Research* 12, no. 3 (2004): 277–335.

Eriksen, Thomas Hylland. *Ethnicity and Nationalism.* Anthropology, Culture, and Society. 2nd ed. London: Pluto Press, 2002.

Fan Hongwei. "Analysis of the June 26, 1967 Anti-Chinese Riots and Myanmar Chinese Society (1967 年緬甸 (6.26) 排華事件與緬華社會研究)." *Taiwan Journal of Southeast Asian Studies* 台灣東南亞學刊 3, no. 2 (2006): 47–72.

———. "The 1967 Anti-Chinese Riots in Burma and Sino-Burmese Relations." *Journal of Southeast Asian Studies* 43, no. 2 (2012): 234–56.

———. "Overseas Chinese during the Period of Industrial Development in AFPFL Burma (1948–1962)" 試論反法西斯人民自由同盟時期緬甸工業發展的華僑 (1948–1962). In *Mianhua shehui yanjiu* 緬華社會研究 (An analysis of Sino-Burmese Society), vol. 3, edited by Lin Qingfeng, 203–18. Macao: Macao Sino-Burmese Mutual Aid Association 澳門緬華互助會, 2004.

———. "A Study on the Changes of Political Status of Chinese Community in Myanmar after World War Two." PhD, Xiamen University, 2004.

Faure, David. *The Structure of Chinese Rural Society: Lineage and Village in the Eastern New Territories, Hong Kong.* East Asian Historical Monographs. Hong Kong: Oxford University Press, 1986.

Fei, Xiaotong, Gary G. Hamilton, and Zheng Wang. *From the Soil, the Foundations of Chinese Society: A Translation of Fei Xiaotong's "Xiangtu Zhongguo."* Berkeley: University of California Press, 1992.

Feltham, Heleanor B. "Everybody Was Kung-Fu Fighting: The Lion Dance and Chinese National Identity in the Nineteenth and Twentieth Centuries." In *Asian Material Culture,* edited by Marianne Hulsbosch, Elizabeth Bedford, and Martha Chaiklin, 103–40. Amsterdam: Amsterdam University Press, 2009.

Feng Lidong. *Mianhua bainian shihua* 緬華百年史話 (A hundred-year history of the Chinese in Burma). Hong Kong: Mirror Post Cultural Enterprises, 2002.

Foucault, Michel. *Discipline and Punish: The Birth of the Prison*. Translated by Alan Sheridan. New York: Knopf Doubleday Publishing Group, 1977.

———. *Language, Counter-Memory, Practice: Selected Essays and Interviews*. Edited by Donald F. Bouchard and translated by Donald F. Bouchard and Sherry Simon. Ithaca, NY: Cornell University Press, 1977.

———. "Space, Knowledge, and Power." In *The Foucault Reader*, edited by Paul Rabinow, 239–56. New York: Pantheon Books, 1984.

Furnivall, J. S. [John Sydendam]. *Colonial Policy and Practice: A Comparative Study of Burma and Netherlands India*. Cambridge: Cambridge University Press, 1948.

———. *An Introduction to the Political Economy of Burma*. 3rd ed. Rangoon: Peoples' Literature Committee and House, 1957.

Gadamer, Hans-Georg. *Truth and Method*. Translation edited by Garrett Barden and John Cumming. New York: Seabury Press, 1975.

Gladney, Dru C. *Dislocating China: Muslims, Minorities and Other Subaltern Subjects*. Chicago: the University of Chicago Press, 2004.

Goh Geok Yian. "The Question of 'China' in Burmese Chronicles." *Journal of Southeast Asian Studies* 41, no. 1 (2010): 125–52.

Goodman, Bryna. *Native Place, City, and Nation: Regional Networks and Identities in Shanghai, 1853–1937*. Berkeley: University of California Press, 1995.

Gravers, Mikael, ed. *Exploring Ethnic Diversity in Burma*. NIAS Studies in Asian Topics No. 39. Copenhagen: Nordic Institute of Asian Studies Press, 2007.

Hall, Stuart. "New Ethnicities." In *Stuart Hall: Critical Dialogues in Cultural Studies*, edited by David Morley and Kuan-Hsing Chen, 442–51. London: Routledge, 2005.

Harrell, Stevan. *Cultural Encounters on China's Ethnic Frontiers*. Studies on Ethnic Groups in China. Seattle: University of Washington Press, 1995.

Harvey, David. "Space as a Key Word." In *David Harvey: A Critical Reader*, edited by Noel Castree and Derek Gregory, 270–93. Malden, MA: Blackwell, 2006.

Hill, Ann Maxwell. *Merchants and Migrants: Ethnicity and Trade among Yunnanese Chinese in Southeast Asia*. New Haven, CT: Yale University Press, 1998.

Hobsbawm, Eric, and Terence Ranger, eds. *The Invention of Tradition*. Cambridge: Cambridge University Press, 2004.

Hosagrahar, Jyoti. *Indigenous Modernities: Negotiating Architecture and Urbanism*. New York: Routledge, 2005.

Huang Chouqing. *Huang Chouqing shiwenxuan* 黃綽卿詩文選 (A collection of Huang Chouqing's prose and poetry). Beijing: China Overseas Chinese Publishing Company 中國華僑出版公司, 1990.

India, Census Commissioner. "Census of India, 1911." Calcutta: Superintendent

Government Printing. https://archive.org/details/censusofindiav12pt1indi (accessed January 8, 2014).

Jones, W. R. "The Image of the Barbarian in Medieval Europe." *Comparative Studies in Society and History* 13, no. 4 (1971): 376–407.

Jordt, Ingrid. *Burma's Mass Lay Meditation Movement: Buddhism and the Cultural Construction of Power.* Athens: Ohio University Press, 2007.

Kelly, R. Talbot. *Burma, Painted and Described.* London: Adam and Charles Black, 1905.

Keyes, Charles. "The Politics of Language in Thailand and Laos." In *Fighting Words: Language Policy and Ethnic Relations in Asia,* edited by Michael E. Brown and Šumit Ganguly, 177–210. Cambridge, MA: MIT Press, 2003.

———. "The Proposed World of the School: Thai Villagers' Entry into a Bureaucratic State System." In *Reshaping Local Worlds: Formal Education and Cultural Change in Rural Southeast Asia,* edited by Charles Keyes, 87–138. Yale Southeast Asian Studies, Monograph No. 36. New Haven, CT: Yale Center for International and Area Studies, 1991.

Khoo Joo Ee. *The Straits Chinese: A Cultural History.* Amsterdam: Pepin Press, 1998.

Knapp, Ronald G. *Chinese Houses of Southeast Asia: The Eclectic Architecture of Sojourners and Settlers.* Singapore: Tuttle Publishing, 2010.

Kuhn, Philip A. *Chinese among Others: Emigration in Modern Times.* Lanham, MD: Rowman and Littlefield, 2009.

Kusno, Abidin. *Behind the Postcolonial: Architecture, Urban Space and Political Cultures in Indonesia.* New York: Routledge, 2000.

Kyaw Aye Thida. "Government to Charge Wine Distributor." *Myanmar Times,* December 15, 2013. http://www.mmtimes.com/index.php/business/9030-government-to-charge-wine-distributor.html.

Kyaw Hsu Mon. "After Arrest in Govt Crackdown, Retailer Points to Alcohol Imports by Tycoons." *Irrawaddy,* December 17, 2013. http://www.irrawaddy.org/business/arrest-govt-crackdown-retailer-points-alcohol-imports-tycoons.html.

Kyaw Yin Hlaing. "The Politics of State-Business Relations in Post-Colonial Burma." PhD diss., Cornell University, 2001.

Lees, Lynn Hollen. "Being British in Malaya, 1890–1940." *Journal of British Studies* 48, no. 1 (2009): 76–101.

Lefebvre, Henri. *The Production of Space.* Translated by Donald Nicholson-Smith. Oxford, UK: Blackwell, 1991.

Lin Qingfeng, ed. *Mianhua shehui yanjiu* 緬華社會研究 (An analysis of Sino-Burmese society). Vol. 3. Macao: Macao Sino-Burmese Mutual Aid Association 澳門緬華互助會, 2004.

Lin Qingfeng and Hong Xinye, eds. *Mianhua shehui yanjiu* 緬華社會研究 (An analysis of Sino-Burmese society). Vol. 1. Macao: Macao Sino-Burmese Mutual Aid Association 澳門緬華互助會, 1999.

——. *Mianhua shehui yanjiu* 緬華社會研究 (An analysis of Sino-Burmese society). Vol. 2. Macao: Macao Sino-Burmese Mutual Aid Association 澳門緬華互助會, 2001.

Lin Qingfeng and Zhang Ping, eds. *Mianhua shehui yanjiu* 緬華社會研究 (An analysis of Sino-Burmese society). Vol. 4. Macao: Macao Sino-Burmese Mutual Aid Association 澳門緬華互助會, 2007.

Lin Xixing. "Miandian huaren jingji bianqian de huangjinsuiyue" 緬甸華人經濟變遷的黃金歲月 (The golden era for Sino-Burmese economic status). In *Mianhua shehui yanjiu* 緬華社會研究 (An analysis of Sino-Burmese society), edited by Lin Qingfeng, 4:201–3. Macao: Macao Sino-Burmese Mutual Aid Association 澳門緬華互助會, 2004.

——. "Miandian huaren jingji de fazhan yu bianhua" 緬甸華人經濟的發展與變化 (Development and changes in the economic status of the Sino-Burmese). In *Mianhua shehui yanjiu* 緬華社會研究 (An analysis of Sino-Burmese society), edited by Lin Qingfeng, 1:30–60. Macao: Macao Sino-Burmese Mutual Aid Association 澳門緬華互助會, 1999.

Lipman, Jonathan N. *Familiar Strangers: A History of Muslims in Northwest China*. Seattle: University of Washington Press, 1997.

Liu, Lydia H. *The Clash of Empires: The Invention of China in Modern World Making*. Cambridge, MA: Harvard University Press, 2004.

Lu, Hsin-chun Tasaw. "Performativity of Difference: Mapping Public Soundscapes and Performing Nostalgia among Burmese Chinese in Central Rangoon." *Asian Music* 42, no. 2 (2011): 19–55.

Lu Wei-Lin. *Huaqiao zhi—Miandian* 華僑志—緬甸 (Overseas Chinese record—Burma). Taipei, Taiwan: Overseas Chinese Publishing Committee 華僑志編纂委員會, 1967.

——. *Miandian Huaqiao gaikuang* 緬甸華僑概況 (The general situation of the Chinese in Burma). Overseas Chinese Youth Books 海外華人青少年叢書. Taipei, Taiwan: Zhongzheng Publishing Company 中正書局, 1988.

Luce, G. H. (Gordon Hannington). "Note on the People of Burma in the Twelfth to Thirteenth Century A.D." *Journal of the Burma Research Society* 42, pt. 1 (1959): 69.

Ma, Laurence, and Carolyn L. Cartier, eds. *The Chinese Diaspora: Space, Place, Mobility, and Identity*. Lanham, MD: Rowman and Littlefield, 2003.

Malpas, Jeff. *Heidegger and the Thinking of Place: Explorations in the Topology of Being*. Cambridge, MA: MIT Press, 2012.

——. *Heidegger's Topology: Being, Place, World*. Cambridge, MA: MIT Press, 2006.

——. *Place and Experience: A Philosophical Topography*. Cambridge: Cambridge University Press, 1999.

Maung Aung Myoe. *In the Name of Pauk-Phaw: Myanmar's China Policy since 1948*. Singapore: Institute of Southeast Asian Studies, 2011.

Maxim, Sarah Heminway. "Resemblance in External Appearance: The Colonial Project in Kuala Lumpur and Rangoon." PhD diss., Cornell University, 1992.

McCarthy, Susan. *Communist Multiculturalism: Ethnic Revival in Southwest China*. Studies on Ethnic Groups in China. Seattle: University of Washington Press, 2009.

McGee, T. G. *The Southeast Asian City: A Social Geography of the Primate Cities of Southeast Asia*. New York: Frederick A. Praeger, 1967.

McGowan, John. *Hannah Arendt: An Introduction*. Minneapolis: University of Minnesota Press, 1998.

McLaughlin, Tim. "Supermarket Entrepreneur Eyes Expansion." *Myanmar Times*, July 31, 2013. http://www.mmtimes.com/index.php/national-news/7653-supermarket-entrepreneur-eyes-expansion.html.

Min Zin. "Burmese Attitude toward Chinese: Portrayal of the Chinese in Contemporary Cultural and Media Works." *Journal of Current Southeast Asian Affairs* 31, no. 1 (2012): 115–31.

Ministry of Religious Affairs. *A Dictionary of Buddhist Terms*. Yangon: Ministry of Religious Affairs, 1996.

Mueggler, Erik. *The Age of Wild Ghosts: Memory, Violence, and Place in Southwest China*. Berkeley: University of California Press, 2001.

Mugerauer, Robert. *Interpretations on Behalf of Place: Environmental Displacements and Alternative Responses*. Albany: State University of New York Press, 1994.

———. *Interpreting Environments: Tradition, Deconstruction, Hermeneutics*. Austin: University of Texas Press, 1995.

Mullaney, Thomas, James Leibold, Stéphane Gros, and Eric Vanden Bussche, eds. *Critical Han Studies: The History, Representation, and Identity of China's Majority*. New Perspectives on Chinese Culture and Society. Berkeley: University of California Press, 2012.

Mya Maung. "On the Road to Mandalay: A Case Study of the Sinonization of Upper Burma." *Asian Survey* 34, no. 5 (1994): 447–59.

Mya Than. "Ethnic Chinese in Myanmar and Their Identity." In *Ethnic Chinese as Southeast Asians*, edited by Leo Suryadinata, 115–46. Singapore: Institute of Southeast Asian Studies, 1997.

Myanmar-English Dictionary. Yangon: Department of the Myanmar Language Commission, Ministry of Education, 2006.

Naquin, Susan, and Evelyn Sakakida Rawski. *Chinese Society in the Eighteenth Century*. New Haven, CT: Yale University Press, 1987.

Oakes, Timothy. "Place and the Paradox of Modernity." *Annals of the Association of American Geographers* 87, no. 3 (1997): 509–31.

Oertel, F. O. *Note on a Tour in Burma in March and April, 1892*. Itineraria Asiatica: Burma, vol. 1. Bangkok: White Orchid Press, 1995.

Okell, John. *Burmese: An Introduction to the Literary Style*. De Kalb: Center for Southeast Asian Studies, Northern Illinois University, 1994.

———. *Burmese: An Introduction to the Spoken Language*. 2 vols. De Kalb: Center for Southeast Asian Studies, Northern Illinois University, 1994.

Ong, Aihwa. *Flexible Citizenship: The Cultural Logics of Transnationality*. Durham, NC: Duke University Press, 1999.

Ong, Aihwa, and Donald M. Nonini, eds. *Ungrounded Empires: The Cultural Politics of Modern Chinese Transnationalism*. New York: Routledge, 1997.

Oxfeld, Ellen. *Blood, Sweat, and Mahjong: Family and Enterprise in an Overseas Chinese Community*. Ithaca, NY: Cornell University Press, 1993.

Pearn, B. R. *A History of Rangoon*. Rangoon: American Baptist Mission Press, 1939. Reprint, Farnborough, England: Gregg International, 1971.

Purcell, Victor. *The Chinese in Southeast Asia*. 2nd ed. London: Oxford University Press, 1965.

Qingfu Gong Executive Committee. *Qingfu Gong baizhounian qingdian tekan* 慶福宮百週年慶典特刊 (Qingfu Gong one hundredth anniversary celebration, special edition). Yangon: n.p., 1961.

Ramsey, S. Robert. *The Languages of China*. Princeton, NJ: Princeton University Press, 1987.

Rangoon Times. "The Chinese in Burma." July 20, 1912.

Reid, Anthony. "Creating the Centre for the Study of the Chinese Southern Diaspora." *Chinese Southern Diaspora Studies* 1 (2007): 172–74.

Renard, Ronald. "The Wa Authority and Good Governance, 1989–2007." *Journal of Burma Studies* 17, no. 1 (2013): 141–80.

Roberts, Jayde Lin. "The Sin Oh Dan Street Lion Dance Competition: A Temporary Space for Cross-Cultural Understanding." In *Transcultural Cities: Border-Crossing and Placemaking*, edited by Jeffrey Hou, 62–74. New York: Routledge, 2013.

Romanucci-Ross, Lola, and George De Vos, eds. *Ethnic Identity: Creation, Conflict, and Accommodation*. 3rd ed. Walnut Creek, CA: AltaMira Press, 1995.

San San Hnin Tun and Patrick McCormick. *Colloquial Burmese: The Complete Course for Beginners*. London: Routledge, 2014.

Scott, James C. *Seeing like a State: How Certain Schemes to Improve the Human Condition Have Failed*. Yale Agrarian Studies. New Haven, CT: Yale University Press, 1998.

Sheng Hua. "Huiyi Mianhua Chunjie Wenyu Guangchang" 回忆缅华春节文娱广 (Remembering the Chinese New Year Culture and Entertainment Carnival). Mianhuawang 缅华网 (Myanmar Chinese website). http://mhhzhh. blog.163.com/blog/static/52160096200810825945223 (accessed June 29, 2013).

Shih, Shu-mei. "Against Diaspora: The Sinophone as Places of Cultural Production." In *Sinophone Studies: A Critical Reader*, edited by Shu-mei Shih, Chien-hsin Tsai, and Brian Bernards, 25–42. New York: Columbia University Press, 2013.

Shih, Shu-mei, Chien-hsin Tsai, and Brian Bernards, eds. *Sinophone Studies: A Critical Reader*. Global Chinese Culture. New York: Columbia University Press, 2013.

Singer, N. F. *Old Rangoon, City of the Shwedagon*. Gartmore, Scotland: Kiscadale Publications, 1995.

Sint Oh Dan Street. Facebook page. http://www.facebook.com/sintohdanstreet (accessed June 8, 2015).

Skinner, G. William. *Chinese Society in Thailand: An Analytical History*. Ithaca, NY: Cornell University Press, 1957.

Smith, Martin. *Burma: Insurgency and the Politics of Ethnicity*. 2nd ed. Dhaka, Bangladesh: University Press, 1999.

Spence, Jonathan D. *The Search for Modern China*. 2nd ed. New York: W. W. Norton, 1999.

Spiro, Melford. *Buddhism and Society: A Great Tradition and Its Burmese Vicissitudes*. New York: Harper and Row, 1970.

Steinberg, David I. *Burma/Myanmar: What Everyone Needs to Know*. Oxford: Oxford University Press, 2010.

Sung, Martin. "Myanmar's Supermarket Queen." CNBC, June 2, 2013. http://video.cnbc.com/gallery/?video=3000172841.

Suryadinata, Leo, ed. *Southeast Asian Personalities of Chinese Descent: A Biographical Dictionary*. 2 vols. Singapore: Institute of Southeast Asian Studies, 2012.

Tagore, Rabindranath. *Japane-Parashye (In Japan and Persia)*. Calcutta: Granthalay, 1940.

Tainturier, François. "The Foundation of Mandalay by King Mindon." PhD diss., University of London, School of Oriental and African Studies, 2010.

Tambiah, Stanley Jeyaraja. *World Conqueror and World Renouncer: A Study of Buddhism and Polity in Thailand against a Historical Background*. Cambridge: Cambridge University Press, 1976.

Tan Sooi Beng. "The Lion Dances to the Fore: Articulating Chinese Identities in Penang and Medan." *Authenticity and Cultural Identity* 65 (2007): 63–78. Published electronically April 28, 2009. http://hdl.handle.net/10502/1955.

Taylor, Robert H. "Do States Make Nations? The Politics of Identity in Myanmar Revisited." *South East Asia Research* 13, no. 3 (2005): 261–86.

———. "The Legal Status of Indians in Contemporary Burma." In *Indian Communities in Southeast Asia*, edited by Kernail Singh Sandhu and A. Mani, 666–706. Singapore: Institute of Southeast Asian Studies, 2006.

———. *The State in Burma*. Honolulu: University of Hawaii Press, 1987.

Thant Myint-U. *The River of Lost Footsteps: Histories of Burma*. New York: Farrar, Straus and Giroux, 2006.

Tinker, Hugh. *The Union of Burma: A Study of the First Years of Independence*. 4th ed. London: Oxford University Press, 1967.

Toyota, Mika. "Contested Chinese Identities among the Ethnic Minorities in the China, Burma and Thai Borderlands." *Ethnic and Racial Studies* 26, no. 2 (2003): 301–20.

Transnational Institute. "Ethnicity without Meaning, Data without Context: The 2014 Census, Identity and Citizenship in Burma/Myanmar." Burma Policy Briefing Series, No. 13. Amsterdam: Transnational Institute, 2014.

Tu Weiming. "Cultural China: The Periphery as the Center." *Daedalus* 120, no. 2 (1991): 1–32. Reprinted in *The Living Tree: The Changing Meaning of Being Chinese Today*, edited by Tu Weiming, 1–34. Stanford, CA: Stanford University Press, 1994.

Turnell, Sean. *Fiery Dragons: Banks, Moneylenders and Microfinance in Burma*. Copenhagen: NIAS Press, 2009.

———. "Myanmar's Banking Crisis." *ASEAN Economic Bulletin* 20, no. 3 (2003): 272–82.

"The Union Citizenship Act, 1948." http://www.burmalibrary.org/docs/ UNION_CITIZENSHIP_ACT-1948.htm (accessed April 28, 2013).

Wade, Geoff. "The Polity of Yelang and the Origins of the Name 'China.'" *Sino-Platonic Papers*, no. 188 (2009): 1–29. http://www.sino-platonic.org/complete/spp188_yelang_china.pdf.

Wang Gungwu. *China and the Chinese Overseas*. Singapore: Times Academic Press, 1991.

———. "Chineseness: The Dilemmas of Place and Practice." In *Cosmopolitan Capitalists: Hong Kong and the Chinese Diaspora at the End of the Twentieth Century*, edited by Gary G. Hamilton, 188–234. Seattle: University of Washington, 1999.

Weinsheimer, Joel. *Gadamer's Hermeneutics: A Reading of "Truth and Method."* New Haven, CT: Yale University Press, 1985.

Wilson, Ara. "Intimacy: A Useful Category of Transnational Analysis." In *The Global and the Intimate: Feminism in Our Time*, edited by Geraldine Pratt and Victoria Rosner, 31–56. New York: Columbia University Press, 2012.

———. *The Intimate Economies of Bangkok: Tomboys, Tycoons, and Avon Ladies in the Global City*. Berkeley: University of California Press, 2004.

Winichakul, Thongchai. *Siam Mapped: A History of the Geo-Body of a Nation*. Honolulu: University of Hawaii Press, 1994.

Wright, Arnold, ed. *Twentieth Century Impressions of Burma: Its History, People, Commerce, Industries, and Resources*. London: Lloyd's Greater Britain Publishing Company, 1910.

Xiao Cao. "Suixianglu: 'Baobo' yici de lianxinag" (Record of random thoughts: My thoughts on "Baobo"). Mianhuawang 緬华网 (Myanmar Chinese website). Posted January 1, 2008. http://mhhzhh.blog.163.com/ (accessed March 3, 2008; site discontinued). Content moved to http://www.myanmarchinese.com/ (accessed December 31, 2013).

Yegar, Moshe. *The Muslims of Burma: A Study of a Minority Group*. Wiesbaden: Otto Harrassowitz, 1972.

Yu Reirong, ed. *Yangguang Guangdong Gongsi (Guanyin Gumiao) yibaiqishijiu zhounian chongxiu luocheng jinian tekan* 仰光廣東公司（觀音古廟）一百七十九週年重修落成紀念特刊 (The 179th anniversary and rebuilding of the Yangon Guangdong Gongsi [Guanyin Temple], special edition). Yangon: Yangon Guangdong Gongsi, 2004.

Yu, Ying-shih. "Business Culture and Chinese Traditions: Toward a Study of the Evolution of Merchant Culture in Chinese History." In *Dynamic Hong Kong: Business and Culture*, edited by Wang Gungwu and Wong Siu-lun, 1–84. Hong Kong: University of Hong Kong, 1997.

INDEX

de Certeau, 24
dialect, 51–53, 60, 62, 71, 74, 76,
    155n69, 164n4

Eastern Language and Business
    Center, 88
eingyi-do, 14. *See also* let-to
eingyi-shei, 14. *See also* let-shei
ethnicity, 4, 9, 17, 24, 47, 48, 89, 90,
    101, 128, 132, 144, 145, 148n5,
    149n14, 150n24, 179n15. *See also*
    ethnic nationality
ethnic nationality, 7. *See also*
    ethnicity
ethos, 4, 5, 7, 20, 57, 77, 92, 116, 148n7
everyday life, 7, 10, 11

Fujian, 14, 21, 35, 39, 40, 42, 51, 52,
    55–57, 59, 61, 62, 64, 65, 67, 71,
    72, 94, 136, 140, 159n45, 160n56,
    163n23. *See also* Hokkien
Fuxing Technology Center, 88

Gadamer, Hans-Georg, 59, 111
guoyu, 74

Hakka, 7, 12, 15, 52, 80, 154n61, 164n4
Heidegger, Martin, 59, 149n11
Hokkien, 7, 12, 14–16, 18, 21, 22,
    29, 30, 32, 36, 39–42, 51–57,
    59–62, 64–67, 69–76, 78, 84, 85,
    90, 91, 93, 94, 104, 105, 107, 111,
    129, 135, 137, 138, 142, 151n28,
    152n41, 154n60, 158n28, 161n2,
    162n8, 163n23,31, 164n4, 165n6,
    166n21,24, 173n56, 174n4, 179n15.
    See also Fujian
Hokkien Gongsi, 60, 62, 65–67, 71,
    94, 163
Hokkien Kuanyin Temple. *See*
    Kuanyin Ting
Ho Sing Brotherhood. *See* Ho Sing
    Gongsi

Ho Sing Gongsi, 33, 36–38, 73, 94,
    120–22, 126
Hock Suan Si, 56, 57*fig.*, 67
home, 8–10, 12, 21, 28, 30, 35, 51, 52,
    55, 56, 60, 65, 67, 70, 130, 140–42,
    144, 145, 150n23
hpoungyi kyaung, 141
Huaqiao Lianhehui, 75
Huaqiao Middle School, 78, 120. *See
    also* Huaqiao Zhongxue
Huaqiao Zhongxue, 72, 77
huashang wenhua, 93. *See also* Chi-
    nese merchant culture
Hungry Ghost Day, 135–38

identity, 3–5, 7, 8, 20, 34, 35, 51, 72–76,
    85, 89, 112, 139, 142, 143, 148n7,
    149n11, 150n19, 152n40, 164n1
in-between, 5, 9, 139
Indian, 11, 13–16, 20, 24, 29–36, 32*fig.*,
    39, 41, 45, 53, 62, 76, 87, 91–94,
    96–101, 142, 143, 153n44,46,
    161n60, 170n2,9, 171n20, 172n37
intimate economy, 95, 171n14

juetougang, 13. *See also* port of last
    hope

Kamma, 107, 173n54
kan, 107, 173n54. *See also* Kamma
kan kaunde, 107, 173n53
kaoshan. *See* kosuan
kapitan, 40, 93, 160n53
Keyes, Charles, 165n16, 168n54
Kheng Hock Keong, 36, 50*fig.*, 51, 61.
    See also Kuanyin Ting
Kien Tek Association, 36, 37*fig.*, 38,
    73, 94, 120, 121, 124, 126, 130, 131.
    See also Kien Tek Tsonghue
Kien Tek Tsonghue, 36. *See also* Kien
    Tek Association
kinship, 8, 32, 34, 51, 69, 158n39
Kiu Liong Tong, 15, 35

port of last hope, 95. *See also* juetougang
Po-sin-tai-tei, 53, 54, 56, 59, 163n23
public realm, 48, 84, 142, 161n66
public space, 45, 48, 112, 137, 156n79, 174n4, 176n23
putonghua, 74

Qingfu Gong. *See* Kheng Hock Keong

Rangoon, 2*map*, 3–15, 18–22, 23–49, 52–54, 56–67, 70, 72–90, 91–106, 108–10, 116–22, 126–27, 129–34, 135, 138–42, 144–45, 147n1, 152n39, 153n44, 156n6, 171n20; colonial, 21, 29–30, 52
religion, 51, 71, 76, 88, 90, 164n1
Rohingya, 100, 143, 144, 149n14, 172n35

secret societies, 33, 36, 39, 94
Sino-Burmese, 4–5, 7–10, 12–22, 29, 33, 35, 39–40, 42, 44–48, 51–55, 57–60, 65, 69, 71–72, 75–90, 91–96, 100–106, 108–10, 112, 113, 115, 116, 118, 120–24, 126, 128–31, 133–34, 135–45, 148n5, 151n28,32, 153n50, 154n60, 155n74, 159n42, 162n8, 166n21, 167n41, 168n50, 169n59, 170n4,5, 175n21, 177n42
Sint Oh Dan, 32, 67, 127, 128, 131–33, 178n45
SLORC, 17, 19, 20, 86, 87, 90, 102, 103, 109, 140, 159n45, 173n55. *See also* SPDC
spatial practice, 9
SPDC, 17, 19, 20, 87, 90, 102, 109, 137, 140, 173n55. *See also* SLORC
Straits Settlements, 13, 29, 39–42, 52, 53, 95, 154n58, 158n30, 159n46, 178n2
strategy, 24, 102
Sun Yat-sen, 8, 37, 52, 73, 74

tactics, 24, 29, 49, 59, 95, 96, 105, 145
tainyintha lumyo, 4, 7
Tai Su Yah, 137, 138*fig.*, 178n2
Taw Sein Ko, 15, 72, 164n6
Tayout, 6, 7, 14–18, 20, 51, 56, 57, 89, 92, 96, 132, 139, 143, 152n40, 168n56; Shan, 15; Shanba, 14, 15
Tayout Hpongyi Kyaung. *See* Hock Suan Si, Kuanyin Ting
Tayout kabya, 12, 152n40
Tayout Tan, 15, 30, 32, 36, 40, 45–48, 51, 53, 54, 59, 64, 70, 72, 75, 82, 96, 100, 106, 117, 120, 122
Tongmenghui, 73
tradition, 10, 59, 65, 111–13, 118–24, 126, 131, 132, 137, 174n2, 175n9,21
Tsingtsiu, 61, 62
Tsing-tsui-tso-su, 38, 53, 56, 59, 163n23
tsi-siok, 62, 71
Tso Su Miou, 53, 56, 57*fig.*, 59. *See also* Hock Suan Si
Tsuantsiu, 53, 55, 56, 61, 62

Wang, Gungwu, 149n11, 151n29

Xiamen, 21, 63, 75, 163n25. *See also* Amoy

Yunnanese, 10, 14–16, 18, 51, 54, 71, 74, 76, 104, 108, 135, 154n60, 173n42

Zeng Guangbi. *See* Chan Mah Phee

CRITICAL DIALOGUES IN SOUTHEAST ASIAN STUDIES

This series offers perspectives in Southeast Asian studies that stem from reconsideration of the relationships among scholars, texts, archives, field sites, and subject matter. Volumes in the series feature inquiries into historiography, critical ethnography, colonialism and postcolonialism, nationalism and ethnicity, gender and sexuality, science and technology, politics and society, and literature, drama, and film. A common vision of the series is a belief that area studies scholarship sheds light on shifting contexts and contests over forms of knowing and modes of action that inform cultural politics and shape histories of modernity.

Imagined Ancestries of Vietnamese Communism: Ton Duc Thang and the Politics of History and Memory, by Christoph Giebel

Beginning to Remember: The Past in the Indonesian Present, edited by Mary S. Zurbuchen

Seditious Histories: Contesting Thai and Southeast Asian Pasts, by Craig J. Reynolds

Knowing Southeast Asian Subjects, edited by Laurie J. Sears

Making Fields of Merit: Buddhist Female Ascetics and Gendered Orders in Thailand, by Monica Lindberg Falk

Love, Passion and Patriotism: Sexuality and the Philippine Propaganda Movement, 1882–1892, by Raquel A. G. Reyes

Gathering Leaves and Lifting Words: Histories of Buddhist Monastic Education in Laos and Thailand, by Justin Thomas McDaniel

The Ironies of Freedom: Sex, Culture, and Neoliberal Governance in Vietnam, by Thu-hương Nguyễn-võ

Submitting to God: Women and Islam in Urban Malaysia, by Sylva Frisk

No Concessions: The Life of Yap Thiam Hien, Indonesian Human Rights Lawyer, by Daniel S. Lev

The Buddha on Mecca's Verandah: Encounters, Mobilities, and Histories along the Malaysian-Thai Border, by Irving Chan Johnson

Dreaming of Money in Ho Chi Minh City, by Allison Truitt

Mapping Chinese Rangoon: Place and Nation among the Sino-Burmese, by Jayde Lin Roberts

The New Way: Protestantism and the Hmong in Vietnam, by Tâm T. T. Ngô

www.ingramcontent.com/pod-product-compliance
Lightning Source LLC
Chambersburg PA
CBHW031131270326
41929CB00011B/1582